BUY, CLOSE, MOVE IN!

BUY, CLOSE, MOVE IN!

How to Navigate the New World of Real Estate—Safely and Profitably—and End Up with the Home of Your Dreams

ILYCE R. GLINK

HARPER

NEW YORK • LONDON • TORONTO • SYDNEY

HARPER

This book is intended as a general guide to the topics discussed and does not deliver accounting, personal finance, or legal advice. It is not intended, and should not be used, as a substitute for professional advice (legal or otherwise). You should consult a competent attorney and/or other professional with specific issues, problems, or questions you may have.

Company names, logos, and trademarks used in the book belong to the companies that own them. There is no attempt to appropriate these names, logos, and trademarks, and none should be construed. Also, there is no endorsement, implied or otherwise, of the companies or individuals listed in this book. They are used to illustrate the types of places, software, Web sites, or information centers where readers can find more information. Finally, company names, phone numbers, addresses, and Web site may have changed since the publication of this book.

For an up-to-date list of Web sites or to contact Ilyce Glink, please visit her Web site, ThinkGlink.com.

HarperCollins books may be purchased for educational, business, or sales promotional use. For information please write: Special Markets Department, HarperCollins Publishers, 10 East 53rd Street, New York, NY 10022.

FIRST EDITION

Designed by Cassandra J. Pappas

Library of Congress Cataloging-in-Publication data is available upon request.

ISBN 978-0-06-194487-1

10 11 12 13 14   OV/RRD   10 9 8 7 6 5 4 3 2 1

For Sam, Alex, and Michael,
without whom my home would be just a house.

Contents

Preface

As a financial journalist covering the residential real estate market, I have always been determined to stay up to date on the latest rule changes and the hottest technical innovations. The last thirty-six months have made that a challenge. They have proven to be some of the toughest in my twenty-odd years covering the wacky world of real estate.

It isn't just that rules have changed. The culture of residential real estate has shifted completely. Since 1994, when the first edition of my book *100 Questions Every First-Time Home Buyer Should Ask* was published, buyers and sellers have become increasingly savvy and sophisticated. It is possible for today's home buyer to know almost as much about a neighborhood's demographics, home sales, and trends as the most informed real estate agent. The Internet has revolutionized how the real estate industry functions day to day, and the buyer—not the seller or the agent—has become the center of the transaction.

The only thing a buyer doesn't have is the wisdom that experience brings to temper the zeal and outsized emotions that come with making the single biggest purchase of your life. For that reason, I still believe home buyers can benefit enormously from using a top-notch real estate agent to help them buy a new or an existing home.

Technology, the 2008 credit crisis, and the greater know-how of buyers, homeowners, and sellers continue to affect and change the U.S. real estate market. This book will help you identify some of the new trends and big changes you'll confront as you buy, own, rent, and sell real estate over the next few years.

Be sure to check out my Web site, ThinkGlink.com, for updates, news, and information. Sign up for my free weekly newsletter, follow me on Twitter (@Glink), check out my YouTube channel (YouTube .com/expertrealestatetips) and connect to my Facebook page (Facebook .com/IlyceGlinkFanPage) to stay on top of this changing universe. If you'd like to share your real estate successes or if you have a question that confounds you along the way, please feel free to e-mail me at Ilyce@thinkglink.com.

ILYCE R. GLINK
January, 2010

 **INTRODUCTION**

When I started writing about real estate in 1988, local newspapers had fat weekend sections filled with ads for new-construction developments, housing listed for sale by real estate agents, mortgages that carried interest rates upward of 10 percent, and homes that were for sale by owner (FSBOs).

At that time, I wrote freelance stories for the local papers about Chicago-area developers who were gobbling up huge tracts of farmland and dividing them into subdivisions with 200 to 400 units each. I wrote about hardscape (the roads, curbs, and other impermeable features of a subdivision landscape plan), the growing interest in maintenance-free communities (where you don't have to mow your own lawn and someone comes to fix the leaky roof), and the increasing variety of limited common elements (like jazzed-up clubhouses and community centers, swimming pools, and covered parking) that developers used to attract buyers. I also started writing about first-time home buyers and the process of buying a home.

In those days, the best and virtually the only way to get information about homes for sale was to make an appointment with a local Realtor (a member of the National Association of Realtors, or NAR). The agent had a thick book that looked like a telephone directory, with newsprint pages; inside were black-and-white photos of the fronts of houses, along with a few details of the listings: the address, price, property taxes, and size and number of rooms. There might also be space for a few words about the property, such as "View of the lake" or "Seller motivated" or "Newer kitchen with gracious entertaining space." Information on how to contact the listing agent and on the commission split would be included as well.

The books were printed once every two weeks. If you were sneaky, you could swipe an old listing book to page through in secret at home. But no one could see you take it, or the Realtor would get in trouble for letting The Book get away.

Your only other option for getting more information about homes for sale was to drive around the neighborhood and look for For Sale signs.

Remembering this makes me laugh, because real estate agents and brokers have long seen themselves as the center of the real estate transaction, and clamping down on the listing book was their way of regulating information. I can't tell you how carefully and thoughtfully my husband, Sam, and I studied the six-week-old information in old listing books with my mother, Susanne Glink, a top Chicago real estate agent for more than twenty-five years, when we were looking for a home.

THE FIRST NEW WORLD OF REAL ESTATE

That was the old world of real estate, and it operated like that for decades. Until the early 1990s, there was no Internet, no Google, no Realtor.com (or other such listing search sites), no Bankrate.com, no Vacation Rentals by Owner (VRBO.com), no Trulia.com, no Craigslist, nor any of the other ways we connect today with information about home buying and selling.

In 1993, as my first book, *100 Questions Every First-Time Home Buyer Should Ask*, was going to press, I got my first e-mail address, at AOL.com. By then, the real estate industry was also going online—although, in some cases, it was dragged there, kicking and screaming.

From the mid-1990s through about 2007, the world of real estate became digitized:

- Listings went online, and Google and other search engines made it easier to find homes that were for sale.
- More recent Internet technology allowed you to wander neighborhoods digitally and get at least a cursory view of what's next to, in front of, and behind a house you're thinking of buying.
- Images of homes for sale evolved from black-and-white to color to digital to 360-degree to interactive photos (in which you click on various points in the house to look at different vistas)—and then to video of the house, property, and surrounding neighborhood.
- Realtor.com became the national virtual warehouse of listings, but hundreds of thousands of real estate company and individual agent Web sites cropped up to help people find them—and millions of homeowners set up their own Web sites. Technology giants like Google, Yahoo, and eBay started their own real estate listing sites, while smaller tech companies created Web applications, or "apps," for various platforms as well as cell phones and smartphones.
- Silicon Valley–based technology companies joined with real estate companies to create mapping software, home valuation technology, real estate tax software, foreclosure listings sites, private label software, and mobile applications like SmarterAgent, which downloads

listing information to any cell phone or smartphone and allows you to search for houses by ZIP code or by real estate company as you explore the area in which you want to buy.

■ Sites like Zillow.com and Trulia.com became top aggregators, mashing up real estate listings with mapping tools and Web 2.0 technologies to allow potential buyers to communicate with one another. These sites made it possible for you not only to find the home you're interested in buying but also to comment on it, locate neighborhood amenities ("Where is the nearest Starbucks?"), and figure out school district boundaries. At Zillow, you can get a "Zestimate," its guess of how much the house is worth, and a number of other sites also provide home valuations. (My advice: Take these numbers with a grain or two of salt—and perhaps an aspirin.)

■ ForSaleByOwner.com, VRBO.com, Apartments.com, and a number of other similar sites were created to level the digital playing field and help homeowners sell or rent their own homes to buyers or tenants who wanted to do more for themselves. (There is a small but growing number of buyers who believe they will get a better deal if they work without a real estate agent, and about 20 percent of sellers believe they will get more money and sell their home faster without listing it with an agent. Web 2.0 tools help these buyers and sellers connect with each other across the world in a way that wasn't possible before.) For those who wanted to rent other people's homes on vacation (instead of staying in a hotel) and live out a dream of living in a castle in Italy, an apartment in Paris, or a cabin in Alaska, sites like HomeAway.com and VRBO.com (Vacation Rentals by Owner) were a boon. They have simply revolutionized the world of vacation rentals.

■ Technology companies figured out how to finance your home purchase on the Web. Sites let you search for interest rates, compare rates among a handful of mortgage companies, have mortgage companies bid on your business, or apply online and have the paperwork sent to you. (The "next big thing" for real estate deals will likely be an "electronic signature" that allows you to sign legal documents via the Internet. While the real estate industry has talked about e-signatures for a few years, the concept now seems to be catching on.)

- One simple idea, Craigslist—created by the world's best customer service guy, Craig Newmark—made newspaper classifieds sections obsolete and gave consumers the opportunity to find whatever they were looking for in the world, including real estate. If you want to rent a condo, find a roommate, or unload some outdated furniture or appliances, Craigslist is the place to go.

THE CREDIT CRISIS, THE HOUSING CRISIS, AND MORTGAGE FRAUD

Technology isn't the only thing that has reshaped the real estate world. More recently, we've experienced this small event called the 2008 credit crisis. Some economists think the crisis began in 2001, just after the September 11 terrorist acts. But I think it started earlier, even as far back as the early 1990s, when interest rates dropped below 7 percent and then went below 6 percent for the first time in decades.

As interest rates dropped, home buyers could afford to buy bigger and more expensive homes—and real estate developers were happy to build them and real estate agents were happy to sell them and collect ever-bigger commissions. The increase in demand caused housing prices to soar. During the 2001 recession, it was the housing industry that prevented the nation's economy from having a complete meltdown. New and existing homes continued to appreciate quickly. New tax laws permitted individuals to keep up to $250,000 (and married couples up to $500,000) in profits, tax free, as long as they had owned their home for at least twenty-four months. As a result, more consumers bought and sold homes and dipped into their burgeoning home equity for the cash they needed to purchase a vacation home or an investment property, or to buy cool toys or pay down debt.

Sometime in late 2006 or early 2007—depending on the part of the country— housing prices reached an incredible peak. Here's what I saw:

- **Home buyers took on mortgages that they were not able to repay.** Buyers who earned $50,000 a year were qualified by mortgage lenders to purchase $500,000 homes. Buyers who didn't earn $50,000 in a job that provided a W-2, or who had a mostly cash business, were qualified to buy million-dollar homes with a good enough credit score using a stated-income or no-doc loan. That meant they (or the loan officer) simply wrote down on the application whatever dollar amount was needed to qualify for the loan.
- **Few, if any, of the loans granted during this time had verifications.** In the real estate industry, verification means someone actually picked up the telephone and checked that the buyer earned enough money or had the necessary financial assets to afford the property. During the run-up to the credit crisis, no one checked tax returns, called employers to verify employment, called bankers to verify how much cash was in the borrower's accounts or when it got there, or even looked at bank, 401(k), brokerage, or other asset statements.
- **Exotic and interest-only loans were standard.** When home prices zoom, thirty-year and fifteen-year loans aren't attractive, because with payments extended out that far, you're paying interest and principal, which can make the monthly payments unaffordable. New, creative mortgages were developed to help home buyers pay for ever-more expensive homes. Interest-only loans became a popular way to boost a borrower's ability to buy a much more expensive

property, since without the principal portion, the payments were far lower than a standard thirty-year mortgage. Another hugely popular financing technique was the pay-option ARM. The interest rate on an ARM (adjustable-rate mortgage) goes up or down usually on a yearly basis (sometimes it adjusts every month or six months) depending on an index (like U.S. treasuries or the London Interbank Offered Rate, or LIBOR) or an outside measure. Almost always, the ARM loan is pegged to the index, and between two and three percentage points are added to that index rate to get the new ARM rate. With a pay-option ARM, the borrower either got an initial teaser rate of 1 to 2 percent—while interest accrued at the real interest rate of 6 or 7 percent—or simply told the lender what he or she wanted to pay. The difference between what you paid and what was owed was tacked on to the end of the loan, a slick move called "negative amortization." (The loans were often referred to as "neg-am loans" for that reason.) At the end of five years, or if your loan balance grew by 10 percent, the loan then converted to a one-year ARM pegged at the current interest rate (or the original rate of the loan). The payments sometimes tripled overnight. When that happened, many Americans defaulted on their mortgages.

- **Home buyers with excellent or even good credit scores were steered into subprime loans.** Subprime loans, which are designed for people who have fair or poor credit, are much riskier and more expensive than traditional loans. Not only do they come with a higher—sometimes much higher—interest rate and higher points (a point is 1 percent of the loan amount) and fees, but they're also often structured as ARMs. Subprime loans put fatter profits into mortgage brokers' pockets, so they were sold to people who didn't need them: home buyers with good or excellent credit.

- **Mortgage fraud and predatory lending were rampant.** In a housing boom (where growth happens organically and can be sustained over the long haul) or a housing bubble (where price is speculative and built on feverish greed), everyone seems to be an expert who profits from inside know-how. As the housing bubble reached its peak in the mid-2000s, everyone had a great story about refinancing—and how much of a "no-brainer" it was—especially your mortgage lender, who was probably earning hundreds of thousands of dollars a year in fees. If you didn't refinance to a new loan and pull out tens of thousands of dollars in cash during those years, you probably spent quite a bit of time at the office water cooler listening to your colleagues brag about the great deals they got. Predatory lending, in which home buyers were sold subprime loans at astronomical fees and interest rates, and mortgage fraud, in which buyers or lenders simply lied on loan applications, was widespread. (The FBI now has more people working mortgage fraud cases than ever before, and their single biggest initiative is catching scam lenders and home buyers.)

- **Buyers bought existing properties or new construction and quickly resold them for a profit.** The "flipping" concept unfolded in several different ways. On the one hand, you might see properties get bid up by "straw buyers" (fake buyers in an auction or multiple-bid situation whose sole purpose is to bid up the price, forcing the eventual buyer to pay more than necessary for the property). Or the buyers would purchase properties for nothing down, do minor (or fake) renovations, and then flip these properties for 100 percent profit—or more—several months later. This happened again and again all around the country. At the height of the market, some buyers would put down money to buy a home or condo that was under construction, and then turn around and resell the contract at a huge profit before they had even closed on that property. The idea was to profit on increasing home values, which were rising in some places like Florida, Arizona, and Las Vegas at a rate of 30 to 60 percent per year. It was easiest to do this with properties that were under construction because of the long lead time (it might take two to three years for the property to be built out) and the fact that buyers had to put down only 5 or 10 percent. This worked beautifully until the housing market crashed, buyers refused to close, and developers were stuck with hundreds of thousands of condos they couldn't sell.

- **Home values shot up at double-digit rates each year, far above the traditional rate of 3 to 4 percent, or just over the rate of inflation.** Affordability came crashing down as home prices were bid up far above the traditional price-to-income ratio. A friend bought several pieces of real estate in a vacation community, mortgaging her primary residence to complete the sales. The properties "doubled in value" virtually overnight and she marveled at her newfound wealth.

- **Homeowners took out cheap home equity loans and home equity lines of credit and began to treat their homes as piggy banks.** The loans were easy to get (every bank on every corner offered them), and they had virtually no closing costs. A friend bought her house for around $400,000 in 2004 and was told in 2007 that her property was worth $750,000. She was able to get a home equity line of credit up to that amount and tapped it all.

- **People were practically inhaling rental properties, then refinancing them to pull out cash.** The demand for information on making a fortune in real estate seemed insatiable. Every month, I would receive a different book to review on real estate investing and flipping. Much of the advice in them was bad; some of it was unethical and even illegal. Learning Annex seminars, held nationwide, featured Donald Trump, Guy Kawasaki, and dozens of "successful real estate investors" willing to sell you their version of a no-money-down program for several thousand dollars a pop. (Unknown to most attendees, many if not all of the so-called "experts" on stage paid a hefty fee to be there.) In 2007, for the first time ever, second homes (including vacation properties and investment properties) accounted for about 40 percent of all homes purchased. (That trend has continued through 2009.)

It was an astonishing time. Mortgage interest rates were low. Everyone in the world was making money in the real estate market and spending those profits just as fast, charging up a storm on their credit cards.

By the fall of 2007, I was feeling a distinct unease about the economy. I talked on my radio show about people being unable to afford much of what they bought. Credit card debt was growing exponentially. Callers told me they couldn't find tenants for the investment houses they had purchased. Then they started having trouble refinancing their rental properties.

In late October, 2007, I was part of an advisory panel put together by Consumer Credit Counseling Services of Greater Atlanta (now called CredAbility.com). The more than a dozen panelists represented mortgage and credit card companies, nonprofits, and media. As we went around the room, I expressed my discomfort with where the economy was headed. I also mentioned that, on the radio, I was being accused of being a pessimist and that my listeners—I particularly recall a conversation with the owner of a Lexus dealership in Atlanta who told me he was having the best month of his life—were assuring me that everything was fine.

George McCarthy, an economist and senior program officer for the Ford Foundation, was sitting kitty-corner from me. He said, "Well, if you're a pessimist, I'm looking at Armageddon." He proceeded to lay out his vision of the massive collapse he believed was directly ahead. "I'm talking about another Great Depression," he said. A few weeks later, the stock market hit its all-time high. By early 2008, it was clear the residential real estate market was headed for disaster.

I'm fairly certain that in hindsight the 2008 credit crisis will be viewed as the worst economic disaster since the Great Depression. Many economists and pundits are already referring to it as the "Great Recession." By the time it's all over, housing prices will fall 40 to 50 percent—or more in some areas. Millions of Americans have watched their net worth decline or even vanish. According to the census, fewer Americans moved in 2008 than in any year since 1998, as home sales nearly ground to a halt. As I write this, at the end of 2009, we're not through it yet. Just recently, one group of economists suggested housing prices won't recover until 2017.

Regardless of when the residential and commercial real estate markets recover, the world of real estate has changed for the foreseeable future. President Barack Obama took office with a mission to right America's financial ship. Since then, he has put secondary mortgage market leaders Fannie Mae and Freddie Mac into conservatorship, spent billions of dollars on stimulus (including an $8,000 federal tax credit for first-time buyers, and a $6,500 tax credit for some trade-up buyers) bought $1.25 trillion in mortgage-backed bonds to push mortgage interest rates lower, and created several programs (some successful, some not so much) to keep millions of Americans from falling into foreclosure.

But the housing market has struggled to find a bottom. And the near-term future for real estate is far from certain.

TODAY'S BRAVE NEW WORLD OF REAL ESTATE

The third piece of the puzzle in the remaking of the American real estate industry is the savvy and sophistication of home buyers—particularly first-time home buyers.

Agents across the country tell me that today's home buyers and real estate investors are much better prepared than those in past years. Much of that preparation is a result of starting their search for a home on the Web.

By the time buyers walk through the door of a property, they've typically seen hundreds of listings online; looked at photos and/or video of the property, street, and neighborhood; and identified neighborhoods they like based on amenities, property taxes, school districts, crime statistics, commuting distance to work, demographics, houses of worship, and other features.

Today's buyers want immediate, unbiased, and unfiltered information about real estate and their neighborhood of choice. They want to communicate with agents instantly and on their timetable, not the agent's. They want to see the interior and exterior of a property electronically, from many angles, and then they'll probably map the neighborhood and take an electronic tour using Google Streetview. It's a process the real estate industry has found it can't control. Savvier agents are trying to embrace it, work on social networking, and figure out how to stay relevant when so much of what they used to offer is available online, 24/7/365.

The combination of technological advances, the housing crisis and its reach into legislation, and increasingly knowledgeable consumers makes up a new world of real estate. While everyone wants to be where we were in 2005, the housing boom proved to be an unsustainable bubble. All that's left is for us to figure out where we are today, and where we'll be five and ten years down the line—and how we're going to make money from our real estate investments.

Let's get started.

ONE

TEN THINGS THAT HAVE CHANGED IN REAL ESTATE, TEN THINGS THAT HAVEN'T

It's late in 2009, and Sarah and Jim are supposed to close on a beautiful and reasonably priced townhome in the next few days. Their city hasn't experienced as deep a drop in home prices as some areas of the country, and foreclosures are mostly limited to pockets of the metro area. Though sales have been slow, home prices have dropped only 10 to 25 percent in the neighborhood where Sarah and Jim are hoping to buy.

Two days before closing, their real estate attorney checks in with the loan officer and discovers that Sarah hasn't filed any tax returns for her business.

Since the credit crisis started, loan officers are verifying everything: income, personal tax returns, assets, credit, retirement accounts, gift letters for cash gifts, business tax returns for self-employed owners—anything you can think of. Verifications are now required by the federal government, which through Fannie Mae, Freddie Mac, and FHA provided financing for more than 85 percent of loans in 2009. Twenty to thirty years ago, banks, savings and loans, and credit unions used to verify everything. You had to prove you were creditworthy, which was more difficult since credit scoring didn't exist as an industry. When credit scoring became more popular, in the mid-1990s, lenders started doing fewer verifications, relying more on credit scores to predict whether a borrower was a risk. Deals were done by pulling a borrower's credit score, filling out an application, and shaking hands on the deal.

But now you can't do a deal on a handshake. The government is now requiring lenders to verify income, assets, and credit the old-fashioned way, by actually calling the bank to double-check that the account exists. This is just one way the government is requiring lenders to roll back many of the new "easier, faster, and cheaper" ways of doing business. Today, home buyers must get documents notarized, prove they have and earn as much money as they say, and allow lenders to contact the IRS to verify information. It takes time and money for the lenders to comply.

The fact that the IRS had no record of Sarah's corporate returns being filed could have spelled the end of their dream to own a home. If she and Jim couldn't get the taxes filed and provide the lender with a copy of the stamped tax return from the IRS as proof, the loan officer told them, the closing would be off. Luckily, Jim and Sarah were able to contact her business's accountant, scramble together a quick return, and get it to the nearest IRS office by the next afternoon.

What Jim and Sarah had to go through would have been an anomaly in the old world of real estate; today, it is replayed again and again as home buyers struggle to understand what they need to do to get their deal done. In order to successfully and profitably navigate the swirling waters of the new real estate industry, you'll need to understand the major trends guiding it. While some things have stayed the same, others have changed dramatically. Here's a look at what they are.

TEN THINGS THAT HAVE CHANGED IN THE REAL ESTATE INDUSTRY

1. You need to have "skin in the game."

Coined by the celebrated investor Warren Buffett, simply put, having "skin in the game" means being an investor in your own company. If you were running a hedge fund, it would imply that you had a sizable amount of cash in the hedge fund, which would grow or shrink based on how well you managed the business. Applied to real estate, it means putting some of your own money into your investment—your home. In other words, you must have a cash down payment.

As home prices soared in the late 1990s and early 2000s, it became tougher for first-time home buyers to scrape together even a nominal down payment. Few buyers looking at a $225,000 home had the traditional down payment of 20 percent ($45,000) just sitting around.

To compensate, lenders created various loan programs that gave buyers the option of putting down nothing, and even let them finance the closing costs. The loans were for 100 to as much as 106 percent of the purchase price and were often structured as piggyback loans, with a first loan for 80 percent of the purchase price set at or close to the prevailing interest rate and a second mortgage for 20 to 26 percent of the sale price at a higher interest rate.

The appeal of these 80/20 loans was as follows: if you got a first mortgage on 80 percent of the sale price of the home, you could avoid paying private mortgage insurance (PMI), which lenders require you to purchase if you put down less than 20 percent in cash as a protection for the lender in case you default on the loan. So if you put down 5 percent in cash, and got a loan for 95 percent of the purchase price, you would have to pay an extra fee each month for the PMI premium. By getting a first mortgage for 80 percent of the purchase price, you could avoid PMI, even when you were getting a second mortgage that covered the rest of the purchase price and brought your true down payment to zero. If you didn't have to pay for PMI, which would be added to the affordability calculation lenders do to figure out how much you qualify to borrow, you could borrow more money.

The problem for borrowers is that PMI is fairly expensive, with an annual fee typically set to 0.5 to 0.75 percent of the loan amount, and the fee rises as the percentage of the down payment falls. If you put nothing down, you're seen as a riskier buyer than someone who puts some payment down. Hence, your PMI premium will be higher if you put 3 percent down in cash than if you put 17 percent down in cash.

With an 80/20 loan, you not only *avoided* paying for PMI, but if you qualify to itemize on your federal tax return, all of the interest you pay on your first and second mortgages (up to more than a million dollars of loans) is tax deductible. Until 2007, PMI wasn't a deductible expense on a federal income tax return, because you typically couldn't deduct insurance premiums. The 80/20 loans were sold to home buyers as a less expensive alternative to buying PMI because interest rates were low and the interest paid on the loans was tax deductible.

The PMI industry lost a great deal of money to the 80/20s, and after extensive lobbying, the tax law was amended. Now, if you earn $110,000 or less per year, you can deduct your PMI premiums through the year 2010. I suspect that this rule change may be extended beyond 2010 so that buyers will again use PMI instead of 80/20 loans. However, because most taxpayers take the standard deduction and don't itemize, this deduction sounds better than it is; most homeowners simply don't use it. (At the moment, lenders aren't doing 80/20 loans at all, but there are a few zero-down loans still available. See chapter 3 for details.)

Why do banks require buyers to have a cash down payment? If things go wrong, a homeowner will be less likely to walk away from his or her mortgage obligations if he or she initially put something down.

In the housing crisis, when homeowners started losing their jobs and their property values plummeted, they stopped making payments on their mortgages. It wasn't long before some were mailing their keys to the lender, which became known as "jingle mail."

When Fannie Mae and Freddie Mac were placed into conservatorship and effectively nationalized, the government stopped allowing these 100 percent loans (except in certain circumstances), and in 2009, the Federal Housing Administration (FHA) raised its down payment requirement from 3 percent to 3.5 percent, deciding that seller-funded down payment contributions would no longer be accepted. (Certain nonprofit companies would facilitate a side transaction between a buyer and a seller in which the seller would "donate" 4 percent of the sale price to the nonprofit, which would turn around and "give" the buyer 3 percent cash to use for a down payment or closing costs, keeping 1 percent for expenses. These transactions became known as "seller-funded down payments." The industry has long known that the less you put down on a property, the more likely it is you will default on your mortgage. With seller-funded down payments, the FHA soon noticed that the default rate was significantly higher than with borrowers who had to put down at least some of their own cash. It gets back to the "skin in the game" mentality.)

Where are we now? If you want to buy a house, you'll need at least 3.5 percent for a cash down payment on an FHA loan, and more if you go with conventional financing. If you need a jumbo loan (more than $417,000 as of this writing), you'll need far more in cash, as much as 50 percent for extremely expensive homes. And if you want to buy an investment property, you'll need to put at least 25 percent down to finance a loan that will ultimately be bought by Fannie Mae or Freddie Mac, which emerged from the credit crisis as the best sources of small-investment real estate financing.

2. Your lender needs to have skin in the game.

Two main problems caused a large part of the credit crisis.

First, mortgages were sold to homeowners who really had no way of paying them back. The loans were then packaged together by Fannie Mae, Freddie Mac, and other secondary market lenders (investors that buy loans from retail lenders who are working directly with borrowers), and sold with seemingly undeserved ratings to investors worldwide.

Second, financial and big Wall Street investment companies used insanely complex financial instruments to try to off-load the risks associated with these toxic mortgages. (Former Federal Reserve Bank chairman Alan Greenspan has said these complex financial instruments confused *him*—and he has a fairly advanced mathematics background.) The problem was, instead of off-loading the risk, these complex financial instruments helped banks overleverage their assets, in some cases by 30 to 1 or even 100 to 1. Since the money men and women of Wall Street believed that only a tiny percentage of the mortgages that backed these securities would fail, they felt comfortable in taking bigger and bigger risks, pocketing fatter and fatter fees. For Wall Street, it was all about fees, profits, and paychecks.

Now the federal government believes that requiring lenders to have an ongoing financial interest in the loans they offer to consumers and sell to investors should keep the mortgage market more stable. While the final number hasn't yet been decided, federal officials now think they should require lenders to hold between 5 and 15 percent of all loans. Officials are also still determining whether lenders should have to hold 5 to 15 percent of each loan they make or the same percentage range of packaged securities. Some industry observers think that lenders should have to hold on to a piece of each loan they originate so less desirable loans don't get lost later on. It seems like this is going to happen, even though lenders say that if they have to hold on to a piece of each loan (or even a percentage of the repackaged loans), they will have less cash available to make mortgages and other loans.

In fact, it's already happening with lenders who do second mortgages, either home equity line of credit (HELOC) loans or home equity loans (HEL). Prior to the credit crisis, if you wanted a HELOC or a HEL, all you had to do was have a pulse and a good credit score. You could walk out of any number of banks with $30,000 burning a hole in your pocket. Now, lenders must keep 50 percent of the HELOC or HEL on their own books, which is why so few want to do these loans at the moment.

You can see how this "skin in the game" requirement will affect how lenders give out future loans. Most likely, credit requirements (see number 3) will continue to tighten as lenders are required to have more skin in the game, because they will have to be sure that they won't lose their investments on bad loans.

3. Credit guidelines have tightened dramatically.

As I've discussed, in the past, if you had a pulse and a credit score that wasn't terrible, you would be able to push your refinance papers through in a couple of weeks—or even, in some cases, a few hours. The lender might give your information a cursory glance, push the button on an electronic appraisal, pull a credit score, and—voilà!—you'd be approved. But since the credit markets froze in 2008, the conservatorship of Fannie Mae and Freddie Mac, and the increase of homeowners who are delinquent on their mortgages, those days are over.

Additionally, homeowners who have undergone a short sale (in which the proceeds from the sale are less than what is still owed on the mortgage, so the lender is short on its investment), a foreclosure, or bankruptcy are being put in the penalty box. Now if you have undergone a short sale, you must wait at least two years to qualify for a Fannie Mae, Freddie Mac, or FHA loan. If you have gone through a foreclosure or bankruptcy, you may have to wait up to five years to apply for a loan. Because Fannie Mae, Freddie Mac, FHA, and other government-backed loans currently account for the vast majority of all loans being granted at the moment, this is a fairly steep penalty. Then again, you might need the time to repair your credit score.

4. The federal government now understands that not everyone should own a home.

In *Outliers,* Malcolm Gladwell writes that one must make seven terrible decisions in a row to wind up in a catastrophic situation. The governmental decision that everyone should be able to own a home led to a bad decision at Fannie Mae and Freddie Mac to create software that was built to say yes to every loan. That led to a decision to base credit decisions almost entirely on credit scores, which have proven to be somewhat unreliable at predicting who is a bad risk in a financial perfect storm—and so on.

Why does the government support homeownership? Over the years (until housing prices collapsed), the government recognized that for the average American, home equity was the largest portion of their net worth. By paying interest and principal each month, the average homeowner participates in a form of enforced savings. Furthermore, because homeowners move less frequently and take better care of their property than renters, homeownership is often tied to neighborhood stability. Finally, and perhaps most important for politicians who are always looking out for the next election, homeowners vote more than renters.

Supporting homeowners and homeownership turned out to be a no-brainer for politicians looking for votes, which is why there are great tax benefits for homeowners, such as the ability to deduct some or all of the mortgage interest and real estate taxes one pays on an itemized federal income tax return. The government decided that homeownership should be not only the American Dream but also the American Reality and pushed Fannie Mae and Freddie Mac to expand their lending in poorer communities and minority neighborhoods. When Congress then agreed to let Fannie Mae and Freddie Mac lend to those with less-than-perfect credit, the firms started pushing local mortgage brokers, S&Ls, and small banks to lend in their neighborhoods. The firms also developed software that automated the underwriting process (which assesses and confirms a borrower's eligibility for a loan), built with the predisposition to say "yes" to every borrower. By packaging these loans and selling the securities around the world, Fannie Mae and Freddie Mac had a virtually limitless supply of funds to give lenders making these loans.

The rate of homeownership rose to nearly 68 percent at the height of the housing boom in 2006, according to the American Community Survey released by the census bureau. Unfortunately, many Americans were living on the edge financially during this time. When the U.S. economy stalled and the unemployment rate soared, married homeowners whose hours were cut at work, or who lost their jobs, went broke trying to cover their mortgage, taxes, and bills on less than two incomes. By 2008, the American Community Survey reported that U.S. homeownership fell to 66.6 percent, as millions lost homes to foreclosure. Today, it seems unrealistic to expect everyone to own a home, although during the housing crisis the government encouraged more than half a million first-time buyers to purchase a home with the $8,000 first-time home buyer tax credit; changed the tax law so that taxpayers who sold in a short sale would not pay income tax on the difference between what they owed to the lender and the sale price (also known as "imputed income" or "phantom income"); and, made numerous other homeowner-favored adjustments to the tax code.

5. "No-doc" or unverified loans are no longer an option.
The banks made another bad decision on the road to catastrophe when they stopped verifying information on mortgage applications. Despite

warnings and the possibility of jail time, people still lie on credit applications.

When used in a very limited capacity, stated-income loans and no-document loans—in which the borrower's income and assets are not supported by documentation—worked for years. These unverified loans were primarily designed for people who owned cash businesses and, because of accounting rules (or perhaps to avoid paying as much tax to the IRS as they should), didn't declare all of the cash they had available to them through the business as income on their federal tax return. In other words, the cash didn't show up on their tax return as income, but there was plenty of cash flow to pay their mortgage, taxes, and insurance. Stated-income loans were also helpful for big-time real estate investors who were able to use their investment properties' depreciation to offset the income on their tax returns, ultimately reducing the amount of income showing on the tax return—sometimes to zero. They may not have owed any income tax, but these real estate investors had plenty of income.

Those willing to pay a higher interest rate and some extra points or fees had their stated-income or no-doc loans easily approved. But the underlying problem with these loans is that the applicant's income and assets aren't verified. During the housing boom, people who earned $50,000 a year were qualifying for $500,000 mortgages by stating on their loan application they had enough income to cover the mortgage, taxes, and insurance. Essentially, they lied or their lender lied on the application. Since no one checked or verified the information, thousands of mortgages were made to folks who couldn't afford them. The amount of fraud can't be overestimated.

Once the government took over Fannie Mae and Freddie Mac and put the companies into conservatorship, there was a new top-down insistence on making sure all loans are verified. Government regulators insisted that all information on loan applications be verified. Since Fannie Mae, Freddie Mac, and FHA account for the vast majority of loans, lenders had nowhere to sell their no-doc loans. Overnight, these exotic mortgages disappeared and homeowners who didn't have the cash or credit to qualify for a conventional or FHA loan were out of luck.

6. Real estate investments are all about cash, too.

From 1995 to about 2005, real estate investing was all about leverage. You could buy a property with nothing down, get cheap financing and tax benefits, and then fix and flip your property for profit. But the credit crisis and the collapse of housing prices have put an end to easy money in real estate for many investors.

Nowadays, financing options are limited for investment real estate. The banks and investors have taken a beating on commercial, industrial, and other types of real estate investments. Fannie Mae, Freddie Mac, and the Federal Home Loan Banks will lend on non-owner-occupied properties, but you may only own up to ten properties including your primary residence and vacation property. If you want to buy dozens of foreclosed properties, you need cash on hand and a previously worked-out deal with a specialized lender. Most of the investors who are doing this have raised private equity funds to buy, renovate, and sell these properties, simply because it is easier and faster than working with a traditional lender. It will be some time before banks lend freely again, especially since the International Monetary Fund (IMF) suggested in 2009 that through the end of 2010, banks around the world will write off another $1.5 trillion in bad investments. Most investors will have to live within the ten-property limit or set up a corporation that can seek out other forms of financing from commercial lenders. The costs to obtain these loans may be considerably higher, if they are even available to the investor.

In the economics of a real estate investment, cash is important. You should be cash-flow positive (with income greater than expenses) or, at the very least, cash-flow neutral (with income and expenses equal). If you do line up lending, be prepared to put down a significant amount of cash, your "skin in the game." Many lenders are requiring real estate investors to pony up anywhere from 25 to 35 percent of the purchase price in cash. Even Fannie Mae and Freddie Mac loans to real estate investors require a 25 percent down payment in cash.

7. House budgets are shrinking.

How far should you stretch when buying a home? For years, real estate agents advised younger home buyers to extend a little beyond their comfort zone. Agents understood that though the monthly cost of a fixed-rate mortgage seems expensive, most younger home buyers will earn more as the years go on, and the cost to carry the home will become more reasonable as a percentage of income. Unfortunately, this understanding was based on a number of factors that no longer apply. First, younger buyers won't always earn more later in their career, and even if they do earn more, many companies have cut their 401(k) plan matches—meaning that employees must set aside more money for retirement, leaving less available to pay housing-related expenses like mortgage, taxes, and homeowners insurance. During the recession of 2007 to 2009, more than seven million Americans lost their jobs. But millions more took pay cuts just to keep their jobs and were earning up to 25 percent less than before. In times of economic strife, job and income loss can weigh heavily on homeownership, making the carrying costs of a home unaffordable.

It may be okay to push home buyers to stretch their budgets a little if their cash flow is neutral, but how much is "a little"? It's clear now that a person with a $50,000 salary shouldn't be buying a $500,000 house, which was the hallmark for exotic mortgages. But how much you push your income ultimately depends on how well you like to sleep at night. For some buyers, spending every cent a mortgage company will lend is fine. But for others, that's cutting it a little too close. The best real estate agents know how much income you need to afford a house and refuse to show properties that are too far outside of those guidelines. The best home buyers have already been preapproved for their mortgage and have spent time thinking about their lifestyle and what they like to do with their money. One of the great lessons in this recession is that it is still a good idea to live below your means.

Many of our parents, grandparents, and great-grandparents never forgot or will never forget the Great Depression. It colored how they treated their money for the rest of their lives. The same may be true for this generation of home buyers after the 2008 credit crisis. Millions of homeowners who watched their home equity get zapped and their net worth evaporate feared for the first time that they would lose their homes and other assets. As our credit card limits are dramatically reduced or even cut off and our home equity lines of credit are shut down, we may now figure out what "deferred gratification" really means.

In boom times, we're willing to stretch a bit, to believe we're entitled to a secure financial future, to grab our share of the American Dream. Now? "I'm getting more statements from Realtors telling me that people are downsizing their budget requirements because they want to be safer going forward," says Lawrence Yun, chief economist for the National Association of Realtors.

8. Smaller homes are becoming more popular than McMansions.

From the late 1970s until 2008, bigger was better in real estate. Everyone wanted a bigger house, with extra bedrooms and bathrooms, a home office, a mudroom, and an outsized kitchen with granite countertops. In response, developers built whole subdivisions of oversized homes on smaller lots. According to the National Association of Home Builders

(NAHB), the average size of a new home grew from about 1,600 square feet in the late 1970s to about 2,300 square feet in 2008.

With the credit and housing crises, the home expansion madness came to a stop. Architect Sarah Susanka's best-selling book *The Not So Big House,* originally published in 1998, again became popular with homeowners who wanted to build smaller homes with more detail and character. (If you're interested in Susanka's work, see our videos at ExpertRealEstateTips.net and ThinkGlink.com.) Now the trend is to downsize homes, because smaller homes are less expensive to own, operate, and maintain. Housing is also the biggest consumer of energy, according to sustainability expert, architect Sergio Palleroni. Our homes eat up many more times the fuel that our cars do. As the green movement grows, there will be bragging rights associated with how little energy your home uses. The smaller-home trend is here to stay.

9. Real estate information is becoming more transparent.

The real estate industry has long operated as though the buyer is a bird in a cage with a dark cloth covering it. In other words, the process and how the professionals were compensated was not particularly transparent to buyers or sellers.

For example, many borrowers believed the mortgage broker worked for them, but the broker was getting a fat fee called a "fee service premium" from the end lender for closing the deal. At best, the broker's interests were neutral. At worst, the broker pushed the borrower to take a more expensive loan. The borrower never understood the full scope of the financial relationship between the mortgage broker and the lender, but new government regulations are working to change this model and disclose all fees paid to related parties in a real estate transaction.

Here's another example: Many sellers were surprised to find at the closing table that the commission they agreed to pay the listing agent for selling their home wasn't automatically shared equally with the buyer's agent. A 6 percent commission paid to the listing agent might be split 55/45 or 60/40, with the smaller share going to the buyer's agent. How did sellers not know this? It wasn't in the listing agreement, and many agents simply didn't share this information with the seller—even though it would have been in the seller's best interest to have a *larger* share of the buyer's agent's commission. (While a good buyer's agent wouldn't necessarily push his or her client to buy a house because of a larger commission, the agent will certainly make sure to show the home just in case the buyer likes it.)

Buyers are continually surprised to learn that in states like Florida, Arizona, Georgia, and California, real estate attorneys are generally not hired to close residential real estate transactions. Buyers and sellers have no legal representation in the single biggest purchase or asset sale they'll ever complete. Rather, the attorney that the buyer pays for actually works for the mortgage company.

If buyers do use an attorney to close their deals, it's likely that the attorney will receive a hefty fee from the title or escrow company (the company that manages the closing transaction for the buyer and seller, and sells title insurance) for signing his or her name to a bunch of papers. This is one reason why title insurance is so expensive. Attorneys who are more transparent charge a proper fee for their services and then pass along to their clients the discount title insurance that companies offer to them, which cuts title insurance fees dramatically. In some states, attorneys make more money as title agents than they do as residential real estate attorneys. (In fact, I just heard from a friend who was perplexed why her attorney received a $600 fee for closing her house plus another $1,400 from the title company, which was disclosed on her HUD-1 settlement statement.)

And although buyers pay for things like appraisals, credit histories and scores, and numerous other items, they're not automatically entitled to get copies of these documents, although now buyers and sellers are entitled to receive a copy of the appraisal done for the property. But that goes hand in hand with mortgage lenders using their own appraisers, credit companies, document preparation companies, and the like in the mortgage process, which can in turn eliminate competition for services and create an incentive for the companies that mortgage lenders use to keep their fees high.

For decades, the real estate industry has operated under the principle that the less information buyers and sellers have, the better it is for agents, lenders, title companies, and all the other folks who eat from the trough. But the real estate tide seems to be turning, as the housing and credit crises of 2008 have heightened awareness in Washington, D.C., and on Wall Street about the catastrophic consequences of a closed information loop. And technology is pushing the industry to become more transparent. The Web site Closing.com allows buyers and sellers to explore all the detailed costs of a closing transaction and to see how much individual professionals and companies charge for their services both in their hometowns and across the United States. A host of Web sites, including Zillow.com, Realtor.com, and Trulia.com allow home buyers to search for properties, read or leave comments on those properties, and shop for mortgage lenders. And then there are sites like mine, ThinkGlink.com, that provide a ton of information about how the industry works, explaining jargon and providing tools that makes it easier to buy, sell, fix up, finance, or invest in real estate.

Hopefully, new rules and regulations from the Department of Housing and Urban Development (HUD) and the Federal Housing Finance Agency (FHFA) will help increase transparency. An example is the new and improved HUD-1 form, which tracks all cash going into and out of a deal. The new HUD-1 form is easier for buyers and sellers to understand. There are also new rules that apply to how appraisals are done to make them more transparent and to help appraisers avoid being bullied by lenders into providing an appraisal that will help close a deal rather than providing the true worth of the property (I'll discuss this more in detail in chapter 3). Transparency in real estate is on an upswing and will allow future buyers to understand far more clearly what they're paying for. What's still unclear is whether the additional transparency will result in lower costs for home buyers and sellers.

10. Homes may not appreciate for years.

Some economists predict that by the time the housing crisis bottoms out, housing prices will have dropped an average of 35 to 55 percent from the peak. By 2009, prices in Phoenix and Las Vegas had already dropped around 50 percent. Not every house in every neighborhood will fall equally in value; some will fall more, and some may not fall at all. It depends on where you live. Traditionally, metro areas that experience explosive growth and price appreciation fall the hardest and fastest. Las Vegas, Miami, and Phoenix enjoyed double-digit home value price appreciation for years. Developers rushed to cash in on the tremendous price appreciation and built thousands of single-family homes, town-homes, and condo buildings. When the market turned, tens of thousands of empty houses, townhomes, and condo units were foreclosed on by lenders, who turned around and started selling them for pennies on the dollar—which is why those markets have seen prices decline harder and faster than markets like Chicago, where home prices appreciated briskly but not insanely.

Unfortunately, housing prices aren't expected to rebound as quickly as the stock market, which bounced up more than 60 percent within six months of its low on March 9, 2009. One economist predicted that property prices wouldn't recover until 2017. There is some precedent for that kind of a slow return: in the late 1980s, housing prices in California collapsed and didn't recover until around 1993 or 1994.

Real estate is an illiquid investment; you can't always sell when you want to, and the home you buy may not appreciate for years. Now is the time to buy a house that you love and want to live in for the next five to seven years, or because you think the house will be a great investment to hold over the longer term.

TEN THINGS THAT HAVEN'T CHANGED
IN THE REAL ESTATE INDUSTRY

Regardless of all the change, a few important truisms of real estate remain. Here is my list of ten things that *haven't* changed during the recent housing crisis.

1. Real estate agents are still a good deal for home buyers.

While the Internet provides great information about homes and neighborhoods, it is not a substitute for the experience and expertise of a qualified real estate agent who understands what you need to do to close on a house purchase. A qualified agent can provide you with context about the homes in a particular neighborhood, because he or she has watched these houses go on and off the market for years. A good agent is a treasure trove of information about more than just the physical property; he or she can talk to you about what is going on in the neighborhood and school district, why the sellers are divorcing, or how the new development going up next door can help you make a smarter offer or be a better negotiator.

This experience is even more important if you're buying new construction. An agent who regularly works with a developer or has watched the developer put up several houses or subdivisions can tell you if buyers are happy with the properties they purchase or, on the flip side, if the builder has had to throw in upgrades or give freebies or discounts to get properties sold.

Best of all, there are no direct savings to the buyer or investor that result from *not* using a real estate agent. The vast majority of buyers and investors don't pay out of pocket for the wisdom and expertise an agent provides. The seller's commission is traditionally split between the listing agent and the buyer's agent. If the buyer comes to the table without an agent, the buyer has no representation or fiduciary agent, and the listing agent would receive the entire commission. Developers build in the cost of an agent when creating their sales and marketing plans, so if you show up without an agent, it's the developer who will pocket the agent's commission, not you. A few buyers who use exclusive buyer's agents (agents who only represent buyers and never take listings, avoiding potential conflicts of interest) may wind up paying the commission out of pocket, but even in these situations the seller will traditionally split the commission or alter the sale price of the home to include the commission.

If you're buying a property that is for sale "by owner" (without a listing agent attached to it), you might imagine you'll save money by not using your own buyer's agent. But this also doesn't hold up. Most sellers don't necessarily know how to price their property, and so they might over- or underprice it. Your agent can bring a tremendous amount of value by helping you negotiate against the seller. And here again, you won't pay out of pocket for this experience and value. If you bring an agent to the table, my experience is that most "by owner" sellers will figure out a way to get your agent paid and be happy to have paid only half a commission instead of a full commission.

2. You'll get the best loan program, interest rate, and terms if you shop around.

Whether you're buying a toaster or a car, you'll get a better deal if you shop around. The same goes for houses. Financing a house may be the most expensive thing you do, next to paying for college. If you take out a $200,000 loan with a thirty-year fixed-rate mortgage for 5.5 percent interest (a historically cheap rate), you'll pay $1,135.58 per month, plus taxes and insurance. The interest alone will run you nearly *$209,000 over the life of the loan*. With those kinds of numbers, it pays to shop around.

Every little bit you save can translate into tremendous savings down the line. Shave a quarter-point off the interest rate of your loan and you'll save more than $10,000 in interest over the life of the loan. When shopping for a mortgage, you'll want to talk with at least five different types of lenders, all of whom your friends or relatives have recently used. Try to find a big national lender (such as Bank of America, Citibank, or Wells Fargo), a locally owned bank that keeps a fair amount of its loans in its portfolio, a Federal Home Loan Bank, a mortgage broker, and a credit union.

Before shopping around, decide whether you want a fifteen- or a thirty-year fixed-rate mortgage or an adjustable-rate mortgage; when you meet with lenders, ask them to provide you with a detailed breakdown of the costs. And remember, getting preapproved for your loan is infinitely better than getting prequalified. (See chapter 3 for more discussion on this point.) Even if you find the cheapest loan, you still need that lender to close your deal. Service counts for a lot when it comes to financing, so don't necessarily choose the lowest-priced lender for your home purchase. Rather, choose the best lender at the lowest price possible.

3. You must figure in the cost of maintaining a home when making an offer.

One of the biggest mistakes home buyers make before putting in an offer is not taking into account the costs involved in maintaining a house. Having a professional home inspection is essential, because it reveals problem areas the untrained eye won't catch, but inspections usually don't happen until after an offer has been accepted. Instead of simply relying on the inspector's assessment, savvy buyers must look for red flags of potentially expensive repair work. And the costs of general maintenance cannot be overlooked when figuring out your homeownership budget.

All houses, new and old, require maintenance. Buyers sometimes think that if they buy a brand-new house, they'll have fewer maintenance headaches. This is not always true, especially if the property has construction defects. But even new houses without construction defects require maintenance—you'll need to mow the lawn, do upkeep on the driveway, and make sure the caulk stays in good shape, among other things. Air conditioners need servicing, as do heating systems, water filters, gutters, septic systems, water softeners, and smoke and carbon monoxide detectors. As with any house, you'll need to check regularly for moisture or pest infiltration problems.

What about condominiums, townhomes, and co-ops? Each of these types of homes has maintenance issues as well, although perhaps fewer compared to a single-family house. How you pay, and how much you pay, will depend in part on the size and type of building. If, for instance, you live in a larger building with many units, you may have a monthly maintenance fee that includes a sum that goes into the building's reserve fund. The reserve fund is used for extraordinary maintenance issues, such as replacing an elevator, tuck-pointing exterior brick, or replacing the furniture in the lobby. If you live in a smaller building, you may have to complete necessary repairs yourself—requiring you to get your neighbors to pony up their part of the cost.

Planning for annual maintenance costs and fees is one part of the equation; but you should also plan for one-time expenses, including the replacement of a hot water heater, air-conditioning condenser units, carpet, appliances, and so on. While hopefully you won't have to shell out for all of these big expenses at once, you should expect the cost of one bigger expense each year in addition to annual maintenance fees.

4. It's still all about location.

Housing prices may fluctuate during bubbles or the arrival or loss of a big employer in a neighborhood, but in a great location, prices will rise faster when times are good and fall more slowly when times are bad. The real estate agent cliché is true: it's all about "location, location, location." (The late *New York Times* columnist William Safire traced the phrase to a real estate agent's 1928 advertisement in a now-defunct Chicago newspaper.)

What makes a neighborhood great? It needs to be in a top school district (this is important even if the buyer doesn't have or plan to have children) as well as safe, well run, and easily accessible to important highways and public transportation. Additionally, the owners who live there must take care of their homes and gardens, and there should be nearby recreation, shopping, services, restaurants, and other amenities.

You can change a house, but you can't change its location, so be sure you really get to know the neighborhood before you make an offer. (In chapter 2, I discuss how "location, location, location" has become even more important for home buyers since the housing crisis.)

5. You must be prepared to spend money on a house you buy in "as is" condition.

A ThinkGlink.com visitor sent me an e-mail about a house she wanted to buy from the bank that was being sold "as is." The house had been foreclosed on, and the bank was clear that it wasn't willing to do anything if a home inspection uncovered problems. Sure enough, the inspector turned up some potentially expensive issues, including a crack in the foundation and an internal plumbing problem. The buyer asked me if she could ask the bank to reduce the price. You can always ask, but expect the answer to be no. Selling a property "as is" eliminates a whole band of disclosure headaches, which is why there is typically no negotiating when it comes to properties that have been taken back by the lender.

When you buy a home in "as is" condition, you take the property in its condition on the day of closing. If there are material defects or structural problems that aren't disclosed, you must deal with them. When buying a house in "as is" condition, you should expect the worst—and expect it to cost you.

Just about all foreclosures and short sales are sold "as is." Other than the financing, the bank or lender has no history with the property and has no way of verifying what's wrong with it—and doesn't want to know. The price you pay for the foreclosure or short sale, often ten to fifty cents on the dollar, is supposed to be cheap enough to compensate for whatever you'll have to spend fixing problems down the line.

6. You can't believe everything you read or see on the Internet.

As helpful as the Internet is, you can't believe everything you read or see online when it comes to real estate. Ever since the first For Sale ads in newspapers, homeowners—and their agents—have been writing descriptive copy designed to pique buyers' interest in the property. A listing sheet that touts a "lake view" or "mountain view" might really mean you have to stick your head out the window and turn it 90 degrees to get that view. The purpose of marketing copy in real estate is simply to get you excited to see a property and to make an offer. Top agents will highlight the best of what a property has to offer, but that may not be the whole story. You have to be skeptical and assume there's more for you to uncover.

This skepticism is important not just when you are searching for homes to buy, but also when you are educating yourself on the ins and outs of real estate or determining the value of your home.

Sometimes the content on real estate sites is just plain wrong. Some sites do a great job of explaining the basics of real estate, while others have bogus information—not that you'd necessarily realize that the information wasn't entirely accurate. (Visit my Web site, ThinkGlink.com /resources, for a current list of my favorite real estate sites on the Web.)

In the case of Web sites that offer home valuation tools to help you figure out how much a property is worth, the technology used may be poor. Or the numbers are based on underlying data that varies greatly from county to county and may not be complete in your area. Or there may be a problem with the mathematical formulas the site uses to calculate the valuation. Of course, you won't know that there's a problem, because you can't access the underlying data. But you can ask your real estate agent to pull comps (recent sales of comparable homes in the neighborhood) for you or visit homes for sale to estimate your home valuation.

7. Seeing a property in person trumps seeing it on the Internet.

You can see a lot online. With Google StreetView, you can virtually move up and down a block. On Microsoft's Bing, you can see an address in 2-D or 3-D and get a bird's-eye view, flying high above the location, then swooping in for a close-up. You can find photos and sometimes video of the house, street, and neighborhood on Zillow.com, on property listing sites like Trulia.com, at a property's own Web site, on the listing Realtor's personal or company Web site, or at Realtor.com. As good as these tools are—and they're getting better every year—seeing photos or video on the Internet isn't nearly as useful as seeing a property in person.

A house's oddities—the train tracks that run just behind the property, or a dump that sits a mere hundred yards outside the front door—can be cleverly hidden by photos or video. Photos don't reveal the bad smells that waft from the dry cleaner down the block, the noise the upstairs neighbor makes while working out early in the morning, or the way the two apartment buildings on either side of the house block the light. You'll see only what the photographer or videographer wants you to see. There is no substitute for walking into the living room of a home you're interested in, sitting on the couch, and imagining how happy (or unhappy) you'd be living there.

8. Being preapproved for a loan is still better than being prequalified.

Knowing that you've locked in your financing, also known as being "preapproved" for your loan, is better than thinking you have one (being prequalified). The difference is that with preapproval, you have a written commitment from the lender to fund your loan, provided that the home appraises at or above the purchase price you are paying for it. Many buyers don't realize there is a difference between being prequalified and being preapproved because the language is similar. Many lenders add to that confusion by using the term "preapproved" when they mean "prequalified."

More specifically, "prequalification" is a wide-ranging industry term that means a buyer has visited a mortgage Web site, or worked with an online calculator to figure out what is in his or her price range, or heard from a mortgage lender in person what size loan he or she can afford to support each month.

"Preapproval" is an industry term meaning that the buyer has actually applied for the loan, the underwriting has taken place, the information on the application has been verified, and the buyer has been approved to borrow up to a specific amount of money, provided the home appraises out in value.

To a seller, preapproved buyers are far superior to buyers who are only prequalified, because the seller knows that preapproved buyers are much more likely to be able to close on the property. Buyers who have been preapproved may have already made an investment, because getting preapproved can cost some money. The lender may charge the buyer an up-front application fee in addition to other fees that are not due until the buyer closes on the loan. And if the buyer fails to close, he or she may still be responsible for these fees and have to write a check to the lender.

If you get preapproved, you should receive a written loan commitment. That commitment should have very few conditions, and what conditions it has should relate to the property you ultimately decide to purchase, such as that the property appraises out and that the title to the property is satisfactory.

9. You alone must be responsible for determining how much you can afford to spend each month.

We live in a world that encourages us to use credit and take on debt. Lenders will grant you a mortgage that adds up to more than 40 percent of your gross monthly income, which will actually be more than half of your take-home pay. As your credit score rises, you'll be given credit cards to max out, and as long as you keep making payments, new applications will arrive. You'll be able to get a car loan, even if your current car is worth less than what you owe. This should be fine as long as you have control over your wallet and your spending habits don't get out of control. But many consumers don't have that control, and the lure of $250 designer jeans, $1,000 handbags, and $35,000 luxury cars is too much to resist.

Only you know how much you can afford to spend each month. You may be able to spend every cent your creditors extend and still sleep at night. Or you may sleep better at night knowing you carry no debt other than your mortgage and perhaps a car loan. The trick is figuring it out for yourself.

10. The world of real estate depends on the phrase "caveat emptor."

Caveat emptor is a Latin phrase that means "let the buyer beware." For a long time, the burden fell to the buyer to beware the dangers lurking in home buying. While most states have adopted written seller disclosure laws (requiring sellers to disclose in writing any known material defects in their property) to help buyers be more aware of some hidden dangers, it is still important to find out how to protect yourself.

If you're buying a home, you'll have to sign all sorts of disclosure forms. Your real estate agent will have you sign an agency disclosure agreement that explains who he or she represents in the transaction. (You may think your agent is your fiduciary, someone who has your best interests at heart, but unless the agent signed a buyer's agency disclosure, the agent might represent the seller even though he or she takes you to showings and discusses your personal finances in detail. Or the agent might be a *dual agent*, representing both the buyer and seller in a single transaction—also known as "non-agency," since the agent technically represents no one's interests.) The lender will have you sign pages of disclosures for the interest rate, the mortgage terms and conditions, and a prepayment penalty if it's attached to the loan. The seller will provide you with a seller's disclosure form that supposedly discloses everything the seller knows or doesn't know about the physical condition of the property, including whether there is lead in the house paint or in the water.

You can see how limited the information might be. That's why, regardless of the disclosures you receive, you have to take responsibility for finding out everything you need to know about a property before you make an offer.

You should:

- Double-check the property's most recent tax bill, so you know what the taxes will be, if all of the seller's tax exemptions have been taken, and when the next reassessment of the property is due.
- Find out crime statistics and demographic information for the neighborhood.

- Walk around the neighborhood at different times of the day and evening to see who lives, works, and plays there.
- Interview several top agents who know the neighborhood and check their references to find one with whom you're truly compatible.
- Read all of the documents pertaining to the purchase and finance of the property.
- Go to the local water department, building department, and public works department to determine whether the property is in a flood plain, requires any permits, or will be affected by any major projects planned by the local government.
- Research the water quality in your area. You should know in advance whether a home you are looking to buy is serviced by municipal water and sewer departments or is dependent on well and septic systems. If the latter is true, and you've never owned a home with these features, take the time to learn how they work; how much they cost to service, repair, and replace; and what you have to do to manage them.
- Check with the local and regional planning departments to see whether a new highway, a commercial development, or even a large residential development is planned for the area in which you want to buy.
- Ask for the homeowners' association budget, financial statements for at least the last year or two, year-to-date expenses, and minutes from the last two years of meetings.

If this sounds like a lot of work, it is. If it sounds overwhelming, then you may need to take a step back and rethink your home purchase ambitions. Buying a home is only the beginning of the true work of homeownership.

Now that you have a sense of some of the important things that are changing, as well as what you can rely on going forward, it's time to dive deeper and see how these apply to the old and new rules of real estate.

TWO

WHAT BUYERS NEED TO KNOW NOW

In chapter 1, we established that the real estate industry has changed more in just the past few years than in the previous twenty or thirty. It isn't that a few things changed; the whole industry seems to have been upended by the collapse of the housing bubble. One thing that hasn't changed is that in order to play the real estate game well—including buying, financing, and closing on your new home—you must know the rules. Some of these rules are tried and true and aren't likely to change; others have come about as a result of the housing and credit crises. If you take the time to learn about the old and new rules of real estate, you *can* have an excellent home buying experience—just like Chris and Kaleigh.

In a town about forty-five minutes north of Atlanta, at the foot of the Blue Ridge Mountains, Chris and Kaleigh got engaged and decided to start a family. At the time, Kaleigh worked at a day care center, while Chris was an electrician who had lost and then found various employment opportunities during the housing crisis. They were living in a tiny three-bedroom, one-bath farmhouse located on property owned by Chris's parents, but when Chris and Kaleigh's daughter, Brooklyn, was born, they decided it was time to find their own home.

To Chris, buying a home was "a progression in life, the beginning of starting a family and providing a safe place to raise a child."

Like most twenty-somethings, Chris and Kaleigh started their search on the Internet. For four months, they looked at various houses online and drove by those that seemed most interesting. When they were ready to get serious, they hired their neighbor, who was a "very professional real estate agent," to help them pick through the houses they found online. They texted her, called her, and e-mailed her. "All the agents have BlackBerrys," Chris recalls. "It was very convenient."

Savvy home buyers will take the time to think about how much money they feel comfortable spending each month on the mortgage, property taxes, and homeowners insurance—not just how much the bank was willing to lend them. Chris and Kaleigh knew they were comfortable spending around $140,000 for their property, and they played with an online mortgage calculator before their agent recommended several lenders, including one whom the couple really liked. "The only thing I had questions about was how much I'd be paying. The lender was very honest, very straightforward," Chris says. "If you don't like your mortgage lender, switch," he advises. "They're not all the same. This one gave us great customer service." Chris and Kaleigh passed on 100 percent financing with a United States Department of Agriculture (USDA) loan in favor of an FHA loan with a 3.5 percent down payment. They qualified for the federal first-time buyer's $8,000 tax credit and opted to get preapproved for their loan.

Many of the homes they viewed on the Internet looked good, and their agent helped them see the not-so-good parts that, as we've discussed, don't always come across on the Web. They made an offer on a house, the seller countered the offer, and they tried to negotiate to a mutually agreeable number. But ultimately, they couldn't come to terms on the price. Then Kaleigh found a special house online. The neighborhood was right and the house, which had been built in 1997, had been updated. It had crown moldings, updated fixtures, and some other niceties added by the owner, a licensed handyman who fixed up the house in his spare time. Much larger than their farmhouse, this home had three bedrooms and two baths (including a master bedroom with a separate shower), vinyl siding, a finished basement, a two-car garage with a workshop, and air-conditioning. It also came with a full termite inspection and treatment. Within a few hours, the agent arranged to meet them at the house for a showing.

The house was listed at $140,000, and Chris and Kaleigh made an offer for $137,000, which was accepted. Their final monthly payment turned out to be less than they expected—$930 instead of $970— "a very nice surprise" for Chris. (The lender later told Chris he was purposely very generous in his calculations so the couple would not get in over their heads.) The inspector spent four hours with the house and found only one small issue to fix: A railing had to be installed on the front steps.

Chris, Kaleigh, and Brooklyn moved into their new home and have never been happier. Ever since they repainted the front door and shutters a vibrant royal blue, Chris and Kaleigh's neighbors have been coming over to share how much they like what they've done to the house.

THE OLD RULES OF RESIDENTIAL REAL ESTATE

Chris and Kaleigh had a successful home-buying experience because they followed timeless rules of real estate (without being aware of them).

Rule 1: Educate yourself on the process.
Chris and Kaleigh went online and read about buying homes, visited many real estate Web sites, and became familiar with what was going on in their local housing market.

Rule 2: Learn the true value of homes in your neighborhood of choice.
Both Chris and Kaleigh looked online at homes that were for sale. They familiarized themselves with their neighborhood of choice and learned how quickly homes were selling and for how much money. They figured out which details were most important, including the size, amenities, price, and condition of each home, and then drove past those that looked most interesting to them.

Rule 3: Don't look at homes you can't afford.
Chris and Kaleigh used online calculators and figured out in advance how much money they could spend, and then they only looked at homes that fell within their budget, saving themselves potential heartache down the line.

Rule 4: Hire a great agent.
As we've discussed, a great agent brings experience and a deep understanding of neighborhood dynamics, which can help balance the emotional nature of the home-buying process. Chris and Kaleigh's agent helped them understand the history of the local housing stock and how they could make that work in their favor.

Rule 5: Build a great home-buying team.
Chris and Kaleigh's agent gave them a list of mortgage lenders and home inspectors she had worked with. The couple wound up using great professionals at every point in the buying process because they shopped around and took the time to make sure the companies they hired were on their game.

Rule 6: Make a fair offer.
Chris and Kaleigh offered just $3,000 less than the list price of the house. Their research showed them that the house was fairly priced

for the neighborhood and was in better condition than similar houses they'd seen. Making a fair offer based on real-life conditions showed the seller they were serious about the property, and the offer was accepted.

Rule 7: Be a good neighbor.

By repainting their front door and shutters, the couple showed they were serious about being homeowners and making a positive contribution to the community. And their neighbors responded just as positively.

Though following these time-tested rules of real estate will certainly help you have a successful home-buying experience, the housing and credit crises have changed the dynamic, requiring an additional set of rules.

THE NEW RULES FOR BUYING

In some areas of the country, neighborhoods and housing prices have been decimated by foreclosures and short sales. Neighbors who lived next door to each other for years have been ripped apart by job losses and "jingle mail" (walking away from a property and mailing one's keys to the lender—hence the term—rather than going through the process of foreclosure). Many homeowners and investors who bought at the peak of the market in 2006 and 2007 have watched their home's value "go under water" (be worth less than the remaining mortgage balance). For some, it's been worse: Their entire net worth has gone negative.

But in every crisis, there is an opportunity for those who are prepared to take action. This may be the best time in half a century to buy a home. The worst economic crisis since the 1930s has brought home prices to the most affordable level in nearly forty years; mortgage interest rates in 2009 touched a fifty-year low. A high unemployment rate means less competition for the homes that are for sale. If you have a job and good credit, the opportunity to buy a home may be as good as it can get.

Here are six new rules that will help guide you as you think about buying real estate today.

New Rule 1: Understand the relationship between income and house price.

Economists have long seen that annual income, interest rates, and house prices are intricately connected. Historically, a family could spend about two and a half times its annual income on a house if interest rates were between 8 and 10 percent, which they were for decades. (It's hard to imagine now, when we have been in an era of super-low interest rates for more than fifteen years, but for a long time, if you were able to finance a home purchase with an interest rate of less than 10 percent, you were doing very well.) So if you earned $40,000 a year, you could afford to buy a house that cost around $100,000. (Extraordinarily low mortgage interest rates change the calculus a bit, which I'll discuss in chapter 3.) In the mid-2000s, the price-to-income ratio shifted drastically from that historical rate. During the housing boom, people who earned $40,000 per year were being qualified to buy houses that cost $400,000. Home buyers were spending up to ten times their income by using exotic mortgages with negative equity or by committing mortgage fraud by putting down a fake salary on their mortgage application.

If you want to be a savvy home buyer in today's market, you need to look beyond your own income when buying a house; you also have to assess the incomes of the homeowners in your neighborhood of choice, which will help you determine where the housing prices in the area are going, and how quickly. For example, if a neighborhood is filled with people who work for the local municipality, housing prices will never really rise quickly, because the homeowners in that neighborhood have incomes that are typically limited by cost-of-living adjustments (COLA); in other words, they will get raises according to the cost of living. COLA is based on the rate of inflation, so salary increases are usually limited to 2 to 3 percent per year. If your neighborhood of choice is filled with CEOs who earn millions, as in the Hamptons in New York, prices may have no basis in reality; they could rise well beyond the rate of inflation or fall by millions of dollars based on factors such as economic fear or estate planning.

You have to look at the price-to-income ratio no matter where in the country you're buying. My husband, Sam, and I have some friends who live in Monticello, Indiana. They have a lovely Victorian house in this relatively sleepy town without a lot of industry. It's farm country, and as you wend your way along the nearby highways, you pass through other rural towns dominated by grain silos and plowed fields.

During the housing boom, buyers bought up attractive old Victorian homes in Monticello and renovated them. And even though everyone still worked basically the same job and had basically the same income, and incomes in town weren't rising, home prices doubled over the ten years leading up to the mid-2000s, appreciating at an average annual rate of more than 7 percent—far above the rate of inflation. Why? A bubble was forming there, as it was elsewhere in the country. Home buyers were priced out of Monticello's market. When the housing market crashed, those inflated housing prices came back in line with what the people in the community could afford ten to fifteen years before the bubble. Monticello's minibubble is instructive because it proves the rule about home prices being connected to income. When the people who worked in Monticello and needed to live there could no longer afford to buy there, the lack of demand caused housing prices to fall. If you had been a home buyer trying to make a decision about buying in Monticello, and you noticed that median home prices were that far out of line with the median income for the town, you might have been much more careful about the offer you were making—or perhaps you might have decided to rent and see whether housing prices would fall.

When deciding how much to spend on a particular house, it's important to look at the price-to-income ratio in light of the credit crisis. One of the little twists in the crisis has been the unpaid furloughs many employers are forcing on their employees. The average employee now works just over thirty hours a week. Even though he gets to keep his job, he must deal with a 25 percent cut in income (because he is working thirty hours instead of forty hours per week), and his home may now be unaffordable. If unpaid furloughs become standard and are not rolled back in the years to come, and new people are hired at lower wages, home prices might not go up at all for the next few years.

In order to figure out the housing price-to-median income ratio in your neighborhood of choice, start by hiring an agent who has worked the neighborhood for a number of years and is smart enough and savvy enough to generally understand the nature and careers of the people who live there. Then find out what kind of salaries they earn, and multiply the average by 2.5. If home prices are a lot higher than the average income, there may be little or no home price appreciation in the next few years, or longer.

New Rule 2: Learn to forecast your income.

If you don't have a job, you won't qualify to buy a house unless you have huge assets that can be pledged as collateral for the property. If you're a first-time buyer, chances are you don't have those assets. If you're a real estate investor, you may have assets, but you probably don't want to pledge them.

Most people who buy homes have jobs. Agents have often pushed home buyers (particularly young first-time buyers) to purchase property that costs a bit more than they want to spend, because the agents know that their clients might soon outgrow the space when they move on with their lives. The reasoning goes that you should spend a little more now so you can stay in your home a few more years before trading up when you are earning more money. But what happens if you don't make substantially more money? You may never feel comfortable with your financial situation if your income doesn't rise faster than your expenses and if you feel pinched from the start by the costs of owning a property, maintaining it, and paying taxes on it.

As a potential home buyer, you must consider all the possibilities when it comes to your income. It may rise, but it also may stay flat. With millions of Americans feeling the pinch in their wallets as a result of unpaid furloughs, it isn't unimaginable that your income may even drop. You might choose to leave a higher-paying job for one that pays less but is more satisfying, or you might buy a house with your spouse when you both have incomes, and down the road one of you may choose to stop working to care for your children. Or one of you might leave your job to start your own business, a risky venture in itself.

If you want to be a smart home buyer, you will learn how to forecast your income and then create a budget based on a realistic assumption of your earning potential. (For more details on how to do this, see chapter 5.)

New Rule 3: Buy your house as a home to be lived in, not an asset to be leveraged.

If the housing crisis has taught us anything, it's the definition of the word "leverage," which is the ability to buy an asset by borrowing against your future stream of income. When you get a mortgage that is for two and a half times your income, economists say you have leveraged your income. If you put down $10,000 on a $100,000 house, you've borrowed ten times the value of your cash down payment for a 10-to-1 leverage ratio. During the credit crisis, banks would often leverage their assets on a 30-to-1 basis.

At some point in time, we stopped thinking about our houses as places to live and started thinking of them as investments and assets to be leveraged, exploited, and traded. Home buyers would purchase and sell homes every twenty-four months in order to take advantage of the federal tax laws that permit you to keep as much as $250,000 (or $500,000 if you're married) in profits tax free when you sell.

While houses *are* assets that can grow in value long term and enforce savings (you save every time you pay down your mortgage and reduce your loan balance), they are primarily a recurring expense. You have to pay your mortgage, property taxes, and homeowners insurance and maintain the property, all of which cost money. It's a lot of work to maintain and improve a house, and decisions about this kind of work should be based not only on how much money you want to spend, or what you can afford, but also on how much responsibility you want to take. In many cases, this last factor explains why some people choose to rent for their entire lives when they have the means to own, or why some choose condominiums or maintenance-free communities over houses.

Depending on where you live, how many foreclosures are in your neighborhood, and other factors, your home may not enjoy any appreciation whatsoever over the next five to ten years, so make sure that when you buy your home, you'll enjoy living there.

New Rule 4: Focus on income if you want to invest in real estate.

Over the past ten years, I have read countless books proclaiming innovative ways to help you get rich by investing in real estate. For the most part, the advice is all very similar: Buy a house; put nothing down with either seller financing or a 100 percent loan from a mortgage lender; spruce up the property with a quick coat of paint, a new toilet, and curtains; and flip it for a fast 50 to 100 percent profit. From 2005 through 2009, roughly 40 percent of all homes sold were to second homeowners or investors rather than buyers who planned to occupy them full-time. Some properties were flipped for enormous profits several times in a year. It's easy to see how these fix-and-flip schemes not only allowed investors to recruit a few straw or fake buyers to whip real buyers into frenzied bidding wars, but also resulted in such a dramatic run-up in prices.

In very few of the books I read did the authors ever discuss a long-term buy-and-hold strategy for real estate investments, nor did they discuss creating a portfolio of rental properties or how difficult, time-consuming, and expensive the job of landlord can be. Most important, they rarely talked about how essential it is to use the income stream from an investment property to calculate its value and plan for the next real estate investment property.

Prior to the housing bubble, long-term real estate investors would search long and hard for a property that would generate enough income in rent to cover the expenses of ownership, maintenance, and insurance. If you bought a house for $100,000 and your expenses were $950 per month ($700 for the mortgage, $150 for taxes and insurance, and $100 for maintenance), ideally you would find a renter willing to pay $1,000 per month in rent. Over time, the rent would rise modestly, and you'd pay off the home and earn income from the property. If the home appreciated in value over ten or fifteen years, you could refinance it to take out some cash or sell it and use the cash for another investment property or two. In the housing boom, investment properties zoomed in price just as owner-occupied homes did, and the focus on income from rent faded as investors bought and flipped properties for price appreciation. But those days are mostly over. Because the housing market will suffer from too much inventory over the next few years, it's important to focus on how much income an investment property will generate, and not solely on price appreciation or the tax loss you'll generate from depreciation. And since property prices have declined so dramatically, it is possible to buy a house and take in enough rent to cover your mortgage, taxes, insurance, and maintenance.

While it is harder to finance investment properties today (remember the ten-property limits of Fannie Mae and Freddie Mac), you can build a substantial portfolio of income-producing investment properties. You'll need to put together a team that can help you understand how much rent landlords are getting in a particular neighborhood and how those rental rates translate into income and indicate a property's true value. Here's an example of how it can work.

In less than eighteen months in 2008 and 2009, a new real estate investor in Atlanta named Michael built a portfolio he estimates is worth $2 million. After his wife, a real estate agent, looked up all of the properties listed in one part of Atlanta that were on the market for $25,000 or less, he started scouting them out. Finding bargains became his full-time job. He and a partner wound up paying cash for a bunch of properties they bought for between $10,000 and $25,000 apiece and then spent near the same amount fixing each one up before renting them for around $800 per month. They invested $25,000 to $40,000 in each unit and made about $9,600 per year in income from each property. The properties will pay for themselves in two to three years, and Michael estimates that by then, values will have recovered somewhat in the neighborhood. He and his partner plan to hold these properties for the long term to generate a significant amount of cash.

New Rule 5: Rethink the concept of location.

Think of the mantra "location, location, location" as a method of evaluation. The first "location" refers to where the property is located in relation to the city or metropolitan area, the second "location" refers to the neighborhood in which the property is located, and the third "location" refers to where the home is located on a particular block (on some blocks, being in the middle of the block is more valuable; on others, the corner takes on a higher value). When you buy a house, you should carefully consider all three locations.

The housing crisis spawned yet another element of location that a potential home buyer must consider: distance to work.

During the housing boom, hundreds of thousands of homes were built in what were once considered undesirable locations: far from city centers, work centers, transportation arteries, and public transportation. Home buyers wanted to live in brand-new four- and five-bedroom homes with granite countertops and other niceties, but could only afford to buy in new communities that were way out there. (The late, great Chicago-based writer, Mike Royko, used to write about the "land beyond O'Hare," as if it were so far away he couldn't imagine anyone actually buying a home there. Today, many of those same suburbs he wrote about are the midway point to some of the newer, farther-away Chicago bedroom communities.)

Here's the thing: if you work in a city like Los Angeles, a home that is sixty to seventy miles away is not in a good location. Not only are you spending two to three hours in the car each day commuting, but you're spending thousands of dollars a year on gas. If everyone else who lives in the subdivision also works sixty to seventy miles away, it could seem like a successful subdivision—perhaps because it sold out quickly—but it is possibly unsustainable. If one thing goes wrong, the entire subdivision could go under.

While that sounds improbable, it happened frequently during the housing and credit crisis. Think about what happened in 2008 when the economy was faltering and a barrel of oil cost about $150. Gas prices at the pump hit $4 a gallon and people literally couldn't afford to drive to work. They quit their jobs (or were fired) and were effectively stranded at their homes sixty miles away from the city center. Without an income, they found that their overleveraged homes were unaffordable. In 2008 and 2009, there were hundreds of outlying subdivisions where the majority of homes went into foreclosure.

Gas prices and distance to work, family, and house of worship continue to be sensitive areas for many home buyers. The fear that gas prices will again increase dramatically hasn't gone away, and it is this fear that makes some of the millions of homes built over the past ten years undesirable for many of tomorrow's buyers.

Over the next few years, it may not pay to be a traditional real estate pioneer, settling in a new or regenerating neighborhood with the expectation of outsized returns when you sell. Rather, you want to pick those close-in neighborhoods that will see their value return and grow more quickly. Chances are that less desirable neighborhoods will be slow to recover, and thus won't see values stabilize and appreciate as fast as prime neighborhoods will.

New Rule 6: Know that all new construction is not created equal.

At the height of the building boom, more than a million new homes were built each year. Contractors and developers believed the party would never end. They sold hundreds of thousands of units off blueprints and charged escalating amounts as they introduced each new phase of a community. For an additional 25 to 50 percent of the purchase price, home buyers put in options and upgrades. The prices for these upgrades somehow managed to appraise out in value with the builder's lender, so buyers were able to get the mortgage amount they needed to cover the total price of the property.

And then it ended. After sales hit an all-time high in 2005 (1,283,000 units), they slipped to just over one million units in 2006, dropped by 25 percent in 2007 (to 776,000), and were down to 485,000 in 2008. Sales of new-construction homes in 2009 wound up at the lowest level since the National Association of Home Builders (NAHB) started keeping track in 1963, except for 1982, when interest rates passed 18 percent.

NEW HOMES SOLD

Year	Number in thousands	Year	Number in thousands
1963	560	1987	671
1964	565	1988	676
1965	575	1989	650
1966	461	1990	534
1967	487	1991	509
1968	490	1992	610
1969	448	1993	666
1970	485	1994	670
1971	656	1995	667
1972	718	1996	757
1973	634	1997	804
1974	519	1998	886
1975	549	1999	880
1976	646	2000	877
1977	819	2001	908
1978	817	2002	973
1979	709	2003	1,086
1980	545	2004	1,203
1981	436	2005	1,283
1982	412	2006	1,051
1983	623	2007	776
1984	639	2008	485
1985	688	2009*	430
1986	750		

Estimated annual sales based on current monthly rate of sales, as of November 30, 2009.

Data provided by the National Association of Home Builders.

In fact, sales slowed so much that even though in mid-2009 there were fewer than 200,000 new-construction homes for sale, the current rate of sale at the time made this number a ten-month supply of stock. Because so few buyers purchased new homes in 2008 and 2009, thousands—or even tens of thousands—of builders turned over their undeveloped, partly developed, or partly sold subdivisions to their lenders and went out of business. This caused more than 130 banks to fail in 2009, with hundreds more on the FDIC's watch list. The once-giant national home builders Pulte and Centex merged in order to survive.

Because the numbers are so frightening, you will have to be extremely cautious about buying in new-construction developments over the next few years as the housing market begins to level off. As I mentioned in the previous new rule, some of the issues relating to location apply to developments in new destinations that may no longer be considered desirable. In new condominium developments in places like South Florida, Phoenix, and Las Vegas, oversupply and foreclosed properties have created a surplus of new and fairly new construction that could make it difficult for housing to appreciate over the next few years, or even the next decade. Developments in areas far from city centers, as also discussed in the previous new rule, were built on the assumption that services would be built out after the community sold out; since they haven't, and likely won't anytime soon, buying into one of these communities could mean you'll be driving longer distances to get the basic necessities of life.

You should also be cautious about buying a cheap new home in a subdivision where the original developer has gone bankrupt. In many of these communities, amenities that were promised—such as clubhouses, tennis courts, swimming pools, and so on—have not been built and may never be built. You may have trouble getting financing for your purchase if not enough of the lots or homes have been sold. A subdivision that advertised home prices "starting in the $350s" before its developer went under may have to sell homes for substantially less if the lender reevaluates the price point to be much lower. That means that any homeowners who bought at the original $350,000 and wanted to sell their property would have to compete with new homes priced at two-thirds below that price or less. To sell, a homeowner might have to take a loss of more than $100,000 on the property. In some new developments, the developer is under extreme financial stress and you might find yourself ponying up for higher monthly maintenance costs to cover the amount the developer should have been contributing—but isn't. You might also find yourself living in a construction zone with unfinished roads, sidewalks, and other infrastructure for a decade or longer.

Even though the price-to-income ratio for existing homes has dropped back in line with historical trends (in 2009, it actually fell below median income), the price of new construction hasn't come down as far. To understand why this might be, it helps to think like a developer who wants to build a new home. In urban settings, one-third of the price of a new home comes from the cost of the land, one-third from construction costs, and the final third is for profit. In suburban or rural areas, the amount paid for land may be less, while the amount paid for construction costs may be more, so the ratio might be a little different.

Economists believe that many developers are just trying to hang on. If new home prices drop by a third or more, developers may not make a penny on their homes. If they drop by 50 percent or more, as they did in some parts of the country during 2008, they could lose so much money they'll go out of business. While it may make economic sense for developers to wait on new projects and sell off their existing inventory, it may not make financial sense for you to pay a higher price for a nearly new home rather than paying much less for an existing home that can be fixed up. (You can find someone to install granite countertops for you in the kitchen and bathrooms.) If you're thinking about buying a developer's home, you have to ask yourself if the development itself is worthwhile and if the location will thrive in the years ahead—or if you would be better off buying in a more established neighborhood where you could renovate the property to suit your own tastes over time.

THREE

THE NEW WORLD OF MORTGAGE FINANCE

Jenny and Bill are two professionals who rented during the boom years, saved their cash to someday buy a home, and then watched housing prices climb out of sight. They adjusted their thinking about what they could buy. But then the housing bubble began to pop. They waited, and as home prices and mortgage interest rates started to come down, they realized they might actually be able to afford to buy something other than a condo in the city where they live.

"Interest rates dropped to all-time lows," Jenny said. "More of our [mortgage] payment will go toward the house." It's comforting to know that even in the post-crisis world of mortgage finance, where so much seems new and different, basic math hasn't changed: Lower interest rates mean you'll pay much less in interest over the life of the loan.

In 2009, mortgage interest rates touched a fifty-year low: At one point you could get a thirty-year fixed rate loan for around 4.75 percent. The federal government was buying up its own offerings, hoping to push the thirty-year rate down even further, to 4.5 percent. That didn't happen, and in fact interest rates stayed at that super-low level for only a few weeks. In the meantime, plenty of homeowners took advantage of the superlow rates and refinanced.

With trillions of dollars being spent to stimulate the economy, the chatter about inflation began, and the bond market did a U-turn. Interest rates went up again to just over 5 percent, and then fell below 5 percent again in October and November, hitting 4.71 percent for a thirty-year fixed-rate mortgage before bouncing a little higher. Let me stop here and make one thing clear:

If you can borrow money for a mortgage at around 5 percent, take it! It's a historically low interest rate.

In 1982, mortgage interest rates were around 18 percent—and people still bought homes. If interest rates were that high today, the real estate market would flatline. (Actually, I'm guessing that if interest rates hit 10 percent, or perhaps even 9 percent, the real estate market would tank.) In 1989, when Sam and I bought our first home (a vintage co-op on Lake Shore Drive in Chicago), the interest rate on our loan was 11.75 percent. Two years later, we refinanced for a bit over 8 percent. In the 1990s, an interest rate under 7 percent was considered fantastic. Then, as the new century began, interest rates fell below 6 percent for the first time in forty years, and the thinking about long-term interest rates began to change. Now home buyers *expect* to get an interest rate in the low 5 percent range.

From a practical point of view, I don't think mortgage interest rates will stay quite this low over the long term. Eventually, as the economy improves, the Federal Reserve Bank will raise interest rates to ward off inflation. And the investors who buy U.S. mortgage-backed securities (or bonds) will demand a higher rate of return to buy the bonds. Why? Quite simply, we've lost the trust of investors around the world, who were sold U.S. mortgage-backed bonds as AAA-rated investments, except that many weren't. Once Uncle Sam backs off buying mortgage-backed securities, economists widely expect mortgage interest rates to rise by as much as 1 percent, as international investors demand a higher return on their investment. The rise and fall in mortgage interest rates is just one piece of the puzzle in the new world of mortgage finance. In this chapter, I will discuss the new rules of mortgage finance, plus give you some insight into what to expect when you finance your new purchase (or refinance your existing mortgage).

FINANCING (OR REFINANCING) YOUR HOME
IN AN ERA OF DECLINING HOME VALUES

I recently heard from Larry, who is wondering how to get out of his own mortgage hell.

He and his wife bought their home more than fifteen years ago. At the height of the boom, it was valued at $215,000. By 2009, thanks to a number of foreclosures in the area, it was appraised at $145,000. His mortgage balance is $153,000, or about 105 percent of the current value of the property.

· The problem that Larry and millions of other homeowners faced in 2009 was the continuing decline of property values all over the country. The decline was faster in some metro areas and slower in others, but in the hardest-hit communities like Phoenix or Las Vegas, home values were decimated, falling by more than 50 percent. Millions of Americans defaulted on their mortgage payments and went into foreclosure or bankruptcy. Thousands of homes were turned back to the lenders via deed-in-lieu-of-foreclosure (where the lender takes the deed to the house instead of filing to foreclose on the property) transactions.

In 2009, economists estimated that a full third of Americans owned properties that were worth less than the mortgage amount, known as being "underwater." Deutsche Bank issued a report that said 27 percent of homeowners with mortgages were underwater, and predicted as many as 48 percent of homeowners would be underwater by 2011. Many of these homeowners might qualify to refinance under President Barack Obama's "Making Home Affordable" plan, which allows homeowners whose loans are owned or guaranteed by Fannie Mae or Freddie Mac to refinance even if they don't have 20 percent equity in the property. In fact, these homeowners can refinance under the plan if their mortgages are worth 125 percent of the loan amount. Larry's house fits that home loan-to-value (LTV) ratio, but unfortunately his loan isn't owned or guaranteed by Fannie Mae or Freddie Mac, and his lender isn't playing along. Larry will probably be stuck with his loan until the housing market improves, or he'll hand over the keys to the lender and walk away, an option more underwater homeowners are considering.

If you're buying a home in an era of declining values, it's the best of times *and* the worst of times:

Financing your home purchase today will be tougher than it was before the housing and credit crises started. If you want to borrow more than the lender thinks the house is worth, don't have enough cash for a down payment, or have poor credit, you could have trouble getting a loan. Options like interest-only loans and negative amortization loans don't exist at the moment I'm writing this. And although credit scores did a poor job of indicating who would be at risk of defaulting in the perfect economic storm that created the credit crisis, they are still largely responsible for determining who will—or who won't—get a loan.

Changes in the appraisal process could spell problems for your financing. Whereas appraisers may have formerly overvalued properties, now they are undervaluing them. This can present problems if the home you want to buy needs to appraise high enough for the financing to work out. (I'll discuss the appraisal process in more detail later in this chapter.)

More foreclosures mean home values will continue to drop. The good news is you can spend less for a better home. The bad news is that once you own your property, its value may fall for a while before the housing market stabilizes in your neighborhood.

THE CHANGING ROLES OF FANNIE MAE AND FREDDIE MAC

Fannie Mae (originally called the Federal National Mortgage Association) was established as a federal agency in 1938 and chartered by Congress in 1968 to lend "liquidity, stability, and affordability" to the U.S. housing and mortgage markets, according to the company's Web site. Freddie Mac (originally called the Federal Home Loan Mortgage Corporation) was chartered by Congress in 1970 for the same purpose and to help create a stronger secondary mortgage market in the United States by providing a bit of competition to Fannie Mae. Both companies were originally set up as government-sponsored enterprises (GSEs), which are essentially private shareholder–owned companies created for a public purpose—in this case, helping Americans finance property. As leaders in the secondary mortgage market, Fannie Mae and Freddie Mac purchase all of the loans banks and mortgage lenders give to borrowers. They turn around and package those loans into investment-grade securities and resell them to investors all over the world. Because of this system, the U.S. mortgage market has never run out of cash. At one time, Fannie Mae and Freddie Mac were deemed so successful that executives from both companies consulted with countries all over the world on how to set up a secondary mortgage market to foster a thriving housing industry.

In 2008, when Fannie Mae and Freddie Mac were facing astronomical losses related to toxic subprime mortgages, the federal government took over the companies, put them into conservatorship (similar to bankruptcy) and provided *hundreds of billions* of dollars in cash to back up failing loans owned or guaranteed by the companies. (Some economists estimated that Fannie Mae and Freddie Mac still had additional losses in the hundreds of billions of dollars to be taken as 2010 started, and as a 2010 New Year's gift, the federal government agreed to absorb all future Fannie and Freddie losses without limit.) Fannie Mae and Freddie Mac essentially became part of the federal government. The Federal Housing Financing Agency (FHFA) was created to oversee the two companies as well as the Federal Home Loan Banks (a system of banks that provides loans to lending institutions) and regulatory responsibility for them was transferred through the Housing and Economic Recovery Act of 2008.

A decision regarding how Fannie Mae and Freddie Mac will be run, or whether they will be allowed to exit their conservatorship, isn't likely to be made before the housing crisis and credit crisis have long subsided. I expect the government to stand behind the debt of each company (the implicit "government-backed" guarantee was one reason why Fannie Mae and Freddie Mac were able to borrow money more cheaply than other companies and rack up incredible profits over the years) and continue to find a way to keep the mortgage market liquid. One likely possibility is that Fannie Mae and Freddie Mac will continue to be part of a government-run agency.

What does this mean for you? The government is now backing the vast majority of loans through Fannie Mae, Freddie Mac and FHA and will continue to do so for the next few years. While all those "government-backed" loans might pose a problem for U.S. taxpayers, if you want to buy a home or an investment property and you have good enough credit and enough cash, you shouldn't have a problem finding financing.

THE NEW RULES OF MORTGAGE FINANCE

While you can get mortgage financing if you have a job and good credit, it still isn't as easy to get financing as it was in 2005, when the joke was that if you had a pulse, you could get a loan. The new rules of mortgage finance are a lot like the very old rules of finance: not only do you need a pulse, but you also have to have a job, sufficient income, cash for a down payment, and cash reserves, and your house must appraise out in value under new, stricter appraisal rules.

Here are the new realities of mortgage finance that you'll face when you apply for a home loan:

1. Lenders require much higher credit scores.

Fair Isaac, a Minneapolis, MN–based company, created the FICO, which is the credit score used most often by creditors evaluating how risky a prospective borrower might be. FICO credit scores range from 350 (on the very low end) to 850. The top tier of credit scores range from 780 to 850. Subprime borrowers generally have FICO credit scores below 600. At the height of the boom, mortgage lenders allowed home buyers with credit scores in the low 500s (and even in the high 400s) to purchase homes. These borrowers weren't getting the best interest rates and terms, but they were able to close on their transactions. Today, you need a minimum credit score of around 580 to purchase a home with an FHA loan, and that number is only going to rise going forward. Most lenders will want to see a minimum FICO score of 620 to 660 for an FHA loan. Want the best rate and terms? You'd better walk through the door with a credit score of 760 or 780 rather than 720. With credit scores, the higher the better, and if you can get your score to 800 or more, you'll have a far easier time getting a mortgage with the best interest rate and terms and the fewest fees.

At Fair Isaac's Web site, MyFico.com, the difference in the interest rate you'll get on a loan if you land in the top tier of credit scores (760 to 850) and the rate you'll get if you're in the bottom (620 to 639) is around 1.6 percent. As the market fluctuates, that number might change, but here's how it breaks down:

Credit Score	Loan Amount	Interest Rate	Monthly Payment	Interest Paid Over Loan Term
760–850	$200,000	4.571%	$1,022.00	$167,855.00
700–759	$200,000	4.793%	$1,048.00	$177,457.00
680–699	$200,000	4.970%	$1,070.00	$185,192.00
660–679	$200,000	5.184%	$1,096.00	$194,646.00
640–659	$200,000	5.614%	$1,150.00	$213,975.00
620–639	$200,000	6.160%	$1,220.00	$239,111.00

Source: Credit score and interest rate information from MyFico.com, December 8, 2009

The 1.589 percent difference between the interest rate you'd get with a top-tier credit score versus the lowest tier could cost you around $71,256 over the life of the loan, or more, if you include the extra fees you'll have to pay along the way. The bottom line is that you should work on building up and maintaining the highest credit score you can, because it'll pay off for the entire term of your loan. (Want to get perfect credit forever? Check out chapter 4, "Fixing Your Credit History and Credit Score for Life.")

2. You need a down payment of at least 3.5 percent for an FHA loan.

In the boom years, you didn't actually need to have cash to buy a house. You could get a zero down payment loan (several options were available for 100 to 106 percent financing that included costs of closing), or you could use a company that arranged for you to get a gift from the seller to fund the down payment required by the FHA. (As we discussed earlier, these third-party companies would get 4 percent from the seller and then turn around and offer the buyer 3 percent—and keep the difference. Because of a higher-than-average default rate for these loans, the FHA has changed the rules to eliminate these seller-funded down payment programs.)

As of January 1, 2009, the FHA began requiring buyers to have more skin in the game. If you want an FHA loan—these currently account for 25 percent of the market, up from the low single digits during the height of the boom—you'll need a 3.5 percent down payment. If you want to get conventional financing through Fannie Mae or Freddie Mac, you'll need at least 5 percent in cash and a very good credit score. The worse your credit score is, the more cash you'll need. You may not be able to get better than a 93 percent loan if your credit score is lower than 720. (As we close out 2009, it is widely expected that FHA will raise its minimum down payment requirement to at least 5 percent, delaying homeownership for thousands of families that haven't saved up enough money.)

3. You need additional cash for reserves and closing costs.
First-time home buyers traditionally have trouble finding extra cash in their budget for a down payment; they can typically manage their monthly payments for mortgage, property taxes, and insurance only because they're used to paying a hefty amount in rent. Today, not only do you need at least 3.5 to 5 percent in cash for a down payment, but you also need cash for reserves and closing costs.

In 2009, lenders were requiring up to six months in cash reserves of your mortgage payment, property taxes, and homeowners insurance premium for a conventional loan (not FHA, Veteran's Administration, also known as VA, or USDA's rural development loans). If, for example, your monthly mortgage, tax, and insurance payments total $1,500, you'll need $9,000 in cash reserves to close on your property. Why so much? Lenders want to know that if you run into financial trouble for any reason (including if you lose a job or get sick), these expenses will continue to be paid on time. The problem is that if you lose your job, you might not find one for six months or longer. Ideally, you'd have six months' to a year's worth of living expenses saved, but not many folks have that kind of cash just lying around.

Having enough cash for closing costs is another concern for home buyers these days. Lenders were once happy enough to finance your closing costs; today, it's extremely difficult to find a lender that will allow you to have a "zero cost" loan that includes your closing costs in the amount financed for a slightly higher interest rate on the loan. You'll need to have cash to pay your closing costs—another reason why it's a good idea to shop around and compare lenders' fees.

4. Acceptable debt-to-income ratios have been slashed.

The debt-to-income ratio compares the monthly cost of the debt you're carrying (mortgage, auto loan, credit card debt, school loans, personal debts, and so on) with the amount of gross income (before tax) you're bringing in each month. At the height of the boom, lenders were accepting up to a 50 percent debt-to-income ratio, which means that if you had monthly debt payments of $2,000, your gross monthly income would have been around $4,000. That translated into debt payments of as much as 60 to 70 percent of your take-home paycheck.

These days, lenders are accepting a debt-to-income ratio of only 30 to slightly more than 40 percent (depending on whether you're getting a conventional loan, a government-backed loan such as FHA or VA, or a special loan through a local housing agency funded with Community Development Block Grant funds). If you factor in only housing expenses (not counting auto and school loans and credit card debt), the total debt-to-income ratio should be no more than 42 percent at the very top, lenders say.

That lower level of debt is "good for our economy. It's good for the person buying the home," said Stan, a senior loan consultant in Orange County, California. Less debt means you're less likely to get into trouble down the line. When your debt payments equal 70 percent of your take-home pay, you're living on the edge. "All you have to do is look in the faces of young couples who are losing their homes because of too much debt. That breaks your heart. It's almost broken our country because of greed," he adds.

5. Prepayment penalties are being eliminated.

Paying off your loan before it's due can save you thousands of dollars in interest. But during the boom, many subprime loans came with steep prepayment penalties that prohibited borrowers from paying their mortgages off early. If you paid your loan off within the first two to four years, because you had the cash, sold the home, or refinanced the mortgage, you would be charged anywhere from 2 to 4 percent of the loan amount. Many borrowers I've heard from over the years who had to pay prepayment penalties had no idea what these were or how costly they'd be—even though they signed prepayment penalty disclosure forms in their loan documents.

Subprime borrowers weren't the only borrowers who had loans with prepayment penalties. Some lenders offered conventional loans with prepayment penalties in exchange for lowering the interest rate by a quarter of a point (a point is 1 percent of the loan amount). While that may have sounded like a smart money move to borrowers who couldn't imagine paying off their loan ahead of schedule, in reality it simply limited their options and opportunities.

Prepayment penalties are now seen (correctly) as onerous for buyers.

It's another complicated, poorly-explained-to-buyers profit center for investors. But with the government looking to streamline the mortgage financing process and make it much more transparent, prepayment penalties are looked at as an unacceptable addition to conventional or government-backed financing. If you need a subprime loan, however, you may still run into them.

6. If you want the best financing, you need to shop around.

When my friends Beth and Mark were shopping around to refinance their primary loan, they were quoted closing costs of several thousand dollars from one lender and $300 from another. (They went with the lowest-cost loan, which also happened to carry the lowest interest rate.) Beth and Mark live in a suburb north of Chicago, but each week on my radio show I'd hear from folks across the country who were experiencing the same thing. Closing costs and fees varied widely from lender to lender in the wake of the crisis, a fact I found rather interesting.

You might think that with Fannie Mae, Freddie Mac, and the FHA guaranteeing the vast majority of home loans, costs from lender to lender would be more or less the same. They're not. In fact, the cost to get a mortgage can vary by thousands of dollars. Some of the discrepancy has to do with how lenders deal with folks who have lower or higher credit scores. But mostly it has to do with profits. Big bank lenders like Citibank, Bank of America, and Wells Fargo need to earn big profits. One way they're earning money is by ratcheting up loan origination charges and fees.

Each lender has the right to set its own interest rates, points, and fees. And you have the right to shop around with a variety of lenders to find the best deal. In my opinion, home buyers should visit several different types of mortgage lenders:

- **A big bank** that does mortgage loans (such as Citibank, Bank of America, J. P. Morgan Chase, or Wells Fargo, and others which I sometimes refer to collectively as big box lenders)
- **A smaller community bank** that does mortgage loans
- **A mortgage broker** (who might work with a bunch of different end investors)
- **An online lender** (like ING Direct or Quicken Mortgage)
- **A credit union** (if you can join one or belong to one)

Credit unions are typically nonprofit and tend to offer excellent deals on home and auto loans. They are government-regulated and are insured for deposits up to $250,000, just like FDIC-insured banks. Most folks don't think about visiting their credit union to check out deals on home or auto loans, but you should. And there are several credit unions, like Delta Airlines's credit union, that are open to the public. Anyone can join. Look for a credit union near you by going to the Web site of the Credit Union National Association (CUNA.org).

7. Condos are harder and more expensive to finance than single-family homes.

You might think that a house is a house to a mortgage lender. Whether it's a condo, a co-op, a townhome, or a single-family house, as long as it provides shelter, qualifies for the tax write-offs, and appraises out in value, it's a property to be financed in the mind of a mortgage lender or an end investor.

Guess again. The credit crisis has refocused attention in some areas on just how bad an investment a condominium can be. Many condos were bought by people who couldn't afford to buy a single-family home. They stretched their budgets to buy a condo, thinking it would be less expensive than a single-family home. But a condo comes with other expenses and issues that single-family homes don't have, such as monthly maintenance costs (known simply in some areas as "assessments" or "carrying costs"), special assessments (extra cash needed for specific maintenance, renovation or improvement costs), condo insurance, and condo reserves.

When the stock market dropped and incomes were slashed and jobs eliminated, condo owners who were affected found they couldn't afford to pay their assessments. So these condo owners—from the senior in Miami whose income was reduced by the 45 percent dip in the stock market to the twenty-something in Boston who lost his job—stopped paying. In some parts of the country, so many condo owners stopped paying their assessments that buildings had to tap into their cash reserves for necessary maintenance and repairs. Or they had to schedule special assessments, which nobody liked.

As a result, lenders are now checking to see how many people in a development are paying their monthly assessments. Lenders say that they will not underwrite the financing if more than 15 percent of owners aren't paying their assessments or are late with their payments, unless the development's cash reserves are enormous. In this market, that means you won't get the loan. In fact, this rule is so important that some lenders tell their borrowers not to even bother looking in a condominium development that has an assessment-paying problem. It's a waste of everyone's time.

There are other financing challenges with condominiums. FHA issued new rules in November 2009 that state it won't finance condos in a multiuse property (that has residential and commercial uses) if the commercial space occupies more than 25 percent of the total square footage. You also won't be able to get an FHA or Fannie Mae loan if a single investor owns more than 10 percent of the total number of units (this applies to units owned by the developer as well, although there are a few exceptions going through). Other lenders' condo rules state that you'll pay a 0.75 percent fee if you finance a condo and don't put down at least 25 percent (this rule was rescinded in 2009 for detached condos). Another challenge relates to buying condos as investment properties. According to Dan, a senior loan officer in Chicago, you cannot finance an investment property purchase with Fannie Mae or Freddie Mac if you already own ten properties including your personal residence (and some lenders won't do the loan if you own a total of four properties). In addition, you have to watch out for how many condos in a condo building are already rented out. If more than 50 percent of the units are rented, you won't be able to get an FHA loan. If more than 30 percent are rented, you won't be able to get Fannie Mae or Freddie Mac financing. To be an FHA-approved condo building, the condo board will have to do a "reserve study" each year, which analyzes how much cash is available for maintenance and repairs. And, if you want your FHA loan to close, you'll need a permanent certificate of occupancy, not a temporary certificate of occupancy.

While some of these rules may ease, change, or be eliminated over time, you can expect to have a tougher time financing a condominium versus a single-family home, especially if you don't put down at least 20 percent in cash. To find the latest rules, go to HUD.gov or search ThinkGlink.com.

8. All the information you provide will be verified.

This is the polar opposite of what was going on a few short years ago. In the heyday of the housing market, stated-income loans, in which nothing was verified, were all the rage. If you put down on your loan application that you worked for Walmart and earned $60,000 as a part-time greeter, that fact—however absurd—wouldn't be checked.

"People inflated their income by a thousand or two thousand dollars a month," recalled Stan, the loan officer in Orange County, California. "Lenders told borrowers, 'You can state your income, you can state your assets. We don't care how much money you have in the bank.' They never verified income or assets on the loan."

Lyndra, a mortgage originator in Baton Rouge, Louisiana, said, "In the late 1990s, the computer underwriting engine was approving loan applications that a human would have never approved."

Thanks to the extremely high rate of default of stated-income loans since the peak of the market, you should expect that every piece of information on your loan application will be verified by someone in the lender's office.

9. If you're self-employed, you'll have to provide even more documentation proving income and assets.

Here's the power of a W-2 form and a paystub: it helps tell a lender how much you earn. Self-employed people rarely have a W-2. Often, their income is shown by a stack of 1099s or cash receipts. It may not be fair, but if you're self-employed, be prepared to come to the table with even more documentation than a salaried employee would; otherwise, you might not qualify for the loan.

Mortgage originator Lyndra said that in the summer of 2008, if she met with someone who was self-employed, was able to put down 20 percent in cash, and had a credit score of 700, she was required only to get a verbal verification that the borrower had been in business for at least two years. By February, 2009, that same customer was also required to provide his or her most current tax return. Some lenders now require copies of the past two years of tax returns—or more—plus a current profit-and-loss statement from the company. (See the next section for a more extensive list of documents that may be required when you finance property.)

10. If you're buying investment property, you'll have to have at least 20 percent in cash.

If you're going to invest in real estate, you must be prepared to put down at least 20 percent in cash if you plan to use a loan owned or guaranteed by Fannie Mae or Freddie Mac. But that's only the beginning. Even if you put down 20 percent in cash, you'll also pay a 3 percent fee, which will either be required up front or built into the interest rate (making it higher), or both. If you put down 25 percent, the fee falls to 1.75 percent of the loan amount, paid up front in cash or built into the interest rate.

Under current guidelines, the GSEs will allow you to own up to ten properties at any one time, including your primary residence and vacation home. But because so many investors bought real estate with very little down, and then walked away when property prices plummeted, lenders are requiring a firm cash commitment in order to provide financing. (And as I previously discussed, some lenders will not finance additional properties if you own a total of four already.)

There are a very few other options for financing real estate investments at the moment, which I'll discuss later in this chapter.

11. Seller financing is making a comeback.

One promising option for investment property or a home you're going to live in is seller financing. In the 1980s, when conventional financing was difficult to obtain and mortgage interest rates were in the double digits, sellers tried everything to attract a buyer. One thing that worked was to offer seller financing. But once conventional interest rates began falling in the early 1990s, seller financing no longer seemed as attractive to buyers, as banks stepped in to offer no-fee and no-cost loans and superlow interest rates. Sellers couldn't compete with what the banks offered, and many sellers had their own mortgages to pay off, so seller financing fell out of favor.

Homeowners who own their homes free and clear can offer to act as the bank for prospective buyers. The seller agrees to finance a percentage of the purchase price, with the buyer making some sort of a down payment (or putting nothing down, if the seller agrees to it). If the seller finds a good buyer, this can be a win-win situation: the seller gets to sell the property and generate a substantial stream of income, and the buyer gets a less costly loan, typically without all the costs and fees a regular lender will charge, and a home.

But as a buyer, you have to be careful if you're planning on doing seller financing. You have to be sure that the seller doesn't have a mortgage on the property, or, if he or she does, that it is small enough to be paid off with your cash down payment. Next, you have to make sure that the loan documents are drawn up properly so they protect you. Your best bet is to hire your own attorney to draft the documents, check out whether the seller has financing, and make sure any loans or liens will be paid off with the closing proceeds; purchase a lender's and an owner's title insurance policy; and ensure that the purchase closes properly and the necessary documents are recorded.

In addition, if you're counting on your regular, on-time mortgage payments to help improve your credit history and score, you'll have to negotiate with the seller to report your on-time payments to the three credit-reporting bureaus. The seller will have to sign up with the bureaus, or the loan may not be reported on your credit history at all.

If you're interested in seller financing, ask your real estate agent to search for properties that include in the listing "seller financing available." Or if you find a property you like that has been for sale for a while and the seller owns it outright, you can ask the listing agent if the seller would be interested in offering seller financing to sweeten the deal.

DOCUMENT CHECKLIST FOR YOUR MORTGAGE LOAN APPLICATION

What can you do to increase the likelihood you'll get the home loan you need? Start by getting your documentation together. According to Erin, a loan officer in Chicago, an easy way to think about what you'll need in terms of documentation is to remember the number 2.

"If you're a salaried borrower, it's actually very standard. You'll need two years of W-2s, a thirty-day history of pay stubs, and verification of employment. For self-employed or commissioned workers, you'll need two years of tax returns. The investor will want a two-year history of residency and a two-year history at your current job. If you're a commissioned worker and the commission isn't guaranteed, the investor will flinch at that," Erin explained.

To apply successfully for a home loan, start by gathering together the following information. The list is long and detailed, and your mortgage lender may not ask for everything on it—or may ask for documentation not listed. But if you want your home loan application process to go smoothly, it pays to get your documentation in order before you ever apply.

1. **W-2 forms for each person who will be a co-borrower on the loan:** You'll also want to provide contact information for the human resources managers, or your direct bosses, so the mortgage lender can verify your income.
2. **Copies of completed federal tax forms for the last two or three years, including any schedules or attachments:** These will be required primarily of self-employed individuals or those who are claiming a history of rental income. Either way, you won't need your state returns.
3. **Copies of one month's worth of pay stubs:** If you're self-employed, you'll need to show profit and loss statements for the current year plus other information that shows how much you've taken out of the business.
4. **Copies of the last two or three bank statements for every bank account, IRA, 401(k), Keogh, or other retirement account or brokerage account the co-borrowers own:** Bring a copy of your most recent statement for any other assets you have. Be prepared to provide six months or more of bank statements upon request.

This may come up if you're using gift money for the down payment or if there is some question as to where cash has come from in an account.

5. **A copy of the back and front of your canceled earnest money check and the escrow deposit receipt:** If you don't get your canceled checks back, then access the electronic version on your account and print it out.

6. **A copy of the fully executed sales contract and all riders:** You'll need the name, address, and phone numbers of both the buyer's agent (if you're using a broker or an agent) and listing broker, and the same information for both your attorney and the seller's attorney (if you're living in a state where real estate attorneys are used to close residential sales).

7. **If you're selling a residence at the same time that you're buying a different one, a copy of the listing agreement and, if the home you are selling is under contract, a copy of the fully executed sales contract:** Be prepared to provide the contact information for the brokers and attorneys for your sale as well, if you're far enough down the line for that. When the property closes, you may be asked to provide a copy of the actual disposition of funds from the escrow account.

8. **If gift or grant funds are involved, proof from the giver (or granter) that he or she had the money to give, such as a copy of a recent bank statement:** If you're receiving a grant, the granter should provide you with a letter outlining the grant and stating that the funds do not need to be repaid. Be prepared to show the paper trail for the grant, including a deposit slip. The giver will have to fill out a gift letter affidavit, available from the loan officer, indicating that the funds were a gift and the giver does not expect repayment. You will need to provide a copy of the check, the deposit receipt, and a bank statement verifying the deposit.

9. Copies of all divorce decrees and property settlement agreements.

10. Copies of a current survey or title insurance commitment for the home you're buying: If these are available when you apply for the mortgage, or if they become available during the purchase process, you may need to provide them to your lender. In most states, the preliminary title report takes the place of a survey, lenders say. But a survey may be required in some states, such as New Mexico.

11. If you're self-employed, complete copies of the last two years of federal business tax returns and a year-to-date profit-and-loss statement and balance sheet with the original signatures: Some lenders will agree to use a letter from your CPA stating that you are self-employed, or a copy of your business license, but have your tax returns and profit and loss handy.

12. A list of your addresses in the last two years.

13. Proof of deposit: If you've made any large deposits (that is, anything larger than your monthly salary) to your bank account in the last three months, be prepared to provide an explanation with proof of where the funds came from.

14. Explanation of funds: If you've opened a new bank account in the last six months, write a letter explaining where the money came from to open the account.

15. Contact information and account numbers for every form of credit you have: Alternatively, many lenders will request your credit history. Pull a copy from each of the three credit-reporting bureaus (Equifax, Experian, and TransUnion) at AnnualCreditReport.com before you apply so you'll see what they see. Pay for a copy of your credit score from Equifax (its Beacon score most closely mirrors the FICO score) while you're there (approximately $8) so you know what you're facing. Or go to MyFico.com and

purchase a copy of your combined credit history from the three credit-reporting bureaus plus a credit score for $39. (A new law requires lenders to have you sign a document permitting them to access your credit history.)

16. **Documentation to verify additional income sources:** If you're receiving additional income from sources such as Social Security, long-term disability, child support, alimony, or even lottery winnings, be prepared to provide proof.

17. **Documentation surrounding a bankruptcy, foreclosure, or short sale:** If you've had a previous bankruptcy, foreclosure, or short sale, make sure you have a complete copy of the proceedings, including all schedules, a letter explaining the circumstances, and, in the case of a bankruptcy, the discharge certificate.

18. **Documentation to prove your identity:** For most loans today, you'll need a photocopy of a picture ID (usually your driver's license or U.S. passport) and, in some cases, a copy of your Social Security card. For VA loans, you will need proof of enlistment (your DD214) and a certificate of eligibility for the loan (details are available at www.va.gov).

19. **If you have any judgments against you that have been paid in full, a copy of the recorded satisfaction of judgment:** If you have a judgment against you that has not yet been paid in full, or if you are currently involved in litigation, you'll need copies of documents describing any lawsuits. You may also be required to settle and pay off any judgments prior to closing on the loan. (Know that if you are being sued and could be at risk of a big judgment against you, it may be extremely difficult to get financing.)

20. **Proof of rental income:** If you're buying a new primary residence and turning your existing home into a rental property, you'll need to show a signed lease agreement as well as proof of receiving the security deposit from the new renter. You should also be prepared

to prove that you have at least 30 percent equity in the existing property.

TODAY'S LOAN OPTIONS: FIXED-RATE VERSUS ADJUSTABLE-RATE MORTGAGES

Home buyers and real estate investors have two basic options when it comes to financing: the conventional fixed-rate mortgage and the slightly less conventional adjustable-rate mortgage (ARM).

Fixed-rate mortgages: Whether the loan lasts fifteen years, thirty years, forty years, or even fifty years, the interest rate and the principal and interest portion of the monthly payment will never change over the term of the mortgage. (And yes, fifty-year mortgages were offered briefly, to allow people to qualify to buy homes that were way more expensive than they could afford.) The amount taken for property taxes and insurance premiums, however, will rise over time as these costs rise. Fixed-rate mortgages are considered the least risky loans you can purchase and have been a staple of home lending for decades.

Adjustable-rate mortgages: The basic premise of an ARM is that the loan has a fixed interest rate for a period of time, and then the loan adjusts into a variable rate that changes every month, every year, or every few years. When the ARM adjusts, you get a new amortization schedule so you know how much you have to pay to get the loan paid off in the years remaining in the term. Typically, the interest rate on an ARM can rise no more than 1 or 2 percentage points per year and has a lifetime cap of 5 or 6 percentage points. To compensate for the risk that the loan's interest rate will rise, ARMs generally offer a starting interest rate that is below that of a fixed-rate mortgage.

ARMs come in all shapes and sizes. In one common type of ARM sold today, the payments are fixed for a period of years (one, three, five, seven, or ten), after which the loan converts into a one-year ARM that fluctuates each year based on the index to which it is tied. Another type of ARM is fixed for a period of years and then converts into a fixed-rate mortgage at the new interest rate. The shorter the initial fixed period of the loan, the lower the initial interest rate.

If you're shopping around for a home loan, you'll take the least amount of risk with a fixed-rate mortgage. These mortgages require you to make fixed payments of principal and interest (the payments do not change through the life of the mortgage). The amortization schedule is set up so that the first few years of payments are almost entirely interest with little principal repaid, and the latter years are almost all principal payments with little or no interest paid. With a higher rate than that of an ARM, a fixed-rate mortgage limits the amount you can borrow unless you extend the length of the loan beyond the traditional thirty years.

Before the housing crisis, if you couldn't afford the house you wanted on an ARM that had principal and interest payments, you could choose either an interest-only ARM or a pay-option ARM. Interest-only ARMs were structured so that you only paid the interest due on the money you borrowed. The payments did not include any principal, although you could choose to pay more each month. But you would never owe more than you borrowed. With pay-option ARMs, interest rates started at 1 or 2 percent, and the difference between the starting interest rate and the actual stated interest rate would be tacked onto the balance of the loan. These are called "negative amortization loans" (also known as "neg-am"), and they essentially allowed the borrower to get a much bigger loan than he or she could afford to pay off.

Today, borrowers are limited in their financing options to a fixed-rate mortgage or one of several types of ARMs, all of which require principal and interest payments each month. None of them are negative amortization loans.

WHAT YOU NEED TO KNOW ABOUT FHA LOANS

The Federal Housing Administration (FHA) was started in 1934 and has helped more than thirty-five million people become homeowners. FHA loans are backed by the full faith and credit of the U.S. government, which means if they fail, the U.S. taxpayer picks up the tab. They were relatively unpopular for a long time, accounting for just a tiny percentage of all loans made over the past twenty years because they were deemed much more complicated and less flexible than conventional loans. Today, FHA loans currently account for about a quarter of the U.S. mortgage market. They're popular because they require a much smaller down payment than Fannie Mae and Freddie Mac loans, and lenders will take a lower credit score. Here's what you need to know about these loans if you're considering applying for one:

- **Lenders are requiring borrowers to have a credit score of at least 620.** Previously, you could qualify for an FHA loan if your credit score was 580 or even lower.
- **Lenders have to be FHA approved.** If you want to get an FHA loan, you'll need an FHA-approved lender. Not all lenders do FHA loans, and those that do are audited every year. You can find one through one of the 2,300 housing counseling programs certified by the Department of Housing and Urban Development (HUD) nationwide; find a program online at HUD.gov, or call toll-free at (800) 569-4287. HUD.gov offers a ""Lender Locator" search function to find an FHA-approved lender by ZIP code. You can access the page here: www.hud.gov/ll/code/llslcrit.cfm.

- **All FHA loans come with mortgage insurance (MI).** If you get an FHA loan, you'll pay 0.5 percent in mortgage insurance, which may rise soon because there has been talk of increasing the amount in order to fill up FHA's reserves. You'll have to pay your FHA MI premium for as long as you have the loan, no matter how much equity you have in the property. With conventional loans, you may be able to get private mortgage insurance (PMI) taken off your monthly bill once the equity in the property reaches 20 to 25 percent (the amount depends on the lender and how long you've had the loan).

- **FHA loans have risk-based pricing.** The lower your credit score, the higher your interest rate. The inverse is true, too: The higher your credit score, the lower the interest rate you'll pay on your loan.

- **The minimum FHA down payment is 3.5 percent.** On January 1, 2009, the FHA raised its minimum down payment to 3.5 percent from 3 percent. However, a buyer may receive gift funds from a family member or friend to come up with that down payment. You may also qualify for down payment programs sponsored by HUD or your local housing authority. To find out what kinds of HUD-funded local programs are available, go to www.HUD.gov/buying/localbuying.cfm. Later, I'll discuss how to search online for down payment programs.

- **Sellers can pay up to 6 percent of closing costs.** This is an excellent way to get the seller to contribute to the pot outside of lowering the price of the property.

- **FHA allows higher debt-to-income levels than conventional loan lenders.** If you have student loans, a car payment, and credit card debt, you might still qualify for an FHA loan even if you no longer qualify for a Fannie Mae or Freddie Mac loan.

- **The property you buy will need an appraisal.** If you're financing with the FHA, the property has to be appraised for three reasons: To find out its estimated market value; to make sure it meets the

FHA's minimum property requirements and standards for health, safety, soundness, and structural integrity; and to make sure it is marketable in the event that you default.

- **As with all purchases, you should get a professional home inspection.** An FHA appraisal is not the same thing as a home inspection, and even though the appraiser is looking for big problems, the appraisal may not alert you to potentially expensive physical problems with the property. Savvy buyers will hire their own professional home inspector to do a thorough assessment of the physical condition of the home.
- **The FHA has requirements regarding a past bankruptcy, short sale, or foreclosure.** Fannie Mae and Freddie Mac also require a waiting period of between two to five years after a short sale, foreclosure or bankruptcy, depending on the circumstances. The rules are changing as I write this, so be sure to check with your lender before you start the financing process.
- **You don't have to be a U.S. citizen to qualify for an FHA loan.** The FHA will insure the mortgages of lawful permanent resident aliens just as it will for U.S. citizens. If you're a nonpermanent resident alien, the FHA will insure your loan as long as you provide proof of a valid Social Security number and a copy of your Employment Authorization Document (EAD) issued by the Bureau of Citizenship and Immigration Services (BCIS).
- **FHA loans are assumable.** If you choose an FHA loan, you may wind up with an extra marketing push when it comes time to sell. All FHA loans are assumable, provided the buyer can qualify for the payments. With interest rates at historic lows, if you ever decide to sell your property, a buyer may be able to pay a small fee and assume the loan. This will save a buyer a lot of cash, making your house much more marketable. The buyer will just have to go through the process of qualifying for the loan, but assuming an

FHA loan would be far less costly than acquiring new financing. To learn more about FHA loans, go to HUD.gov.

WHAT TO DO WHEN YOU DON'T HAVE A DOWN PAYMENT: OPTIONS FOR 100 PERCENT LOANS

For many years, 100 percent mortgage loans were a fast ticket to home-ownership for first-time buyers who didn't have a lot of cash (or any cash) for a down payment. The credit crisis has almost completely wiped out zero-down mortgage loans, as investors are still reeling from all the toxic loans approved during the housing boom. But there are still two ways to finance 100 percent of the purchase price of a property: with a VA loan or with a USDA Rural Direct Housing loan.

VA Loans

VA loans are backed by the full faith and credit of the federal government through the Department of Veterans Affairs. The VA housing guaranty of 25 percent (the government assumes payment of the top 25 percent of the mortgage in case of default) protects the lender should the veteran default on the mortgage and allows the veteran to finance up to 100 percent of the purchase price, as long as the property falls within the price limits for the county set by the VA. (In 2009, county price limits ranged from $423,750 in places like Weber County, Utah to $1,094,625 in San Mateo County, California.)

- **Eligibility**: VA loans are available only to those who have served at least 90 days on active duty during wartime service (including World War II, the Korean War, and the Vietnam War) and been discharged with something other than dishonorable conditions. In addition, you must have served at least 181 days of continuous service during peacetime, with the same discharge requirements. If you served fewer days but were discharged because of a service-related disability, an approved medical condition, an involuntary reduction in the number of armed forces, or "at the convenience of the government," you may also be eligible for a VA loan.

If you're on active duty now, you'll qualify once you have served 181 days (90 days during the Gulf War), with some exceptions. A Selected Reserve or National Guard member with a long enough service history (Selected Reserve personnel must have served a minimum of six years, with points earned for weekend drills or active duty for training and received an honorable discharge; National Guard members must have served at least six years and been honorably discharged) would also qualify for a VA loan, as would an "unremarried spouse of a veteran who died while in service or from a service disability" or the spouse of a service person who is missing in action or a prisoner of war, according to the VA Web site (homeloans.va.gov).

"Individuals with service as members in certain organizations, such as Public Health Service officers, cadets at the United States Military, Air Force, or Coast Guard Academy, midshipmen at the United States Naval Academy, officers of the National Oceanic & Atmospheric Administrations, merchant seamen with World War II service, and others" may also be eligible. For more details on VA loan eligibility, go to www.homeloans.va.gov/elig2.htm.

If you are eligible under these guidelines, you'll need a certificate of eligibility (which will no longer display your birth date; you'll have to prove that fact to the lender with another form of identification). In some cases, your lender will be able to access your certificate of eligibility online using special software. Otherwise, you'll need to download and complete VA Form 26-1880 (available online at www.vba.va.gov/pubs/forms/vba-26-1880-ARE.pdf) and send it to the VA Loan Eligibility Center, P.O. Box 20729, Winston-Salem, NC 27120, along with proof of military service.

- **Qualification:** Although you may have a certificate of eligibility from the VA, you still have to qualify financially for a VA loan. That means you have to have a credit score of 620 or higher. A past bankruptcy also plays a role in your ability to be qualified. If you went through a bankruptcy that was discharged two years ago or more, the lender may ignore it. But if it was discharged within the past twelve months, you probably won't qualify for a VA loan.

- **Costs:** Even if you are eligible for a VA loan, it will be expensive, especially if you don't have any cash for the down payment. While the whole point of a zero-down loan is to avoid shelling out any cash, the VA requires regular military veterans who are using their entitlement for the first time to pay a funding fee of 2.15 percent of the purchase price if they want to borrow 100 percent. If you put down 5 to 10 percent, the funding fee drops to 1.5 percent. If you put down more than 10 percent, the funding fee drops to 1.25 percent.

  For a subsequent purchase—a second use of the benefit—the funding fee rises to 3.3 percent for a zero-down payment loan. Similar funding fees are charged for cash-out refinances. Of course, if you have 3.3 percent to pay as a funding fee, you may opt for an FHA loan instead.

- **Good Lenders:** Lenders that offer conventional loans may also offer VA loans. To find a good lender with expertise in VA loans, start by checking with the VA regional loan centers (www.homeloans.va.gov/rlcweb.htm). Each center has a Web site as well as a brick-and-mortar office, and is set up to help veterans, active-duty personnel, and Special Reserve and National Guard members with purchasing, financing, and retaining a home (if you're behind in your payments on an existing VA loan, they can help).

  You can contact the loan administration department at any of the regional loan centers for information on bidding on property, short sales, VA discharges, deeds for old installment contracts, or the status of a claim. The loan production department handles questions on eligibility, loan processing, credit, guarantees, and assumptions, according to the Web site. The appraisal department can answer questions on what kinds of properties will be approved for a VA loan.

When shopping around for a good VA lender, all the rules outlined earlier in the chapter on finding a good lender apply. Start with a couple of reputable lenders in your area; check in with a local bank or savings and loan, particularly if it is an active residential lender that works often with VA loans; and contact a mortgage broker in your area as well as a national mortgage lender. A credit union may or may not work with the VA.

Most VA loan rates are not advertised the same way conventional loan rates are advertised. Ask each of the lenders to quote you the VA rate, and then ask them to tell you what fees they charge in connection with the loan. While VA loans can carry higher fees than conventional loans, you'll want to make sure the lender isn't adding any fees to the loan transaction. If the lenders do add fees, then you'll be able to compare them on equal footing.

The key is to find a lender who has had plenty of experience with VA loans *and* has a great reputation for customer service. Just because a lender only does VA loans does not mean that the lender is a good lender.

USDA Rural Housing Direct Loans

A Rural Housing Direct Loan, also known as a "Section 502 loan," falls under the U.S. Department of Agriculture's Rural Development Guarantee Loan Program (www.rurdev.usda.gov). It is a 100 percent–financing product that does not require private mortgage insurance (PMI), has no "declining market" considerations in the appraisal process (meaning that it doesn't penalize you if home prices are declining in your neighborhood), accepts a credit score of 620, and does not require that the buyer have cash reserves. In addition, borrowers may spend up to 41 percent of their gross monthly income on their mortgage, taxes, insurance, and total debt payments. With a loan of this type, you can borrow up to 102 percent of the purchase price, which includes the 2 percent funding fee (or, if you're refinancing, 100.5 percent, which includes a 0.5 percent funding fee), and sellers or other third parties may contribute cash toward a down payment.

While USDA Rural Housing Direct Loans may sound appealingly straightforward, strict income, debt, location, and loan term requirements must be met.

- **Income requirements:** These loans are available only for households that are low income or very low income. Low income is defined as between 50 and 80 percent of area median income (AMI); very low income is defined as below 50 percent of AMI. (Moderate income is between 80 and 100 percent of AMI.) To be considered for the program, you must be able to pay between 22 and 26 percent of your gross monthly income. To find out what the income limits are for your area, go to www.eligibility.sc.egov.usda.gov/eligibility/incomeEligibilityAction.do.
- **Debt requirements:** To qualify for this loan, you'll need to meet strict debt-to-income ratios. Unlike FHA loans, Rural Housing Direct Loans count currently deferred student loans in your debt-to-income ratio.
- **Location requirements:** These loans are available only in certain areas of the country, including rural areas and communities of less than twenty thousand. Communities that have been the victim of a natural disaster may also qualify. To find out if your neighborhood of choice is eligible for a USDA loan, go to www.eligibility.sc.egov.usda.gov/eligibility/welcomeAction.do. (There is some talk in the

mortgage industry that the USDA may open up the program to more areas of the country by changing the population requirements.)

- **Loan terms:** USDA loan terms run for up to thirty-three years, or up to thirty-eight years for those with incomes below 60 percent of AMI and who cannot afford a thirty-three-year term. If you're trying to finance a manufactured home or mobile home, which must be permanently installed and meet the HUD Manufactured Housing Construction and Safety Standards and Housing and Community Facilities Programs (HCFP) thermal and site standards, you'll be able to finance for only a thirty-year loan term.

- **Changes to USDA Rural Development Loans:** In the wake of the credit crisis, the USDA began offering buyers a 2/1 buy-down program. A buy-down mortgage allows the home buyer to pay at a lower interest rate than is currently being offered for a specific period of time, typically three to five years. The seller pays the difference between what the interest rate should be and what the buyer is paying. For example, if the mortgage interest rate is 5.75 percent, the buyer might pay only 3.75 percent for the first twelve months and 4.75 for the second twelve months, and then start paying 5.75 percent in the third year of the loan. In a 2/1 buy-down, the buyer's starting interest rate would be 2 percent below the true interest rate for the first year, and then 1 percent below the true interest rate for the second year. In the third year of the loan, the buyer would pay the true interest rate associated with the loan. As is the case with buy-downs, the seller makes up the difference in interest to the lender.

According to Shannon, a senior loan officer in Dunwoody, Georgia, the USDA used to allow buyers to qualify for the entire at the buy-down rate (in our example, 3.75 percent). Since the housing and credit crisis, buyers must qualify at the note rate (5.75 percent in our example) rather than at the lower rate that might be offered in a buy-down program.

GETTING A JUMBO MORTGAGE

As long as you have a credit score of at least 620, enough income to pay your loan note and taxes and insurance, and some cash reserves, you shouldn't have a problem getting a mortgage for $417,000 or less. But if you want a jumbo loan—that is, a mortgage for more than $417,000 but less than $650,000—you'll have a tougher time in this post-crisis world.

Before the 2008 credit crisis, if you wanted a loan between $417,000 and $650,000, you'd need a decent credit score and 5 percent down in cash, and to be willing to pay a slightly higher interest rate. A jumbo loan would cost you maybe a quarter of a point more than the going conventional loan. A super-jumbo loan—a mortgage for more than $650,000 but less than $1 million—might cost half a point.

When the credit markets froze in 2008, the federal government put Fannie Mae and Freddie Mac into conservatorship in order to keep the secondary mortgage market functioning. But neither Fannie Mae nor Freddie Mac bought single-family home mortgages for more than $417,000. (There were, and are, higher limits for multifamily buildings of up to four units, and now there are jumbo-conforming loans: in "high-cost" areas—mostly in Southern California and the Northeast—Fannie Mae and Freddie Mac will buy home loans up to $729,250.) Meanwhile, investors started taking a bath on their toxic jumbo mortgages, killing any appetite lenders had for bigger home loans.

Today, if you want any sort of jumbo loan, you'll need to put down 20 to 25 percent or more in cash and have two to six months of cash reserves, a credit score in the 700s (at this writing, a very few lenders will take a credit score of 660), and a pile of documentation at the ready. And you should expect your loan to carry a significantly higher interest rate, perhaps by a half percent or more.

"Jumbo buyers were typically allowed to show little documentation—[it] is the complete opposite now. We, as an industry, now actually ask jumbo borrowers for more information than some FHA buyers, which doesn't make any sense to consumers. But from a bank's point of view, a bad $1 million loan is a lot worse than ten bad $100,000 loans when you consider the amount of time it could potentially take to get that one loan off the books in the future," says Dan, a Chicago-based mortgage banker.

While the jumbo loan market is a fraction of the size of the conventional loan market, it is key for home buyers who earn $200,000 to $600,000 per year. But the government doesn't want to be seen as helping the "rich," and if you can help out ten people instead of one, it is a better use of tax dollars. So the government has essentially left the jumbo market to thaw on its own. And, slowly, it seems as though more jumbo mortgage options have become available.

Dick, a mortgage broker in San Francisco, says it will be a while before a secondary market for jumbo loans develops. What should you do if you need a jumbo loan now and you don't live in a high-cost area?

Your best bet is to go to a big commercial bank. Some banks will issue a first mortgage for $417,000, and a second mortgage or home equity loan for whatever is needed above and beyond the first mortgage. The interest rate on the first loan will be at the conventional interest rate, while the second mortgage will carry a much higher rate. But don't expect to get everything you want. The best you might do is finance up to 75 percent of the purchase price with a jumbo loan, with perhaps an additional 10 percent second mortgage (for a total loan-to-value ratio of 85 percent).

The key to finding a good jumbo mortgage is to work with a mortgage banker or broker who does a lot of them. Since there isn't much of a secondary mortgage market for jumbo loans at the moment, you're looking for a bank that will hold the loan in its portfolio.

If you're going to apply for a jumbo loan, here's what you can expect:

- **You'll need a credit score of at least 700.** The lowest credit score accepted these days for a conventional loan is around 660, but you'll pay higher fees and a much higher interest rate, lenders say. And few lenders will do a jumbo mortgage for someone who has a 660 credit score.

- **You'll need a lot of cash for your down payment and reserves.** You'll need at least 20 to 25 percent down in cash and six months of cash reserves. (The bigger your loan, the more cash you'll need in reserve.) Most lenders will ask for 25 percent down, but if you borrow more than $1 million, you might have to put down 30 percent or more.

- **Your interest rate could be as much as 1.5 percent higher than conventional interest rates.** If conventional borrowers are paying 5.5 percent on a thirty-year $417,000 loan, a jumbo borrower could expect an interest rate of 6.5 to 7 percent, lenders say. You might have to consider an ARM rather than a fixed-rate mortgage, since interest rates on a 5/1 ARM (fixed at a slightly lower interest rate for the first five years of the loan, at which point the loan converts into a 1-year ARM) will be lower than on a thirty-year fixed-rate mortgage—but not by much, and you'll be taking a risk that the rate will adjust up in five years. If you get a jumbo loan, you'll also have higher fees.

- **You'll need to have your paperwork ready.** Dan, the mortgage banker in Chicago, says he is now collecting the borrower's last two pay stubs, last two months of statements of all asset accounts, and last two years of full federal *and* state income tax returns. "We can't get away with limited documentation on jumbo loans anymore," he says.

- **You may have to go through several rounds of verifications.** Not only will the lender call your employer and perhaps even your banker during the application process, but the lender may make a second round of calls just before the closing to make sure you're still employed.

- **You may need to pay for two appraisals.** Lenders will want to have a good read on the property's actual value. To get that, they may ask you to pay for two separate appraisals.

There are two pieces of good news about jumbo loans. First, you can still get a jumbo loan, although it won't be as easy as it was before the crisis, and you won't be able to finance as much. Second, it shouldn't take much longer to get a jumbo mortgage approved than it would a conventional or FHA loan, lenders say. But you could run into trouble (and significant delays) if the property you're buying doesn't appraise out in value. (See the end of this chapter for details on what has changed in the world of appraisals.)

HOME BUYER CLOSING COSTS AND FEES

Over the last several years, many things have changed in real estate—and not for the better. For one, the costs to purchase a home, especially closing costs, have gone up. Not only have traditional closing costs skyrocketed, but there are also many new fees you'll have to pay. In addition to your mortgage lender's fees, other common closing costs include title insurance fees, recording fees, inspection fees, and city, county, and state transfer taxes. So be prepared to pay when the time comes to close on your new home.

Here's a detailed look at the many closing costs you might have to pay when you buy a home. Not every closing cost listed here will apply to your deal, and the fees and closing costs you pay may be higher or lower than the range I've provided, depending on where you live and the particular home you're about to purchase. Who pays these fees typically varies from state to state and may vary from city to city within a single state. It can be easy to wind up paying certain fees that are not your responsibility if you don't realize (and no one tells you) that the custom in your area is for the seller to pay them. The savvy home buyer will be aware of what he or she is responsible for paying, and which costs and fees are legitimate and apply to the deal at hand.

1. **Lender's points and loan-origination fee:** These points and fees usually run from 0 to 3 percent of the loan, although they can be higher. A point is 1 percent of the loan amount. Lenders will typically charge points in exchange for giving you a lower interest rate, so if you see a point charged to you, it should be because you're getting a lower rate. Due to the financial crisis, some additional fees—usually in the form of points—are being charged to borrowers for purchasing condominiums and certain other properties that have had high foreclosure rates in the past. Unfortunately, these new loan-origination fees won't decrease your interest rate but will just add to the fees to close on your purchase.

   When shopping around with different mortgage lenders, you need to make sure you're shopping for the same mortgage product. If you're looking at a thirty-year fixed-rate loan with one lender, look at that same loan with another lender and then compare points and loan-origination fees—one may be half a point cheaper and charge you thousands less in fees. The process is more difficult when shopping for an ARM. A five-year ARM will have a fixed interest rate for the first five years that will adjust in the sixth year and generally on a yearly basis thereafter. With that adjustment come the finer points of your loan: the interest rate may be tied to the U.S. Treasury rate or LIBOR (the London Interbank Offered Rate), and how much it rises will depend on which index it is tied to; the adjustment may be limited to two percentage points at the end of the fifth year or may increase up to six percentage points; and different lenders will add anywhere from 1.75 percent to 3.25 percent to the adjusted rate.

2. **Loan processing fee:** Many lenders charge a loan processing fee. It can range from $200 to $800 and is in place to compensate the lender for processing your loan.

3. **Loan application fee:** This fee, which typically runs from nothing (some lenders do not charge an official loan application fee) to $500, gets the lender started on your loan application. Frequently the fee is applied toward other costs the lender will incur in processing your loan. In some cases, it covers the appraisal and the credit report, with any excess payment applied to other lenders' fees.

4. **Lender's credit report:** Expect to pay $10 to $100 or more for each credit report pulled. While the pricing for credit reports has come way down, some lenders still charge a rather high amount for pulling them, although sometimes subsequent "credit pulls" are less expensive than the initial charge. If there is a co-borrower on the loan (such as a spouse, partner, or other family member), these fees will be higher, to cover the cost of pulling two (or more) sets of reports. In some cases, a lender will pull an updated credit report on you right before the closing to make sure your credit history has not deteriorated. If you and your spouse or partner are both named on the loan, and the lender pulls two sets of credit reports on each of you, your credit report cost could total as much as $400.

5. **Lender's underwriting fee:** The lender charges this fee to finalize the loan by having the lender's underwriting department give it a final review. It may cost between $75 and $600. Not all lenders charge an underwriting fee, but many do.

6. **Lender's document preparation fee:** This fee, for preparing the

documentation needed in the closing, can cost $50 to $250 or more. In some cases, it is paid to a third-party document preparation company.

7. **Lender's appraisal fee:** The lender will hire an appraiser to determine whether your property is worth what you're paying for it. This appraisal will cost $225 to $750 or more, depending on the value of the property. For some high-priced properties, lenders will require two appraisals. When that happens, the fee usually doubles, because the lender typically hires two different appraisers.

8. **Prepaid interest on the loan:** This cost depends on what day of the month you close and how much you're borrowing. If you choose to close in the first days of a calendar month, you'll have to pay a higher amount of prepaid interest than you would if you closed in the last days, because the interest due on your loan is paid per day until the end of the month in which you close. So you'll be covering all the days in the month from your closing date through the last day of the month. If you close on the last day of the month, you'll need only one day's worth of prepaid interest in cash at closing.

9. **Lender's insurance escrow:** The lender expects that your home— the lender's collateral for the loan—will be insured at all times, so that the loan can be paid off or the house rebuilt (with the lender's permission) in the case of a total loss of the property. At closing, the lender will require the homeowners insurance policy to be paid in full for at least one year. The lender will also want two months of the annual premium up front to ensure that enough money is collected on a monthly basis during the term of the loan to pay the insurance premium on a yearly basis. If the policy costs $1,200 per year, you'll need to come to the closing with that $1,200 unless you paid for the insurance policy before the closing and gave

proof of payment to the lender. In addition, you'll need to give the lender $200 to put into the escrow for future homeowners insurance policy premiums that come due.

10. **Lender's insurance escrow for condominium owners:** In a change since the housing crisis, lenders are requiring that condominium buyers own a homeowners insurance policy that includes contents coverage. As with a single-family house, the lender will require you to buy your condo insurance policy prior to the closing or pay for the policy at the closing. You'll also have to escrow funds with the lender for the ongoing insurance premiums.

11. **Lender's tax escrow:** If you have a tax escrow, you'll need to make sure that your lender has sufficient funds on hand for the next tax bill. For example, if your annual real estate taxes are $1,200, and the next tax bill, for the first half of your taxes, is due one month after the closing, the lender will want to have the amount that will be due plus two months' reserve on hand, or $800. The amount the lender will require in escrow also depends on the location of the home. In some parts of the country, winter taxes are higher than summer taxes. In other parts, real estate taxes are paid at irregular intervals.

12. **Lender's tax escrow service fee:** This onetime fee of $40 to $125 is paid to the lender to have a company set up the annual monitoring and payment of your real estate taxes.

13. **Title insurance cost for the lender's policy:** Expect to pay $150 to $1,000 or more, based on the purchase price of the house. In some parts of the country, the seller picks up most or all of the cost of the owner's title insurance policy, and the lender's title insurance policy can be piggybacked onto it. But if you are buying in a state in which the buyer pays for both the owner's title insurance policy and the lender's title insurance policy, the amount you pay can be substantial. Some states set the title insurance rates, and

those fees are nonnegotiable; in other states, the fees are negotiable—you would be wise to determine what your state allows. For comparison purposes and to educate yourself further on title insurance, check out Closing.com.

14. **Title insurance cost for the owner's policy:** If you choose to buy an owner's policy—and I absolutely think you should—the cost will run from $150 to $1,000 or more, depending on the price of the home. (In some areas of the country, the seller picks up this cost. Make sure you find out what the local custom is in your neighborhood of choice.) If you buy only a lender's title policy, and someone makes a title claim to the property and you lose the house, only the lender will get a check. You need to buy a separate owner's policy so that you will be fully compensated for the loss of the property in the event that someone has a successful title claim. (Visit ThinkGlink.com/title-insurance for dozens of stories and videos about title insurance.)

15. **Cost of special endorsements to the lender's or owner's title insurance policy:** An endorsement is an amendment to the title insurance policy that offers specific or additional coverage over a special item. Based on the type of property you are purchasing, the lender can require that you add special endorsements to the title, such as an environmental lien endorsement, an adjustable-rate mortgage endorsement, or even a condominium endorsement. In states where these endorsements are required and available, they can cost $150 each or more, depending on the type of endorsement and the title company's fee schedule in your state.

16. **House inspection fee:** A house inspection can cost from $250 to $1,000 or more. A basic inspection may start at $250, but the cost can quickly increase if you add a radon test, a water-quality inspection, a pest inspection, a septic system inspection, and a lead inspection.

17. **Title company or closing agent fee:** This closing fee, which is separate from the cost of a title insurance policy, can run from $200 to $1,500 or more, depending on the value of the home and the value of the mortgage you are obtaining. The fee is paid to the title company or closing agent to work through the paperwork for the closing. (The title company or the closing agent will not represent you or the seller in the transaction but will act as an intermediary to facilitate the transaction, or work on behalf of the lender.)

18. **Recording fee, of deed or mortgage:** When you purchase a home, you receive the title to the home in the form of a legal document that must be recorded with the local recorder of deeds office in the county in which the home is located or other office responsible for such documents. Expect to pay a recording fee of $25 to $150.

    In addition, if you borrow money, the lender will have a mortgage or trust deed to record. The mortgage or trust deed is the document that gives the lender the right to foreclose and sell the home to satisfy the debt you took out. The recording fee varies from state to state, but you should expect to pay at least $100. In some states, you will have to pay a mortgage tax (a percentage of the loan) to record the document. For example, if your mortgage loan is for $250,000 and the mortgage tax is 1 percent, the recording fee tax will be $250.

19. **Local city, town, or village property transfer tax; county transfer tax; state transfer tax:** These charges vary from locality to locality and are usually either a flat fee or based on the sales price of the house. For example, in Chicago, the buyer picks up the city transfer tax, a hefty $3.75 per $500 of sales. The fee is generally up to $10 per $1,000 of sales price.

20. **Flood certification fee:** This fee, which you'll pay for the lender to determine whether the home you're buying is located in a flood

zone, is $10 to $50. If your home is in a flood zone—and these zones are being redrawn by FEMA all over the country—your lender may require you to buy flood insurance. You can find out more about flood insurance at FloodSmart.gov.

21. **Attorney's fee:** If you need an attorney to help you close your deal, the flat-fee rate generally starts around $500.

22. **Condo or co-op move-in fee:** You may have to pay up to $500 for this building charge. The fee is typically paid to the condo association or co-op corporation. In addition to the fee, which is revenue to the condo association, you may also have to put up a security deposit, in case your movers cause any damage to the property.

23. **Association transfer fee:** Often required for condominium and townhome buyers, this fee can range from a minimal charge to more than $500. In some cases, it is billed to the buyer. Make sure you know whether it is the building custom to have the buyer or seller pay this fee.

24. **Co-op apartment fee:** This fee is often charged for the transfer of the shares of stock in a co-op transaction; it can be a flat fee of between $50 and $300 (or more, especially in New York), or be based on the purchase price. In some cases, it is billed to the buyer. In some co-ops, this may be referred to as a "flip tax," or you may have a single larger fee to cover the transfer or shares and the sale of the property.

25. **Cost for credit checks for condo and co-op buildings by the board:** You can expect a cost of $25 to $150 per credit check.

26. **Move-in deposit fee:** Some condominium associations and co-op corporations charge a deposit for the right to move into the building. In some cases, this deposit is refundable; in others, it is an outright fee paid to the association. It can run from $50 to $2,000.

27. **Assignment fee:** Some lenders immediately sell the loan they just gave you to an investor or another institution, in which case the lender may charge you an additional fee to assign the loan. The

cost can be as little as $25 but may be more if the fees in your state to record or file the documentation of assignment are high.

28. **E-mail and delivery fees:** Many title companies and closing agents charge a fee, as little as $10 to as much as $100, to receive documents by e-mail from lenders. Closing agents and title companies defend this charge as a fee to cover the costs of maintaining the e-mail server and the cost of printing documents and overseeing the loan package preparation. Title companies and closing agents may also charge a fee to send your signed loan documents back to your lender.

29. **Notary and other fees:** Some states have enacted laws that require additional paperwork to transfer the title of a home. If that additional paperwork has to be reviewed and signed by a notary public, you may have to pay a fee to the notary. In some states, the fee is nominal, while in others it can be $25 to witness your signature on a document.

All of the fees that you are charged should show up on your HUD-1 form. They should also be detailed in the good faith estimate (GFE) that your lender is required by law to provide you within three business days of submitting your loan application to the lender. (Savvy home buyers will ask the lender to give them a GFE before they complete the loan application.)

You can find updates to this list online at ThinkGlink.com/closing-costs. If you're selling a property, you can find updated seller closing costs at ThinkGlink.com/seller-closing-costs-updated.

CHANGES IN THE APPRAISAL INDUSTRY

At the heart of the credit crisis is a question of value: What is a piece of real estate worth?

Appraisers are professionals who help us estimate the value of a particular asset, whether it's a vase from the Ming dynasty, an antique car, or a piece of real estate. I use the word "estimate" because you can't really know what an asset is worth until you sell it—and that's the rub for real estate. In other sorts of appraisals, such as for a high-value piece of art, the appraiser generally goes to work before the Manet goes up for auction. When it comes to real estate, the appraiser is called in after an offer to purchase has been accepted by the seller and the details of price have been worked out.

You might ask why an appraisal is needed after a willing buyer and a willing seller come to terms on a deal. It's a great question. The real estate industry has argued that an appraisal of the property's price *after* the final offer has been accepted is a waste of time and money. On the other hand, buyers and sellers have often agreed on a price that has nothing to do with the true value of the property. Lenders want to know if the price that's been agreed to has any basis in reality before they fund the loan, and so they engage appraisers to determine the true value of the property—and the home buyer foots the bill.

Appraisers are supposed to be independent third-party consultants who are hired to figure out, based on empirical evidence, what a piece of real estate is worth. But I've watched the industry for the past twenty-plus years, and here's how it often works:

1. **The buyer and seller strike a deal.** They agree to a price, a closing date, and so on. The buyer informs the lender of the deal.
2. **The lender hires an appraiser to make sure the property is worth what the buyer wants to pay.** More to the point, the lender hires an appraiser to make sure there is enough value in the property that the loan-to-value ratio required by the terms of the buyer's financing is sufficient.
3. **The appraiser contacts the listing agent for the property.** The

listing agent provides the appraiser with some background information, often including the comps (the sales prices of comparable homes in the neighborhood that have recently sold) that the agent used to price the property to begin with. Agents will also often provide comps for the neighborhood that prove the property sold for the right price.

4. **The appraiser tours the home.** Often, the agent will meet the appraiser at the property to ensure that the appraiser fully "appreciates" the property and doesn't miss anything. The appraiser will usually create a sketch of the home's floorplate, measure the exterior of the home (and sometimes the interior rooms), take photos and note special rooms of interest or upgrades to the property.

5. **The appraiser may do some of his or her own research.** This might consist of driving around the neighborhood, or pulling some comps. The appraiser may talk to other brokers, as well.

6. **The appraiser turns in the appraisal to the lender.** Prior to the housing and credit crises, the appraised price of the property almost always turned out to be *exactly* the same as the sales price— to the dollar. What were the odds of that happening? (Post-crises, lenders are finding appraisals to be unpredictable at best, which I'll discuss further in a moment.)

7. **The lender funds the loan.** With an appraisal in hand "proving" that the property is worth what the buyer wants to pay, the deal can close.

The Big, Fat, Ugly Truth About Appraisers and Appraisals

The appraisal industry has been pretty upset over the years about claims that its appraisers don't actually do the independent work they're paid to do. The industry believes that the media have given appraisers a black eye. The truth is that when it comes to properly appraising a property, the real estate industry set itself up for failure long ago.

I've spoken to many appraisers over the years about how they do their jobs, and I'm convinced that the best ones try to do truly independent appraisals. Unfortunately, appraisers have faced a significant amount of arm-twisting from lenders who only wanted appraisals that would show the property appraising out in value. And why wouldn't they? If the property doesn't appraise out in value, the lender is out of luck—and so are the buyer, the seller, the buyer's agent, the seller's agent, and even the escrow or closing company. In fact, everyone involved in the transaction (except perhaps a lawyer paid separately by the buyer or seller, which is the case only in a few states) needs the property to appraise out in value for the deal to close, and to make money on it.

Some of the most honest appraisers I know have spoken for years about the "blacklist" kept by some mortgage companies, containing the names of appraisers who turned in one too many appraisals with the "wrong" number. Imagine the pressure an appraiser would be under to come in with the right number. Even in a situation where there were no comps or the comps were a lot lower than expected, the right number had to magically appear on the bottom line. As an appraiser, why risk losing a significant percent of your business? It's easier to simply play your prescribed role in the deal and bring the appraisal in right where the lender, agents, buyer, and seller want it to be.

This whole real estate appraisal system worked out pretty well while properties were going up in value. Whether the property was up 2 percent or 20 percent, rising home values meant that everyone was covered.

And Then Came the Credit Crisis

Appraisers played a key role in the housing boom, and in retrospect it's easy to see why. As buyers and sellers started moving at a more frenzied pace, appraisers put the stamp of approval on ever-higher prices. Mortgage fraud also boomed, as the FBI noted that some bad-apple agents, lenders, and appraisers worked in cahoots to get superhigh prices for homes that were essentially teardowns—and then walked away with the profits, leaving home buyer—and in some cases the investors who bought those loans from the lender—holding the bag.

The housing crisis and credit crisis have in part come down to toxic loans. Even before the home value meltdown, many houses weren't worth what appraisers said they were, even though buyers made offers that sellers accepted. Buyers were bidding more because creative loans (such as pay-option ARMs and interest-only mortgages) gave them the financial firepower to spend more. Loans were made against property that wasn't worth what someone was paying for it.

And then came the crash.

Once home prices started falling, houses stopped appraising out in value. When a property doesn't appraise out in value, a buyer can either back out of the deal (because the financing falls through) or come to the table with more cash to get the loan-to-value ratio back in line. But buyers who once relied on creative financing techniques didn't have cash for a down payment or closing costs, let alone to make up a 5 to 10 percent shortfall in the appraised price of the property. It's hard to know exactly what the tipping point was, but somewhere a buyer finally said, "This is crazy. I'm not buying that house." Once there was a change of mind-set, the boom was over and home prices were in a free fall.

New Rules for Appraisers and Appraisals

There's plenty of blame to go around in the housing crisis, the result of a boom so big it can't be explained in economic terms other than a simple one: greed. But the federal government was worried enough about the role appraisers played and the true independence of their advice that it created the Home Mortgage Valuation Code of Conduct (HVCC). Effective May 1, 2009, the HVCC was the product of an agreement between New York Attorney General Andrew Cuomo, Fannie Mae and Freddie Mac, and their new federal regulator, the Federal

Housing Finance Agency. The goal of the agreement was to enhance the independence of appraisers, improve the accuracy of appraisals, bring more transparency to the process, and add protections for home buyers and lenders.

The HVCC essentially puts a layer between mortgage lenders and appraisers by creating a system in which lenders have to go through an appraisal management company to hire an appraiser. Instead of the lender contacting an appraiser directly, the lender must now call the appraisal management company, who will then randomly assign an appraiser to do the appraisal.

While this sounds like a perfect solution to the problem, in practice there have been tons of problems stemming from the cost structure and a mismatch of appraisal experience and expertise:

Cost: Adding another layer to the process means another hand in the pot. Appraisals already cost home buyers anywhere from $225 to $750. With a new player in the transaction, the appraisal management company, the cost of an appraisal could go up by as much as $100 to $250—something the government doesn't want. Instead of the lender taking the hit, the appraiser's fee is being cut significantly while the home buyer is often asked to pay a slightly higher price. Many good appraisers aren't willing to take a lower fee, so the appraisal management company will bring in someone cheaper.

Experience and expertise: As a result of the fee reductions leading some local appraisers to turn down a job, out-of-area appraisers may have to travel fifty miles or more from where they work and live to do an appraisal. This is a terrible deal for buyers and sellers because the appraiser may not be very familiar with the area being appraised. Why is it important to have an appraiser who knows the area in which you are buying? It's the same reason you want to hire a real estate broker who has sold in your neighborhood of choice for years. They have the experience and expertise to understand the housing stock in a neighborhood and have seen single-family homes and condos go on and off the market for years. They may even be aware of upgrades and improvements that have been made to the area over the years. But someone who doesn't know the housing stock is left to simply look at the comps prepared by the agent or look them up him- or herself on the local multiple listing service site or elsewhere on the Web.

As a result of the HVCC, many houses are being underappraised, lenders believe, rather than fairly appraised. Then again, the record number of foreclosures being sold in 2008 and 2009 might have something to do with home values plummeting.

Dan, the mortgage banker in Chicago, says that one of the biggest problems for buyers is appraisers' inexperience and lack of knowledge about how to appraise condos. "Appraising single-family houses is completely different from condos when you consider that a lot of information is gathered from management companies for condo appraisals," he says. "Experienced condo appraisers/appraisal companies know the right people to speak with at the management companies. They know what questions to ask. Inexperienced appraisers leave things off the reports or want to charge more money to get the information for reporting. They would require delays in getting the reports to us [potentially delaying the closing] as well as cost buyers more—both of which were never issues before the HVCC [because more experienced appraisers know what information local lenders require]. When errors are found in the appraisals, lenders cannot contact appraisers anymore; we have to work through appraisal management companies, which could cause further delays."

HVCC has caused additional problems, lenders say. The appraisal management companies who coordinate orders for lenders don't necessarily monitor the experience or required travel distance of appraisers, nor do they seem to have an established tracking system to monitor the error rate.

Lenders say it's clear that the lawmakers who wrote the HVCC never thought of the "local" aspect of real estate. Instead, they wrote the law with a broad brush and thought that every appraiser should be able to appraise every property. Beyond that, many industry leaders believe that appraisal management firms will focus on doing the cheapest and fastest appraisal, but still charge the conventional amount—and pocket the difference.

In general, appraisal industry leaders think HVCC missed the boat by not focusing enough on appraiser competency, undercutting the relationship between honest appraisers and mortgage lenders, increasing the influence of appraisal management firms, and encouraging the continued use of computerized automated valuation models (AVMs) and broker price opinions (BPOs) provided by real estate agents and brokers as a less-expensive option to appraisals.

In fact, the appraisal industry is so up in arms about how HVCC is *not* working that legislation was introduced to put a moratorium on the code for eighteen months, during which time the legislation will be redesigned.

Handling the Challenges of Appraisals

Whether HVCC goes away entirely or comes back in a different form, it's clear that the government wants to step in and somehow regulate how appraisals work in the real estate industry.

But no matter who does the appraisal, if you're buying a home in an era of declining values, you may have a problem with your property appraising out in value. Millions of foreclosures and short sales have kicked home valuations off a cliff. A savvy buyer will make sure the property can appraise out before making an offer. That means you have to be extremely aware of what's going on in your neighborhood of choice, what properties are selling for (not what they're listed at), and how much you should spend before you make an offer.

FOUR

FIXING YOUR CREDIT HISTORY AND CREDIT SCORE FOREVER

How likely is it that you're going to default on a debt? Miss a mortgage payment? Fail to pay at least the minimum balance on your credit cards? In short, how big a risk are you?

These are the questions that creditors—companies that lend out money—ask themselves every day about prospective borrowers. To help them answer these questions, mortgage lenders, credit card companies, and school and auto loan finance companies rely on certain tools, such as the FICO credit score, which was invented by Fair Isaac, a Minneapolis, MN–based provider of "credit scoring, decision management, fraud detection, and credit risk score services," according to its Web site, FICO.com. And it isn't just creditors who want to see how well you're managing credit. Prospective employers and insurance companies will often pull a copy of your credit history and score to decide whether to hire you or sell you insurance.

In this chapter, I'll discuss how to fix your credit history and credit score forever. It may sound like an impossible task, especially if you don't have good credit right now. I'll be honest: there is no magic bullet, no way to instantly fix your credit history and raise your score. (Anyone who promises that is trying to scam you, which I'll address later in this chapter.)

Before we get started, let's look at some basic definitions.

Credit-Reporting Bureau: Your credit information is collected by entities called "credit-reporting bureaus." The three main credit-reporting bureaus in the United States are Equifax, Experian, and TransUnion; there are also smaller bureaus and regional bureaus, but most creditors rely solely on these three main credit-reporting bureaus. They each maintain vast databases of information updated by creditors every day. Your credit history and credit score is culled from the data collected by the credit-reporting bureaus, and the credit-reporting industry is highly regulated by the federal government.

Credit History: Credit-reporting bureaus collate the vast amount of data they collect by Social Security number. Your credit history is essentially a collection of all the financial information assigned to your Social Security number. It includes:

- **Personal information:** Your name, current and former addresses (my credit history lists my last three addresses plus my current house), and employment history, as well as any alerts, a personal statement (you can use up to one hundred words to explain a credit situation or a piece of negative information), and other identifying information.
- **All credit accounts:** These might include mortgages, credit cards, and department store and gas charge accounts. Credit accounts are often characterized as "mortgage" (including home equity loans and home equity lines of credit), "installment" (for which the number and amount of payments are predetermined and fixed, such as a car loan or school loan), "revolving" (in which you charge a variable amount each month and are required to pay it off, such as a credit

card), or "other." You'll also see in this section whether the accounts are open or closed (sometimes referred to as "active" or "inactive").

- **Payment history**: This section notes whether you pay on time or late, the minimum balance or in full, or not at all. Often, you'll see the phrase "paid as agreed," which indicates that you are meeting the payment terms of your credit account.

- **Negative information**: This section includes any negative information about your credit history including late payments, delinquent accounts, accounts that have been closed with a balance, charge-offs (in which the creditor assumes your debt as a loss, closes the account, and either continues to collect payment from you or sells your account to a collection company), collections, or other credit problems you're having.

- **Court judgments**: These judgments against you might include wage garnishments or liens.

- **Accounts in collections**: Any debts that have been turned over to a collection agency will be listed here.

- **Inquiries**: These include soft inquiries, in which a company pulls your credit history for its own information, and hard inquiries, in which you give a creditor permission to pull your credit history and score. Soft inquiries do not count against you (meaning, they don't reduce your credit score), while too many hard inquiries might. You can pull your own credit history as often as you like without it counting against you.

- **Disputed information**: This section contains information that you've officially disputed, and any resolutions.

- **Other information**: Each credit-reporting bureau collects the same basic information about your major credit accounts, but sometimes one bureau will pick up different pieces of information here and there. (That's why I suggest you get a copy of your credit history from each of the three bureaus once a year; I'll talk more about that later.)

Credit Score: A credit score is akin to an SAT score. Just as colleges use your SAT score to predict how successful you'll be in college, creditors use your credit score to predict how successful you'll be as a borrower: to figure out how likely it is that you'll pay back your loan on time or default. Some credit card companies have identified a "sweet spot," a credit score where consumers are likely to accumulate credit card debt instead of paying it off each month.

The most popular credit score in use is the FICO score. Fair Isaac created a mathematical formula to arrive at this score that was innovative and disruptive—it completely changed the way companies analyze prospective borrowers for risk. The invention of the credit score also led to the creation of a hugely profitable industry. Each of the three credit-reporting bureaus has its own version of the FICO score, and they've also come together to create a brand-new score called the "Vantage score." The FICO-based scores run from 300 to 850; the higher the number, the better your credit. The Vantage score goes up to 999; a score in the 900s is an A, a score in the 800s is a B, and so on. And now, Fair Isaac has the FICO 08 credit score, which supposedly is a better estimator of which consumers are likely to default on their debts in a weakened economy. You can expect credit scoring models to continue to evolve over time.

Credit scores have changed the world of lending, in many ways for the better:

- **Credit scoring helps consumers get loans faster.** It's easier to decide whether someone qualifies for a loan and how much to charge them by simply looking at their credit score.
- **Credit scores (and credit histories) level the playing field.** Color, race, national origin, age, sex, marital status—none of these stars of past financial discrimination come into play. You're judged solely on how much credit you have, how you use it, and how wisely you manage your credit accounts.

- **Credit scores are time sensitive.** Negative information counts less as time goes on and you add more positive information (such as on-time payments) to your credit history.
- **Credit is more widely available, and interest rates and loan fees are cheaper, than in countries where credit scoring is not as developed.** The U.S. credit markets are far more developed than in Europe, Asia, or Latin America.

But credit scoring models aren't perfect. Credit scores failed to predict what would happen to a Grade A credit borrower who lost his or her job and fell on hard times during the housing and credit crises. The streets of America are littered with foreclosures that once belonged to families who had excellent credit.

HOW CREDIT SCORES ARE CALCULATED

I will focus primarily on the FICO score in this chapter, because most of the other scores are based on the FICO score model, and it is the most widely accepted credit score in use today—more than 70 percent of mortgage lenders and creditors use it to determine credit worthiness. FICO scores are generated by taking your financial data and assigning it to one of five scoring areas, which contribute in different amounts to your total score:

- **Payment history, 35 percent of your total credit score:** Your payment history is the record of how you pay your bills: whether you pay late or on time or at all; how much you owe; whether you have defaulted on payments or lenders have charged off your balances; if you have adverse public records (including lawsuits, liens, judgments, and wage attachments) and collection notices. Your payment history also shows how late any payments are—whether thirty, sixty, or ninety days—and how long it has been since you've had a late payment.

- **Amounts owed, 30 percent of your total credit score:** This category shows the number of accounts with balances owed, how much you owe on each account, and the total amount owed compared with the total amount of available credit on each account.

- **Length of credit history, 15 percent of your total credit score:** This area analyzes how much time has elapsed since you opened each credit account and since your last credit activity. (If you have credit cards but never use them, that small fact could ding your credit score, since lenders like to see you actively managing several different forms of credit.)

- **New credit, 10 percent of your total credit score:** This category includes information about how many new lines of credit you've opened up, when you opened them, and how many times and how long it has been since prospective creditors have inquired about your credit. Steps you've taken to reestablish new credit after a major financial problem, such as a bankruptcy or foreclosure, are also analyzed here.

- **Types of credit used, 10 percent of your total credit score:** Information on all the different types of credit you have—mortgages, installment debt, revolving debt, and other sorts of debt—is collected here. This category also analyzes how frequently you use your different types of credit. (Having a mortgage you pay on time and credit cards that you use each year, even if you pay them off in full each month, will help your credit score.)

WHAT IS THE DIFFERENCE BETWEEN GREAT AND FAIR CREDIT?

FICO scores range from 300 to 850, with 850 representing an optimal credit history. But just because you don't have an 850 credit score (and

I've never met anyone who had a FICO score above 830), doesn't mean you don't have very good or even good enough credit to get the mortgage or credit card you want. Here's how the range is broken down and how lenders view the scores:

Credit Score	Mortgage Interest Rate Differential	Sample Interest Rate*
760–850	Best available	4.974%
700–759	+ 0.22%	5.196%
680–699	+ 0.18%	5.373%
660–679	+ 0.21%	5.587%
640–659	+ 0.53%	6.017%
620–639	+ 0.49%	6.563%

*Interest rates and the differential between credit scoring levels may change based on what credit scores various lenders or end investors will accept. These numbers should be viewed simply as a guide, with the general understanding that the higher your credit score, the lower the interest rate you'll pay to your creditors.

Source: MyFICO.com, July 10, 2009.

The difference between the best available interest rate (4.974 percent on a conventional thirty-year fixed-rate mortgage) and the interest rate available to someone with a 620 credit score (6.563 percent) is 1.589 percent. Here's what that difference would look like for a $200,000 thirty-year fixed-rate mortgage:

Credit Score	Monthly Payment	Interest Over Term of Loan
800	$1,070	$185,367
620	$1,272	$258,079

By having great credit versus fair credit, you'd save yourself $72,712 in interest over the life of the loan. (You can play around with these numbers yourself at ThinkGlink.com/tools.)

It's important to note that some FHA loans will provide borrowers who have a 620 credit score with a much cheaper interest rate than what I've shown here. That's why you should shop around and make sure you talk with different types of lenders about different sorts of loan programs. However, the bottom line is the same: the higher your credit score, the less you'll pay in interest rates and fees over the life of your loan.

WHAT YOU NEED TO KNOW ABOUT CREDIT SCORE CALCULATIONS

When assessing your credit score with an eye toward improving it, keep in mind these important rules:

1. **Bad financial moves will hurt your credit score, but how much differs from person to person.** Whether you get a foreclosure notice or are simply late in paying your bills, it will hurt your credit history and score. But each piece of bad news doesn't affect your score equally. If we grade negative information on a scale of 1 to 10, with 10 being the most damaging to your credit score, bankruptcy is a 10, foreclosure might be a 9 or an 8, and a late payment might be a 4 or a 5.

   Even these grades vary from consumer to consumer, depending on the rest of your credit history. If you have an extremely strong credit history and are late paying a credit card bill (maybe because you went out of town and simply forgot), you'll have caused less damage to your credit score than if you have a poor credit history (perhaps because you've gone bankrupt) and miss the same payment.

At ThinkGlink.com, one of the most asked questions is "How much will a bankruptcy"—or foreclosure, short sale, or late payment—"hurt my credit score?" The answer is that I have no way of knowing; it depends on you and your individual mix of credit accounts, and how well you managed those accounts up to the point where you got in trouble financially. It's entirely possible that if you have to file for bankruptcy, and your credit score was 750 before the bankruptcy filing, your credit score might drop 150 to 200 points. If your home is foreclosed upon, your credit score might drop 100 to 150 points. But if your credit score is 500 and you go into bankruptcy, it might only drop thirty to fifty points.

2. **If you want to raise your credit score, change your mix of credit accounts.** My friend Judi is a smart, talented television reporter. One day, she told me that her friend had advised her to buy a car and take out a car loan just to improve her credit history. She wanted to know what I thought, because she had enough money saved to pay cash for the car.

I'll tell you exactly what I told her: Don't take on additional debt in order to raise your credit score. Whether you pay 5 percent or 15 percent interest on that loan, it's a steep—and unnecessary—price to pay for a higher credit score.

Instead of increasing your debt, consider changing your mix of credit accounts if you want to raise your credit score. For example, if you don't have any credit cards, or if you have only one, add another credit card account to the mix. (I'd advise you to choose one that doesn't have an annual fee and gives you something for nothing. You can look up credit card deals at CardRatings.com, CardWeb.com, or Mint.com.) Then use your credit cards a few times a year, paying off the balance in full at the end of each month.

(Optimally, you'll have four to five lines of credit open and active at any time. These should be a mix of credit accounts, including mortgage, home equity line of credit, car loan, school loan, and credit cards. But if you had a mortgage and paid it off, don't refinance your house just to have an open line of credit.)

By getting another credit account, you've increased your available amount of credit and decreased the ratio of debt-to-credit used (a higher ratio can ding your credit score). These factors, plus your on-time payments, will help raise your credit score over time.

3. **Longevity of credit is extremely important.** One of the credit behaviors lenders prize is properly managing credit you've had for a long time. My oldest piece of credit is a Discover Card that I opened up in the last 1980s. I have never paid late, I don't carry a balance, and I have a large amount of available credit on the card. Having this account active (and in good shape) tells creditors that I know how to manage credit over a long period of time, and it boosts my score. That's why I'll never cancel the account. Although I opened up a Visa credit card a couple of years after I got my Discover Card (and I now have a walletful of other credit cards as well), canceling the Discover Card account today could send my credit score down ten, twenty, or even thirty points because it is my oldest piece of credit. Why risk it?

Canceling cards or accounts that have been open for ten years or longer can be a real drag on your score—but so can closing credit accounts that are three to five years old. If you're constantly opening and closing lines of credit, it tells lenders that you aren't able to manage credit effectively—*even if that's not the case!*

As long as we're on the subject of credit longevity, opening up a rash of new credit accounts can also damage your credit history and lower your score. Even if you open up just one new account, it can lower your score temporarily by twenty to fifty points, depending on the relative strength of your credit history. (I recently tested this out by opening up a new Visa credit card and watched my score fall thirty points. It rebounded several months later.)

I'm often asked if closing a just-opened or never-activated account will damage a person's credit score. The answer is that closing an account you just opened shouldn't really hurt your score, provided you don't close the account with a balance on it (a big no-no), but I wouldn't make a habit of it.

4. **Your credit score is calculated using only the information in your credit history.** What information isn't involved in calculating a credit score? According to MyFICO.com and the Fair Credit Reporting Act (available at the Federal Trade Commission's Web site, FTC.gov), credit scores do not include the following:

- Age, race, national origin, marital status, sex or sexual preference, or religion.
- Your salary, occupation, title, employer, or employment history. These items are on your credit history but are not used to calculate your score.
- Where you live, what type of housing you live in, and how much you paid for it (if you own it); however, whether you pay your mortgage on time is typically factored into your score.
- The interest rate you're being charged on a particular account. But the amount of debt you have, the monthly payments you make, and whether you make them on time do count.
- Child support, divorced spouse support, and rental agreement payments.
- Consumer-oriented inquiries (when you pull a copy of your own credit history) and soft inquiries (when a potential creditor pulls your history without your requesting it).
- Whether or not you are participating in a credit counseling pro-

gram, such as a debt-management program, homeownership program, or budgeting program. A credit counseling program can in fact help you raise your credit score. Most people have very low credit scores upon entering a debt-management program. Being in an approved program will help you raise your score over time, because you will be paying off your debts on time each month and lowering your debt-to-credit ratio.

HOW TO REPAIR YOUR CREDIT HISTORY AND
RAISE YOUR CREDIT SCORE FOREVER

Before the credit crisis, home buyers who were viewed as less desirable in the eyes of lenders still had options for getting a home purchase financed. Now they're finding they don't. Either they've been self-employed for less than two years, their credit history isn't long enough, or their credit score isn't high enough. If your problem is having just a so-so credit score, here are some things you can do to repair your credit history and raise your score forever.

Identify mistakes and errors. In a study released in 2004 by the National Association of Public Interest Research Groups, 79 percent of all credit histories were found to contain mistakes. While most of the mistakes were small—typos or incorrect dates—a full 25 percent of the credit reports studied contained mistakes significant enough that a lender would reject the credit application:

- Fifty-four percent contained personal demographic data that was misspelled, was long outdated, belonged to someone else, or was simply wrong.
- Twenty-two percent of the credit reports were missing credit cards,

loans, mortgages, or other consumer accounts that would have demonstrated the credit worthiness of the borrower.

- Thirty percent of the credit reports were listed as open accounts that had been closed by the consumer.

Since most credit reports have some sort of error, you should pull a copy of your report from each of the three major credit-reporting bureaus and scrutinize them for any mistakes, including a wrong or misspelled name or address, an incorrect Social Security number or birth date, accounts that aren't yours, late payments you made on time, late payments that are more than seven years old, credit inquiries more than two years old, bankruptcies more than ten years old, and duplicate collections.

Dispute inaccurate information. Once you've identified the errors, the next thing to do is dispute them in writing with the credit-reporting bureaus. You may dispute online (the best and fastest method), over the phone (not the best choice, so I don't recommend it), or by mail; the three major credit-reporting bureaus have information on their home pages about how to do it. Most important, gather together the data you'll need to prove that the information on your credit report is wrong. While the credit-reporting bureaus are supposed to investigate and remove any errors within thirty days, sometimes it takes longer (and sometimes you have to make your request for an investigation more than once), so it's helpful to get them everything they need up front.

Make all of your payments on time. People in the credit world tell me that the single best thing you can do to improve your credit score is to make all of your payments on time each month. Whether you're paying the minimum or paying your balance in full, the payment needs to be made on or before the due date. Snail mail is unpredictable (and don't get me started on the cost of a stamp), so your best bet is to open an online account with all of your financial institutions that will give you 24/7 access, as well as online accounts for your credit cards, gas cards, and any other bill you pay regularly. Set up online reminders so you know when to pay these bills, or schedule payments so that they are made automatically. If you do this, you'll never miss another payment, and your credit history and score will benefit forever.

Get current on your accounts. If you've missed payments, you need to figure out a way to catch up and to start paying on time each month. Call your creditor as quickly as possible and let the customer service department know exactly why you missed a payment (you lost the bill, lost a job, were in the hospital, were traveling for business, were on active duty with a division of the armed forces) and when they can expect another check from you. Most creditors won't report you as late to the credit-reporting bureaus until you're fifteen or thirty days late with your payment. So if you're only a couple of days late, get on the phone right away and find out how much you'll need to pay to get the account current. You might even want to pay a little extra to ensure that you won't get into further trouble by inaccurately calculating the amount you'll need to pay to get current. If you're more than thirty days late, you've damaged your credit score, but getting current or at least having a plan in place with your lender before you hit the sixty-day mark is extremely important. Every day you avoid calling your lender or creditor will cause you more problems down the road—and will damage your credit history and lower your score further.

Pay your bills in full each month and pay off your debts. You should not only pay your bills on time, but also strive to pay your bills in full each month and pay down your debt. Paying in full each month should be your absolute priority. Paying off your debts will also give a big boost to your credit score, because you'll have lowered the total amount of debt you carry relative to the amount of available credit you have. What shouldn't you do? Transfer your balance from card to card without paying it down. If you're going to do a balance transfer to get a lower interest rate, you'll want to use that lower rate to pay down your debt as quickly as possible, which in turn will raise your credit score.

Get your debt-to-credit ratio in line. Aim to keep your debt-to-credit ratio below 25 percent. In other words, if a credit card has a limit of $10,000, never run a balance on it of more than $2,500. If you do, your credit history will take a hit. For example, if you have a $9,500 debt on that $10,000-limit credit card, your debt-to-credit ratio is 95 percent. That looks bad to prospective creditors, who will see it as a sign that you don't know how to properly manage your credit accounts. If you have to carry debt of $9,500, you're better off spreading it over a few cards so that your credit history and score suffer less.

Limit credit inquiries. Avoid filling out a lot of applications for new credit. Every time you fill out an application for credit (whether it is a gas card, a department store charge card, a major credit card, a car loan, or a mortgage), the lender will pull a copy of your credit history and score. Too many credit inquiries in a short period of time will ding your score because lenders will think you're desperate for cash and may quickly draw down on all of your available credit.

Don't shop around too long for a mortgage or car loan. If you take too much time to find a mortgage or car loan that works for you—and, in the process, get too many hard inquiries on your credit history—your credit score will suffer. How much time do you have? If you're looking for a car loan, you have about fourteen days to shop around and secure financing without your credit score taking a hit. If you're looking for a mortgage, you have about thirty days. It's hard to say who came up with these numbers, but creditors do follow them.

Limit lines of credit. At most, you need no more than half a dozen lines of credit: a couple of major credit cards, preferably including at least one that offers you something for nothing (cash back, miles, and so on), and a department store or gas charge card, if necessary. When you have too much available credit relative to your income, it starts to damage your credit history and score. Why? Let's say you have $100,000 worth of available credit. The risk-assessment folks at big credit card companies assume that someday you'll need to use it, and when that day comes, maybe you won't be able to pay everything back. (What we've seen is that in a financial perfect storm, such as the 2007–2009 recession, consumers use their cards for basic necessities and default more on their debts as they lose their jobs and their ability to pay their bills.) Try to limit your lines of available credit to half a dozen great ones and cancel the rest. (Just don't cancel your older accounts or those that have a balance—see below for details.)

Never cancel an account with a balance on it. If you close an account that has a balance on it, a prospective creditor will see it as an indication that you can't manage your money—or that another creditor felt you couldn't manage your money and shut down the account for you. This kind of action makes prospective creditors—who are continually pulling copies of your credit history and score to see what's happening in your financial life—very nervous, so nervous that they might choose not to extend credit to you. If you want to get rid of an account that has a balance, either pay off the balance in full and then close the account or transfer the balance to another card and then decide whether to close the account or keep it open. Remember that long-standing accounts that are paid on time and don't have a balance can often bolster your credit history and score.

Negotiate for "paid as agreed" status on debts and collections.
Having a charge-off or unpaid balance on a closed account is a big
negative for your credit history and will lower your credit score. But
there may be an opportunity to mitigate the damage. If you have a
charge-off or a balance on your account and you negotiate to pay it off
for less than the full amount, you want to make sure that your account
reflects the transaction in the best way possible. Try to get the creditor
to agree—in writing—to report the account as "paid as agreed" or "paid
in full." Reporting that the account is "paid as agreed" will show these
negatives in the best possible light and that will help your credit history
and score recover more quickly.

**Pull a free copy of your credit history from each of the three credit-
reporting bureaus once a year.** AnnualCreditReport.com is the *only*
Web site where you can get a free copy of your credit history once
a year directly from the three credit-reporting bureaus. Other "free"
credit Web sites may ask you for a credit card number, or might hit
you up with offers for credit after providing you with a copy of your
credit history and score. And while your credit history is free at An-
nualCreditReport.com, you'll be asked to pay around $8 for a copy of
your credit score (the cheapest price on the Web). Some states, like
Georgia, allow you to get multiple copies of your credit history from
each of the credit-reporting bureaus every year. You can get these
reports online or through the mail. (See "How to Contact the Three
Major Credit-Reporting Bureaus" in this chapter.) If you don't live in
a state where you can pull multiple copies a year, the best thing to do
is to pull from a different credit-reporting bureau every four months
to help you monitor your credit history throughout the year without
paying a penny.

While you're taking these steps to clean up your credit for good, keep a few things in mind:

1. **Closing an account or a line of credit doesn't make it go away.** Your closed or inactive accounts will stay on your credit history for seven to eleven years from the date of the last activity, depending on the manner in which they were closed (for instance, if you closed an account with a balance still on it—even if you paid it off shortly thereafter) and the reasons they were closed.
2. **Your financial history will follow you.** Certain other items will remain on your credit history for years to come:

   - Public records (such as judgments, liens, lawsuits, overdue child support, and bankruptcies): seven to ten years
   - Unpaid tax liens: indefinitely (or until they are paid off)
   - Inquiries (hard and soft): two years
   - Late payments: up to seven years
   - Collections: seven years from the date that the account became past due

   Most items will be cleared within ten years, so it's possible that if you really screw up your credit in your twenties, by your thirties you'll be able to have great credit—or at least good enough credit to get the financing you want.
3. **Your best bet is to rebuild your credit history gradually over time.** You'll want to open new credit accounts responsibly and make sure that you pay those bills on time and in full each month. If you're coming out of bankruptcy and can't get a major credit card, start with a secured credit card offered by your local bank. With a secured card, you put a sum of money into an account and are allowed to charge up to that amount. For example, if you put

$1,000 into the account, you can charge up to $1,000. (If you default on the payment, the bank can seize the $1,000 in the account to pay off the bill.) After you've had the secured credit card for a period of time, you can add a gas or department store charge card, and then a major credit card.

CREDIT REPAIR SCAMS TO AVOID

If you are in a situation where your credit is badly damaged, you might be tempted to believe that the right company or individual can fix your credit in an instant. According to the Web site of the Federal Trade Commission, www.ftc.gov, the most successful phrases for credit repair companies are as follows:

> *"Credit problems? No problem!"*
> *"We can remove bankruptcies, judgments, liens, and bad loans from your credit file forever!"*
> *"We can erase your bad credit—100% guaranteed."*
> *"Create a new credit identity—legally."*

Unfortunately for consumers, there is no quick fix when it comes to repairing your credit. As we've discussed at length in this chapter, only you can fix your credit history and score, and only over time. If you fall for one of these lines, you could get into even bigger trouble with your credit history and score—while being out several thousand dollars. How do you know if a credit repair company is a scam? Here are some red flags:

- **The credit repair company wants you to pay in full before it provides any services.** Under the Credit Repair Organizations Act, companies have to provide all of the services promised before you fork over the dough.

- **The company doesn't fully inform you of your rights under the law or tell you what you can do yourself, for free.** All of this information is available at ftc.gov, on the Web sites of the three credit-reporting bureaus, and at ThinkGlink.com.

- **The company tells you to avoid contacting the three credit-reporting bureaus and asks that you correspond only with the company.** Sound a little controlling? That's how a fraudulent credit repair company keeps you from finding out that what it is doing is illegal.

- **The company tells you that accurate information can be removed from your credit history (whether it is positive or negative).** You're being sold a big, fat lie.

- **The company tells you it can give you a new Social Security number and start you off with a new credit identity.** This is completely false. What these companies do is pull an Employer Identification Number (EIN) for you to use instead of your Social Security number. The biggest problem with this is that if your wages and credit are tied to this new number, when it comes time for you to retire, part of your work history won't be factored into your monthly payments.

- **The company tells you it will clean up your credit history in thirty days.** This means they're going to dispute every piece of negative information, whether or not it is accurate. While the dispute is ongoing, the negative information will be temporarily removed from your credit history. But once it is confirmed, it will be back.

- **The company encourages you to lie or falsify documents in order to "clean up" your credit history.** According to the FTC, it's a federal crime to "lie on a loan or credit application, to misrepresent your Social Security number, or to obtain an Employer Identification Number from the IRS under false pretenses." You could be charged and prosecuted for mail or wire fraud if you use the mail, telephone, or Internet to apply for credit with false information.

How do you know if a credit repair organization is legitimate? Here's a checklist to follow:

- A credit repair organization must give you a copy of the "Consumer Credit File Rights Under State and Federal Law" brochure before you sign a contract.
- Your contract should specify payment terms, including the total cost; a detailed description of the services the company is performing for you; an estimate of how long it will take to achieve the required results; any guarantees offered by the company; and the company's complete contact information (name, business address, phone, and Web site).
- The company should not perform any services until it has your signature on the contract.
- You should be told that there is a three-day waiting period during which you can cancel the contract (in writing) without paying any fees.

The bottom line is that you're the best person to repair your credit history and score. You'll do it slowly, over time, while learning good money-management habits. If you follow the tips in this book—paying your bills on time, and in full, while paying down debt and practicing good credit management—your credit history will rise over a period of twelve to twenty-four months. *No one else can make this happen for you.* If your debt is overwhelming, contact the National Foundation for Consumer Credit (NFCC.org) or CredAbility.com, a national network of award-winning nonprofit credit counseling agencies, for information on quality budget counseling and debt-management programs.

WHAT TO DO WHEN SOMEONE ELSE DAMAGES YOUR CREDIT

It's bad enough if you damage your own credit. But it's really annoying when your credit history and score are damaged not by your own behavior but when someone steals your identity and uses your credit illegally.

When this happens, you can place a fraud alert on your credit history that lets the credit industry know that you may have been the victim of an identity theft. You can place a fraud alert on your report for ninety days, during which time creditors are not supposed to approve new credit accounts tied to your Social Security number without reaching you by phone to verify that you're you—and not someone simply posing as you. Once you place a fraud alert on your credit history, the three credit-reporting bureaus are required by law to send you a copy of your credit history. (If you ask, they will print only the final four digits of your Social Security number on the report.)

If you have a valid police report to prove that you have been a victim of identity theft, you may extend your fraud alert for up to seven years; creditors will have to contact you by phone before issuing credit during those additional years. With an extended fraud alert, you should be able to get two additional copies of your credit history, and your Social Security number will be removed automatically from prescreened credit and insurance offers for five years.

If you're a member of the military, you can request an active-duty alert, which is similar to a fraud alert but lasts for twelve months. With this alert, your Social Security number will also be removed from credit and insurance offers for two years.

To place a fraud alert, you simply have to contact any one of the three major credit-reporting bureaus and ask them to do it. It may take up to forty-eight hours for the alert to appear on your credit report. The bureau you call is required by law to contact the other two bureaus, who will then place a fraud alert on your credit report with them as well. The fastest way to place an alert—or basically do anything with the three credit-reporting bureaus—is to do it online.

HOW TO CONTACT THE THREE MAJOR CREDIT REPORTING BUREAUS

To place a fraud alert or to obtain a free copy of your credit history, contact the credit-reporting bureaus at the following phone numbers and addresses:

Equifax
To receive your free Equifax credit report visit www.equifax.com
/fcra or call 800-685-1111 or write to:
Equifax Information Services
P.O. Box 740241
Atlanta, GA 30374
To obtain your credit score, which costs $7.95, call
toll-free 877-SCORE-11, or write
Equifax Information Services LLC
PO Box 105252
Atlanta, GA 30348

Experian
P.O. Box 9554
Allen, TX 07013
(888) EXPERIAN (397-3742)
Experian.com

TransUnion
(800) 680-7289
Transunion.com
TransUnion
P.O. Box 6790
Fullerton, CA 92834

To request a copy of your free credit report from each of the three credit reporting bureaus once a year, you can go online to AnnualCreditReport.com. If you want to get your reports texted to your cell phone, call toll-free 877-322-8228. If you want to receive them through the mail, go to the Web site, download the form from this page (www.annualcreditreport.com/cra/order?mail), fill it out and mail it to: Annual Credit Report Request Service, P.O. Box 105281, Atlanta, GA 30348-5281.

If you decide you no longer want the fraud alert on your credit history, you can remove it by making a written request (either in a letter or on a fraud alert form, available on some of the credit bureau Web sites); provide a copy of a government-issued ID (driver's license, passport, state ID) and a copy of a utility bill, a bank statement, or an insurance statement; and mail it to the credit-reporting bureaus. (For more information on what to do if your identity is stolen, visit ThinkGlink.com/identity-theft.)

CREDIT OR SECURITY FREEZES

Fraud alerts are a temporary way to provide heightened security on your credit history. But having a fraud alert doesn't mean your credit history will be safe from identity theft—or that all creditors will follow the rules and call you to verify your identity before issuing new credit.

As a stronger protection against identity theft, states started passing new laws several years ago allowing consumers to freeze their credit history. A credit freeze, also known in some states as a "security freeze," literally stops all activity in your credit history. While you can still pull a copy of your credit history, no one else can, so creditors cannot issue new credit at all. To apply for new credit, you have to unlock or unfreeze your credit history (some credit experts say "lift" your freeze) and then refreeze it after you get the credit you need.

With a credit freeze, it's impossible for someone to steal your Social Security number and use it to open up new credit accounts. However, some threat of identity theft still remains—someone could get hold of an existing credit card and use it to charge up a storm, for instance—but no one will be able to buy a car and get a car loan posing as you.

Creditors don't like the idea of credit freezes because it can take some time to unfreeze your credit, so they lose out on some sales opportunities. For example, you might be walking around in a store that is offering a 10 percent off coupon if you sign up for a store credit card. If your credit is frozen, you won't be able to take advantage of that coupon, or sign up for the credit card—much to the retailer's chagrin.

The three major credit-reporting bureaus initially fought credit freezes but have managed to turn them into somewhat of a profit center. If you buy a credit-monitoring service from one of the bureaus (see a later section for information on these), it often comes with the ability to easily freeze and unfreeze your credit.

If you don't go with a credit-monitoring service, however, it's slightly more of a pain to implement and manage a credit freeze. And unless you're a victim of identity theft, a member of the armed forces, or, in some states, a senior citizen aged sixty-five or older, you may pay as much as $10 in fees to freeze your credit. (It costs nothing to remove a security freeze, because it's in the credit-reporting bureau's own financial interest to do so.) Experian, Equifax, and TransUnion all publish information on their Web sites explaining security freezes and the costs of implementing, lifting, and removing a security freeze.

If you don't need new credit, I think credit freezes are a good idea to keep identity theft at bay. But regularly checking your credit history will do the same thing.

To place or remove a credit freeze, contact the three major credit-reporting bureaus in writing at the following addresses:

Equifax Security Freeze
P.O. Box 105788
Atlanta, Georgia 30348

Experian Security Freeze
P.O. Box 9554
Allen, TX 75013

TransUnion Fraud Victim Assistance
P.O. Box 6790
Fullerton, CA 92834

HOW TO PROTECT YOURSELF AGAINST IDENTITY THEFT

Here are ways you can reduce your risk of identity theft:

1. **Protect your personal information.** Put a lock on your mailbox (but make sure mail carriers have a big enough slot to deliver mail) and remember to pick up your mail as soon as possible. Cross-

shred your bills. Carry only the information you need. Use effective ("strong") passwords for your online financial accounts.

2. **Protect your Social Security number.** Don't carry your Social Security card—ever. Request alternate identification numbers and don't use your Social Security number as a password.

3. **Opt out of companies sharing your personal data.** Make sure you call (888) 5-OPT-OUT to stop creditors from sending you pre-approved offers. Then opt out of information sharing at your bank and other financial services policies—otherwise you're giving your financial institution permission to sell your personal information to third-party partners.

4. **Avoid "phishing" or "pharming" schemes.** Never reply to an e-mail or a pop-up ad or an IM that asks for personal information like account numbers or passwords, and never click on the links in these messages. Be very careful of tweets you receive through Twitter asking for personal information. Watch out for Facebook friends who ask you to follow links to suspect sites. You should just assume these are all fraudulent, even if they look real. If you are interested in the offer and want to determine if it's real, contact the company separately.

5. **Be a savvy Internet user.** Never use your debit card when shopping online; deal only with reputable companies; and check the privacy and security policies of Web sites you frequent. Most important, be sure to install firewalls and virus-detection software on your computers and keep them updated daily. (I think firewalls and virus-detection software are a *must* for all computer users.)

6. **Keep track of your financial accounts.** Check your accounts during the month for fraudulent charges and report suspicious charges immediately. Make sure you get your statements and bills on time (keep track in your calendar or with an online reminder), and call

your creditor if you don't. Creating online accounts makes all of this easier and faster—and paying online is generally a smart idea.

7. **Monitor your credit report.** As we've already discussed, you can get a free credit report from each of the three credit-reporting bureaus once a year. Go to AnnualCreditReport.com.

8. **Take control of your credit history.** If your identity has been stolen, consider putting a fraud alert on your credit history or perhaps even using a credit or security freeze to prevent further theft.

9. **Just say no.** If someone asks you for personal information that seems unnecessary for the transaction, don't give it to them. Don't let anyone take your credit card someplace you can't see, even for a moment. When you go to a doctor's office and have to fill out paperwork, don't put down your Social Security number. (Medical identity theft—where someone steals your Social Security number and personal information in order to get medical care or medical reimbursements at your expense—is a growing problem. I've created a bunch of helpful videos on medical identity theft at www .ExpertRealEstateTips.net.)

10. **Be active.** Talk to your employer about what policies it has in place to protect your identity. Write your congressional representative to request tougher laws that better protect consumers' personal information.

CREDIT-MONITORING SERVICES AND OTHER TOOLS

How closely should you monitor your credit history and score? According to the three credit-reporting bureaus, you can't monitor them too closely. Each credit-reporting bureau offers a credit-monitoring service for a monthly fee. While the details of each monitoring service differ, they essentially provide the following:

- Unlimited access to your credit history and score from the company where you purchase the service
- Limited access to your credit reports from the other two bureaus
- Information about your credit history and score and what you can do to improve them
- Information on how your credit history and score compare with those of the general public
- Text or e-mail alerts to changes in your credit report or score
- The ability to freeze and unfreeze your credit report (depending on which service you purchase)
- Identity theft insurance in varying amounts
- 24/7 customer service by phone
- Online dispute capabilities
- Online fraud alert placement capabilities

The price you'll pay for these services ranges from $9.95 per month to more than $14.95 per month. You have to decide if you're comfortable with a higher level of credit monitoring and if you want to pay for that service, or if you can manage your own credit using the free credit reports you can get each year from AnnualCreditReport.com.

I'd like to see more options for credit monitoring, such as the option to build my own credit-monitoring service and price it accordingly, or to choose services and features à la carte.

Do you need to pay up to $180 per year for a credit-monitoring service to have a great credit history and score? No, but it can be helpful, and it's a lot less expensive than paying a fraudulent credit repair company thousands of dollars to mess up your credit even more.

FIVE

WHAT CAN YOU AFFORD TO BUY?

t was 2007, and Lyn and Todd were ready to buy a home where they could raise their six-year-old twin daughters. Lyn had been offered a teaching position in Dutchess County, New York, near where she grew up and where her extended family still lived. Her husband found work at a local bank. They weren't sure exactly where they wanted to live, so they rented a house and spent their weekends walking the girls through different neighborhoods, checking out the playgrounds, and visiting coffeehouses to pick up the local flavor.

Lyn and Todd knew it would take some decent planning to figure out what they could afford. Home prices in Dutchess County—just as everywhere else in the United States at the time—were extremely high. The stock market was rising to record heights (and would hit a high in November, 2007), and sellers in the area didn't see the writing on the wall. They were hanging on, expecting their home values to keep rising forever. And, of course, New York State isn't exactly the land of cheap living. Between income taxes, real estate taxes, and the occasional slice of pizza, half a person's income can easily be eaten up. Lyn and Todd weren't really in a hurry to buy, and home prices were so high it wasn't worth it to them to jump into the real estate market. So they spent their time getting their financials in order.

"We used inheritance money to pay down our revolving debt, and we made sure we knew our credit scores. We did make a budget, which in New York is even more important, since property taxes are so high. We needed to make sure we took into account that tax number when thinking of our monthly mortgage payment," Lyn explained. One of the houses they liked cost $285,000, but the property taxes were $6,100— just over 2 percent of the asking price.

By early 2008, they were watching the stock market begin to slide, and then the housing market started to unravel all around them. Panic was in the air. "When home prices started going down around us, we pounced," Lyn said.

They put together a great home-buying team: they found a real estate agent they liked at an open house she was hosting, a loan officer who worked at the bank where Todd was employed, an attorney from Lyn's father's firm. They applied for an FHA loan and ultimately locked in at 4.75 percent for thirty years; they'd pay closing costs with funds borrowed from Lyn's 401(k). But the local housing stock was an issue. Even with home prices dropping, the houses they could afford were all fixer-uppers. The interiors looked as if they hadn't been touched in decades.

"We were prepared for that, and even welcomed some that needed work, and were very willing to trade space—both acreage and square footage—for a house that was in perfect condition. But—wow—there were still some crappy houses out there that needed a *lot* of work. And we had to be in a decent school district for the children, so that, too, added to the search," she recalled.

Lyn and Todd didn't find any foreclosures that were affordable, but they did see a house they liked that was owned by a relocation company and had been vacant for two years. "It had had a bid on it and gone to contract about a year and a half [prior], but the home inspection found mold, and the relocation company refused to remediate it. So the buyer backed out. Fast-forward to now: the company finally realized that in this market, and even back then, no one was going to buy a house with a mold problem. So, as luck would have it, the relocation company decided to remediate the mold right about the time we went to see the house," Lyn said.

Working with the relocation company was a slow process, and, at the same time, the lender said that because the house was built before 1978, it was a likely candidate for having lead paint. A condition of Todd and Lyn's loan was that any chipping exterior paint would have to be sanded off and repainted. Since the relocation company wouldn't spring for that, Lyn and Todd spent a few days working on the exterior in order to qualify for the house.

And then, before they knew it, it was time for the closing.

What made it work, Lyn realized, was the time she and Todd took to really scope out the neighborhood and calculate exactly how much they could afford to spend on the costs of owning and maintaining their home. They realized they were priced out of the market for a new house but wanted to have a beautiful home, so they set aside some of their annual budget for projects that would improve their home over time.

Lyn and Todd's experience in sorting out their financial issues and strengthening their family balance sheet is the same that millions of other home buyers go through each year—— particularly in light of the negative financial effect the recent recession has had. This chapter will help you analyze your financials so you know exactly how much you have to spend on your purchase and how to calculate all the real costs involved in owning property.

CALCULATING YOUR INCOME, ASSETS, EXPENSES, AND LIABILITIES

Figuring out how much you can actually afford to spend on a house—which is perhaps different from what a lender tells you that you can afford—requires spending a little time with a pencil and paper calculating how much you earn, how much you have, how much you spend, and how much you owe; in other words, analyzing the four chambers of your investment life: income, assets, expenses, and liabilities. How you manage each of these allows you to realize a golden financial future—or not. Here's a look at each:

- **Income:** Everything you earn, including your salary, commissions, bonuses, interest income, dividends, alimony and child support, rental income from any investment properties you own, and profits from your business.
- **Assets:** Equity (value of the property minus the mortgage you owe) for any homes or investment properties you own, stocks, bonds, mutual funds, retirement accounts, cash on hand, precious metals, and anything else you own that might have value, such as artwork, jewelry, or collectible cars. (When calculating your assets for the purposes of a mortgage, lenders generally will not include your furniture, the cars that you drive to and from work, or your clothing.)
- **Expenses:** Food, clothing, shelter, utilities, transportation, education, entertainment, house of worship (tickets or tithing), child care, mortgage or rent, vacations, insurance policies, lawn care, car repairs, debt service (that is, interest or fees paid on any outstanding debts or loans), afternoon coffee runs, and so on.
- **Liabilities:** What you owe, including school loans, car loans, mortgage, and credit card debt.

You should know exactly what you owe and what the interest rate is on the debt you're carrying. (One way to build wealth is to watch out for ways to pay less interest on debts you owe so that you can pay them off faster and be debt-free sooner.) If you spend more than you earn, your debts (liabilities) will be high. You'll pay so much to service your debts that you won't be able to put aside cash to build your asset base. What you need to do is add up your current debt load and figure out how much you're paying each month to service the debt (paying at least the minimum amount due). If your monthly debt service is more than 10 percent of your gross monthly income, you should focus on paying down your debt so that you can more easily qualify for a loan. (With a high debt load, you might not qualify at all.)

Let's start the process of figuring out how much you can afford to spend by taking a closer look at your daily, monthly, and annual expenses.

EXPENSES: HOW MUCH DO YOU SPEND IN A YEAR?

If you don't know how much you spend in a year and aren't even sure whether you spend more or less than you earn, now is the time to start writing down every cent that leaves your pocket.

I recommend writing down every cent you spend because even people who have a great memory have trouble remembering how much they spend in a day. There's just too much going on in most of our daily lives. Whether you whip out a sixty-cent pad of paper or track each day's expenses on scrap paper and later transfer the information to your computer, the process of writing down your daily expenses will make you a much more thoughtful consumer.

But as you're getting started writing down your daily expenses, you'll need to look backward to help figure out some of the weekly, monthly, and annual expenses you've been paying. Here are two tricks I use that might be helpful.

First, categorize your major expenses into daily, weekly, monthly, and annual expenses, such as in the sample chart below. If you set up the chart as an Excel spreadsheet or use Google Docs, each day you enter your expenses you'll be able to automatically calculate your costs going forward—and that should help you figure out what you've spent earlier. To calculate your monthly expenses, multiply your weekly expenses by fifty-two (weeks) and then divide by twelve (months) to come up with an annualized "monthly" expense number. For annual expenses, like insurance or tuition, you'll want to divide by 12, so you have a monthly figure. Keep track of daily expenses for two to three months, then add the average of those months in as part of the monthly expenses.

Daily Expenses	Weekly Expenses	Monthly Expenses	Annual Expenses
Coffee	Groceries	Rent/mortgage	Life insurance
Lunch	Gas for car	Utilities	School expenses
Dinner	Entertainment	Phone/wireless	Subscriptions
Transportation	Child care	Cable	Charity
Snacks	Landscaping	Property taxes	Dental bills
Drinks with friends	Laundry	Health insurance	Vacations
Books/CDs/DVDs	Dry cleaning	Homeowners insurance	House of worship
Pharmacy	Housecleaning	Retirement contrib.	Savings
Gifts	Care for aging parent	Auto loan/lease	Other insurance costs
Babysitting		Tuition	
		Debt service	
		Health club	
		Clothing	

My other trick is to go back over my monthly credit card bills, checkbook, and any receipts I happened to stuff into my pockets and analyze where I spend money over a day, over a month, and over a year. This is easy for me because I prefer to charge (and receive cash back or miles) rather than pay cash. You can also do this by examining your bank statements, if you pay by debit card or by check.

Here's another option: Track your expenses on a daily basis with software. I track everything in Quicken (for house expenses) and Quick-Books (for business expenses). You can also use Mint.com or Quicken Online, or any of the free Internet budgeting sites that allow you to set up your bank and credit accounts so that your monthly expenditures flow directly into the budget. Some of these programs allow you to link your credit and bank accounts directly to the software so you don't have to manually enter most of your expenditures. They'll also update your bank totals every time you open up the program. All you'll have to do is set up the accounts online (which will take a bit of time initially) and then enter the cash receipts for items you purchase separately.

Once you have a daily figure for every expense, add up the figures and multiply that number by 365 to get an approximation of what you spend each year. (If you want to know what you spend per day, divide your annual expenses by 365, your monthly expenses by 12, and your weekly expenses by 7.) Ideally, you'll want to know what your annual expenses are and how these expenses compare to your gross annual income and take-home pay. If what you spend annually is less than your annual household income, great—you get to move on to adding up the costs of owning, operating, and insuring a home.

If, however, you spend more than you earn, you've got a big problem to solve before you can think about establishing a budget for your home purchase. How are you going to cut expenses so that you can afford to buy, own, and maintain your new home?

Cutting Your Budget

When advising people on how to cut their expenses, most financial experts will say, "Slice 10 percent off what you spend each year" and leave it to you to figure out where to make the cuts. I have the complete opposite view: I make a list of necessities and then add in what I can afford. My starter list includes the following:

- Food
- Shelter (including rent or mortgage, property taxes, and insurance)
- Utilities (including cell/wireless but not cable)
- Child care and children's expenses
- Transportation
- Insurance
- Medical expenses

That's it. No gifts, no contributions to a house of worship, no weekly or monthly maid service, no entertainment—just the basic necessities of my life. Some people think this is extreme. Then again, some folks believe life without cable isn't worth living. (If you are one of them, we'll have to agree to disagree.)

When trimming expenses, it's much easier to start with necessities and then add where you can, rather than just cutting into a budget, which can cause problems for families who don't agree on what needs to be cut. Once you understand how little you actually need in order to live, you can start to build from there.

So take out a piece of paper and a pencil (or use Excel) and tally up these basic monthly expenses. Subtract that number from your take-home pay. If you have any cash left, here's what you should add in next, in order:

- Debt service other than your mortgage, including credit card debt and student loans (minimum payments only)
- Emergency savings
- Retirement contribution, preferably to your company 401(k) or a Roth IRA
- Down payment savings—you can switch retirement contribution with down payment savings for a while, but it's important to do both

I host a top-rated radio talk show on WSB radio in Atlanta on Sunday mornings, and many of my listeners feel strongly that tithing or contributions to a house of worship should be at the top of the basic necessities list. I believe that while it would be nice to put donations at the top, charity begins at home. I feel you need to take care of yourself and your family first, by providing a place to live, food on the table, lights, health insurance, and coverage for medical expenses. Then you need to pay down your debt and build up your emergency savings. You can spend what's left where you need to.

The reality is that just about everyone's funds are limited, and some are desperately short. When cutting your budget and living with spending limits, instead of thinking about what you're giving up, focus on what you're potentially getting: a new home. You're trading something that's less important to you (cable TV, perhaps) for something that's incredibly important to your long-term happiness and financial well-being (real estate). Figuring out what you absolutely *need* in order to live versus what you *want* will help you prioritize your financial life and get you focused on the only goal that matters.

ADDING UP THE COSTS TO OWN,
OPERATE, AND INSURE YOUR HOME

Something is always going wrong with my house. While I was writing this chapter, the microwave broke. I put my mug of water into the microwave, and when the time was up, I opened the door—and the microwave kept running. (As I was making my final changes to these pages, the dishwasher broke!)

Before we had the microwave problem, the garbage can track inside my kitchen cabinet broke and had to be replaced. Earlier in the year, our refrigerator stopped keeping things cold, so that had to be replaced as well. (The cost of replacing it was actually less than the cost of the original ten years ago—a nice surprise.) Our kitchen sink faucet broke, and we found a fabulous replacement for less than $200. Then, we spent $300 to fix one of the burners on the stove that had stopped working.

Did you know that smoke detectors work for only a few years before needing to be replaced? In the fifteen years we've lived in our house, we've replaced the whole set at least three times. The seal on the picture window in my office has broken and been replaced twice as well. We've had new gutters installed and put heat wires on the roof to help keep ice dams at bay. The toilet in our son's bathroom lasted forty-odd years but needed replacing this summer.

And all this is in addition to the ongoing house maintenance.

In the summer, we have weekly—or semiweekly, depending on the amount of rain—landscaping chores. It takes my husband, Sam, about an hour to mow the lawn, plus extra time for us to trim the bushes, weed and water the flowers, and sweep up the plant debris. In the winter, he puts a plow on the tractor and removes the snow. Once a year, we blacktop the driveway (it gets scraped up by the snow plow). If we didn't have siding, we'd have to repaint the exterior of our house about every three to five years (siding was an easy choice after we calculated the cost of painting). Next year, the side door leading from the garage to the driveway will have to be replaced.

Inside the house, we have to change all kinds of filters and batteries, repaint rooms and replace carpeting from time to time, spray for ants in the spring, watch for leaking in the fall, and so on.

Our rental properties aren't cost-free, either. We've had good tenants and bad, clean ones and those who kept the place less than clean. Between each lease, the apartments need painting. One tenant's dog scratched up the hardwood floors in one of our units so badly that we had to have the floors redone. And although we tell our tenants to change filters and batteries and take the lint out of the dryer, not all of them do—some see those chores as a landlord's job. (See the following section for a longer list of costs you may encounter when you own rental property.)

My point is simple: It's expensive to own and maintain property, and you can easily go broke if you underestimate the costs. Here's what you can expect to pay:

- **Mortgage, real estate taxes, homeowners insurance premium:** Often called "PITI" (principal, interest, taxes, and insurance) for short, these expenses are either paid as one payment each month (if you escrow your taxes and insurance premium) or as a monthly check for the mortgage and an annual or a semiannual check for taxes and insurance.
- **Homeowners association fees, co-op assessments, monthly maintenance fees:** If you live in a condo, co-op, townhome development, or single-family-home subdivision, you'll have to pay some sort of regular fee to cover the maintenance and expenses of the common areas.

- **Utilities:** These include gas, electricity, cable or satellite, Internet service, garbage removal, water, and sewer (these last two may be billed together).
- **Repairs to and maintenance of the exterior and interior of the property:** These costs include everything from window washing and tuck-pointing to replacing appliances, carpet, batteries, and filters, and pest control (particularly in some parts of the country).
- **Landscape care:** You'll need to plan for lawn and garden care in warm weather months and snow removal (in areas that get snow) in the winter.

Some people are of the opinion that preventive care is not worth the expense, or that a small problem, if it doesn't inhibit daily life, is a problem that can be ignored. The problem with not taking care of problems when they're small is that they only get worse. In 2008, an incredible hailstorm seemed to position itself directly above my friend Fred's neighborhood in Glenview, Illinois. He didn't think much about it, but the following year his insurance company sent out inspectors to check his roof, which turned out to have sustained so much hail damage that the shingles looked like Swiss cheese. The entire roof needed to be replaced (which his insurance company paid for), but those damaged shingles could have caused extensive, and much more expensive, damage inside the house. (The moral of this story is always check your roof after a major hailstorm.)

The bottom line is that home maintenance requires vigilance—and a ready checkbook. The most cost-effective way to manage your home's ongoing maintenance is to learn how to do it yourself. My husband calculates that he has saved us at least $5,000 a year in home-maintenance costs by learning to do much of the work himself. That adds up to more than $100,000 in the twenty-plus years we've been homeowners. Think about what you wouldn't be spending if you mowed your own lawn, replaced your own toilets, fixed the squeaky doors, sprayed for insects, and so on.

If you've never owned a home, talk to your homeowner friends about what they spend on all of these expenses. Ask them for a list of everything they've had to spend money on in the past year and then adapt it for the type of property you plan to buy. If you currently own property, go through your checkbook or credit card statements to figure out what house-related expenses you've had in the past year. If you track your expenses with Quicken, create a "house" category, and these expenses will pop up automatically. Even if you plan on doing all your maintenance work yourself, it's helpful to know what to expect.

THE COSTS OF BUYING AND OWNING INVESTMENT PROPERTY

In general, the costs of buying and owning investment real estate are similar to those of buying and owning a primary residence. You don't want to skimp here just because you're not planning on living in the property. First, if your tenants are unhappy, you'll be unhappy because they'll be constantly calling you to fix things. Second, life can change at the drop of a hat. You might wind up living in this property at some point in time.

Before you buy, you'll want to make sure you know about any potentially costly problems with the property—for the sake of your tenants and your wallet. To do this, hire a professional home inspector who specializes in the type of property you're buying. (A professional home inspector will work for a condo, a townhome, a single-family house, or even a small building with four to ten rental units. For something larger, you may want to hire a commercial building inspector or someone with experience inspecting commercial or industrial buildings.) You should expect to pay at least $400, depending on the size and complexity of the inspection.

Of course, you may not be able to inspect the property before making an offer. This happens with some foreclosure auctions. In that case, you'll have to make an educated guess about the condition of the property and make the best deal possible. Sam and I bought an investment condo near where we live in 2000. It seemed like an amazing opportunity, but we bought the property at an auction, without having toured the inside. It was a new building (the unit we bought already had a tenant), and I hadn't heard of any problems with it. In fact, the property had several big, expensive problems that we had to shell out thousands of dollars to fix. An inspection might not have caught the property's water drainage issue, but it might have caught some other issues. (Later, I describe what happened at that auction and how you might want to protect yourself.)

Keep in mind that sometimes the bigger the property, the more expensive the problems. In some cases, it's just that smaller problems are replicated over four or more units and wind up costing a lot of cash up front to fix.

Some longtime friends of mine own dozens of investment properties with thousands of apartment units. Some of the buildings also have retail or office space. These real estate investors are successful in part because they have a profile for the buildings they know (or expect) will be profitable. And they know they may have to pay up front to make adjustments to their units that will pay out over time. For example, they make each tenant responsible for his or her own hot water heater and electric heat—removing one cost item from the landlord's balance sheet and transferring it to the tenant's bill pile. It's a smart move, but it requires that my friends invest in advance to fix up each unit. That's one of many costs that they factor into the calculation to help them determine whether a building is worth a particular price.

In addition to spotting potentially expensive problems and factoring in any necessary adjustments before you purchase the property, you'll also have to figure out a budget for ongoing maintenance. Will you paint the walls each time a new tenant moves in? Will you clean the carpet? Will you polish the floor? Will you have the windows washed and the furnace inspected and cleaned each year? Will you buy new air-conditioning window units for each apartment when the old ones break?

If the property is large enough, you may want to hire someone to be the building caretaker, which is another expense. This person would ideally live on-site or in the neighborhood, so that he or she can be on hand to take care of those pesky 3 a.m. calls to fix a clogged toilet. An investor I know who primarily invests in buildings on college campuses hires a graduate student to handle these chores. The graduate student lives on-site either for free (if the property is large enough) or at a greatly reduced rent. In addition, the graduate student receives a small monthly stipend for handling the routine maintenance of the property and keeping an eye on the student tenants.

Here's a list of potential expenses you may encounter when you buy and own rental property:

- **Mortgage and real estate taxes.**
- **Property and umbrella liability insurance premiums:** For investment real estate, you'll want to have not only property insurance, but also an umbrella liability insurance policy, in case someone gets injured on your property (if, for example, your tenant, or a visiting friend of your tenant, trips on the stairs and breaks a leg). If you decide to hold your investment properties in a limited liability company (LLC) or an S Corporation or a C Corporation, you will want to purchase property and liability insurance that names the company or corporation as the insured. In addition, you may want

to purchase an additional umbrella policy for yourself, just in case someone sues you and is successful in coming after you personally (not just your companies). If you're going to hold your investment properties personally, you'll definitely want to carry a large amount of umbrella liability insurance. Your insurance agent should be able to help you determine the appropriate amount based on the size of the property.

- **Homeowners association fees, co-op assessments, monthly maintenance fees:** You may be able to charge enough in rent to cover these, but if not, they're your responsibility.
- **Utilities:** The tenant may pay some of these directly, and others will be a part of your tax bill. (Be sure to factor in the cost of the utilities you'll pay when calculating the rent you'll charge.)
- **Repairs to and maintenance of the exterior and interior of the property:** This covers everything discussed in the section under maintaining a primary residence, plus carpet cleaning, repainting between tenants, repairing items damaged by the tenant, and re-placing any items that "disappear" when the tenant leaves. (One way to stop these disappearances is to have an exit interview with the tenant in which you tour the property together with a checklist of every item in the unit; if anything is missing or damaged, the cost comes out of the tenant's security deposit. You can provide a copy of the checklist, with costs assigned to the items on it, to the tenant when he or she moves in. That way, the tenant is on notice of how much it will cost at move-out time if something is broken or lost.)
- **Landscaping:** If you purchase a condominium as an investment property, landscaping typically won't be your responsibility (or your tenant's). Instead, you'll pay a monthly maintenance fee that will pay for the building management company to take care of the com-mon elements of the property. With a single-family home, make sure your rental agreement lists the items that the tenant is respon-

sible for doing, including maintaining the landscaping, and changing lightbulbs, filters, and batteries. If the tenant fails to maintain the landscaping, or if there is a problem caused by the tenant's failure to change a lint filter in the dryer, for example, one option is for you to do it and bill the tenant for the cost.

■ **Special taxes and fees:** As an investment property owner, you can expect to pay higher property taxes, because you won't be able to use the homeowners' exemption on investment property. Also, some homeowner associations charge owners who rent their properties extra fees because they believe that non-owner-occupied property costs more to manage.

■ **Repairs to get the unit in rentable condition:** This is the big number for most rental properties. If you're buying a unit that needs extensive repair work before you can rent it, it's important that you factor those costs into the purchase price. But it's always possible that those anticipated expenses (such as painting, carpeting, replacing some appliances) will mushroom when you start making other repairs. (This is why having a top-notch inspector as part of your home-buying team is so valuable.) Unless you're a contractor, it will take some time and practice for you to figure out exactly how much it will cost to get an investment property into rentable shape.

■ **The X factor:** The "X factor" is a line item in your investment property budget for the unknown—and something always pops up. Some investors use a percentage (such as 2 percent or 5 percent of the maintenance budget), and some just add in a fixed cost (such as $1,000 or $5,000), depending on the size of the maintenance budget. This column covers issues such as having to replace a furnace or hot water heater.

As you grow and learn as a real estate investor, you'll develop your own formula for success. But you'll always have to watch your expenses.

When it comes to owning investment real estate, every time you spend money, it's coming out of your own pocket, so finding better and cheaper ways to maintain your property will benefit you in the long run.

MAKING TRADE-OFFS AND COMPROMISES

Unless you have more money than you need, you'll have to make some trade-offs and compromises when you buy a piece of real estate. What will those trade-offs be? It's hard to know before you find the property you want to buy, but being prepared for what you might confront will only help you make a decision when the time comes. One exercise I suggest is making a wish list and a reality check. I talk about these in my book *100 Questions Every First-Time Home Buyer Should Ask* as a way of figuring out what you're willing to trade off.

A *wish list* is a list of everything you've ever wanted in a home, from the number of bedrooms and bathrooms right down to the type of granite in the kitchen. When you make this list, be sure to include items such as distance to work, school district, recreational opportunities, home office, etc.

A *reality check* is a list of everything you can't live without. For example, you might want a four-bedroom single-family house with four and a half baths (wish list), but what you really need is a three-bedroom town house with two and a half baths (reality check). The operative word is *need*, because in the post–housing crisis world, most of us have to focus on our needs and not our wants.

Once you complete the wish list (and I'll be disappointed if it doesn't have at least twenty items on it), then you can tackle your reality check or list of needs. If you're buying the property with another person (spouse, partner, parent, child, friend, and so on), make sure that person also completes a wish list and a reality check.

The next step is for each person to sort his or her lists. Start with your wish list. The first item on the list should be the item that is most important to you. The first item on your reality check should be the one thing you truly cannot live without. Once you prioritize your lists, you and whoever else is buying the property with you should sit down and compare them.

The trading off and compromising part of buying real estate starts at this point—once you know what you need and what you want (and what your spouse or partner needs and wants) and the difference between the two, you can figure out what should be on your joint wish list and reality check. That's right: you need to combine your individual lists into one master list representing what you both truly want and need in the property you buy.

Why is this important? You and your spouse or partner (or whoever is buying the property with you) will be working (most likely) with one real estate agent. Your master wish list and reality check will help the agent understand what you're looking for in a piece of real estate, which will help narrow the choices.

Of course, the time will come when you have to figure out which of a number of properties will work best for you. Your wish list and reality check will allow you to compare these properties on an apples-to-apples basis and make trade-offs, such as amenities for room sizes, or school district for number of bedrooms, or distance to work for additional recreational opportunities.

For example, let's say that you and your spouse have listed a short commute to work at the top of both your wish list and your reality check. You've also listed three bedrooms and a good school district near the top. You're looking at two properties, one of which is a two-bedroom, two-bath house within a thirty-minute commute to work for you both; and the other home is farther away but has three bedrooms and two baths and is located in a better school district. Your master lists might dictate that the first home is the right one for you because of the commute. But if you think about the longer horizon, you'll have better price appreciation in the better school district, and you're getting a house that is the size you really need. Because you've been thoughtful in prioritizing your wish list and reality check, you and your spouse or partner will be able to have a thoughtful, productive discussion about which way to go.

Even if you're buying on your own, you'll need to make some trade-offs and compromises, because almost no one gets to have everything he or she wants in a property. You may want a top school district but can afford only a two-bedroom house. If you want a larger house, you might have to settle for a second-best or third-best school district. (Just remember: the one thing that's really difficult to change is a property's location—very few people will actually move a house to another location.)

Understanding your wants and needs is a key part of figuring out how much you can afford to spend. It's incredibly helpful to know where you can trim a want in order to make room for a need. Hopefully, you'll get some of what you want and everything you need in the next home you buy. When it comes to real estate, you generally have to buy the house you can afford and over time turn it into the home you see in your dreams.

SIX

DOWN PAYMENT AND RESERVE MONEY: WHERE TO FIND IT AND WHERE TO STASH IT

We saved for a really long time," recalls Krista of the 3 percent down payment she and her husband, Phillip, scraped together. What they saved wouldn't have been enough for a down payment in their old neighborhood in California, but when she and Phillip moved to Colorado, they found a neighborhood they liked that was extremely affordable. They closed on their 1,800-square-foot, three-bedroom, two-and-a-half-bath house in December, 2008 and looked forward to starting a family there.

Like Krista and Phillip, most home buyers have trouble not with paying their monthly mortgage, real estate taxes, and insurance, but with coming up with cash for a down payment. If they've been rent-ers in the past, they're used to paying monthly checks; it's saving and accumulating enough for a cash down payment and the reserves that mortgage lenders now require that's the problem—especially when sav-ing for a down payment alone can take years.

In this chapter, we'll look at how much you need to put down to-ward a home purchase in today's market, where to find that money in your budget, and where to get help if you can't. We'll also look into smart places to stash your cash as you're building up funds for a down payment. Let's start with the numbers.

HOW MUCH CASH DO YOU NEED?

As we've discussed, the biggest change in real estate since the housing crisis is that prospective home buyers need cash, and plenty of it. Zero-down loans have virtually vanished (except for VA loans and USDA loans, which we looked at in chapter 3), as have 106 percent loans, which folded all of the closing costs into the purchase price.

Today, you'll need at least 3.5 percent for a cash down payment with an FHA loan (as much as 5 percent if you're closing in 2010 and beyond), plus more cash for closing costs and reserves.

At least the market isn't as it was in the 1930s and 1940s. According to Walter Moloney, a spokesman for the National Association of Realtors, if you wanted to buy a home during the Great Depression and its aftermath, you had to put down 50 percent in cash and pay off the rest of the house on a ten-year amortization schedule. (Today, that would be like buying a home with a 50 percent down payment and using a home equity loan!)

Of course, finding and saving even 3.5 percent to put down on a house is hard enough. For home buyers used to instant gratification—and when everything from new cars to flat-screen televisions is available to take home today (provided you have the credit), how could you not be?—the idea of stashing away cash for years in order to buy a home is difficult for some to grasp. We're all so used to getting what we want when we want it that the concept of *delayed gratification*, or having a goal and working toward it, seems a little, well, quaint.

And yet we've arrived at a place in time where if you want to buy a $200,000 house, you'll need the following:

- $7,000 in cash for the down payment, or 3.5 percent, for an FHA loan. You'll need more if you want a conventional loan through Fannie Mae or Freddie Mac.
- One to six months of housing expenses (mortgage, taxes, and insurance) in cash (these are the so-called "cash reserves"). On a $196,500 loan at 5.5 percent, that's $1,115 per month just for the mortgage. If we assume another $450 per month for taxes and homeowners insurance premiums, you're looking at a total of $1,565 per month to set aside for reserves.
- Closing costs of anywhere from 2 to 6 percent, or $4,000 to $12,000.

SOURCES OF CASH FOR YOUR DOWN PAYMENT AND CLOSING COSTS

So where can you go to come up with this cash? Your loan officer doesn't care where you get it—he or she just wants to make sure that the cash you use to buy the home is really yours. Your down payment can come from a variety of sources:

- **Savings:** Your loan officer will want to verify that the cash has been in your account for at least six months to ensure that it's "seasoned"— in other words, that it's really yours and not a short-term loan from someone.
- **Investments:** You can either use the income from investments or sell them and cash out. Remember that you may owe taxes the following April 15 for any profits realized on the sale of the investments. You'll pay tax at your marginal tax rate on your short-term profits, and long-term capital gains tax on profits from assets you've held at least a year, so be sure to set aside the cash you'll need to pay those taxes or adjust your withholdings.

- **Home equity:** You can tap the equity from a property you own, including your current primary residence, your vacation home, or an investment property. The easiest way to do this (if you have a significant amount of equity in these properties) is with a home equity loan. For vacation homes and investment properties, it's much more difficult to do a cash-out refinance—in which you refinance your mortgage by taking out another one for more than you owe—and you won't be able to do one if your primary home is currently on the market or has been within the last six months.

- **Gift funds:** FHA rules permit any family member or friend to give you the gift of cash. However, your lender will require you to get a gift letter stating that the funds are a gift and do not need to be returned. Gift funds should be in your account at least three to six months before you need them to "season" the cash. The longer the cash is in your account, the better it is for you.

- **IRA distribution:** First-time buyers may use up to $10,000 from an IRA to "buy, build or rebuild a first home," according to IRS Publication 590 (download this for free at IRS.gov). Most first-time buyers use their IRA distribution for a down payment. While you'll have to pay taxes on the cash you withdraw, you won't have to pay a penalty if you're under the age of 59½ .

- **A 401(k) or other company-sponsored qualified retirement plan:** I'm not a big fan of borrowing from your 401(k) plan for your down payment (I think you should keep that cash growing for your golden years), but if your company allows it and you've exhausted all your other options, go for it.

- **Social lenders or P2P lenders:** P2P (or person to person) lenders allow you to borrow from a group of people who select you based on personal information (who you are, what your credit score is) and why you need the cash (school loan, car loan, home loan, and so on). The current borrowing limits are probably too small on today's

P2P sites to get enough to buy a property, but you can get enough for a down payment. Top P2P sites include Prosper.com and LendingClub.com. If you and a family member or friend want to do a private loan to purchase your house, you can use a P2P site like VirginMoney.com, which will facilitate the loan process for a flat fee (that is much less than you'd pay a conventional lender), provide the paperwork, and then set up an automatic withdrawal from the borrower's bank account each month.

- **Down payment assistance programs:** Income-based programs are often available through your local housing authority (see the following section for more details) or sometimes through a local nonprofit housing agency, though each program runs for a limited period of time.

DOWN PAYMENT AND MORTGAGE ASSISTANCE PROGRAMS

Sometimes first-time buyers need a little helping hand. Since the government has deemed homeownership to be a community benefit, Community Development Block Grant (CDBG) funds are passed down from the federal government to state housing authorities and agencies to create down payment and mortgage assistance programs. These programs are usually income based or location based, meaning you have to either earn less than the prescribed amount or live or work within the prescribed area. Often you cannot purchase a house that costs more than a certain amount. You may be required to live in the house as your primary residence for a number of years, and in addition to attending required homeownership classes, you may be subject to other requirements and restrictions. The interest rate on loan programs (as opposed to outright grants) is typically well below the market interest rate.

These housing programs can be structured in a number of ways. You might see a program that offers a "silent second mortgage" to help the borrower qualify for an FHA program or a county-funded low-income mortgage payment. You might also see a matching grant program, where the housing agency gifts funds matching the cash the buyer has accumulated for a down payment. Other programs buy down the interest rate of the buyer's mortgage or offer a below-market interest rate. And still other programs are structured as forgivable loans, where a portion of the loan is forgiven each year over three, five, or ten years.

One thing to know about these programs is that they come and go fairly frequently. Housing agencies are given grants or a specified amount of cash to fund a specific program, and when those funds have been doled out, the down payment or mortgage assistance program closes until new funds have been secured. Program details and requirements are also subject to change.

Here are a few examples of local programs that were running in 2009 (please note, these programs may no longer be operating, but other similar programs might).

County of Orange Mortgage Assistance Program
Affordable Housing Clearinghouse (the county's nonprofit service
    provider)
(949) 859-9255
Program details: Orange County, California, offers a "silent second mortgage loan program for low-income first-time home buyers." Home buyers must contribute 1 percent of the purchase price. The mortgage assistance program contributes up to $40,000 as a silent second mortgage, which means that the funds can be used as a down payment and will not require any repayment until thirty years have expired (the assumption is that you will have finished making your primary mortgage payment by then), you sell or transfer the property, or the property is no

longer your primary residence. The interest rate is 3 percent, computed as simple interest.

Who qualifies: The program is available to first-time buyers who either have never owned a home or have not had ownership in a principal residence during the prior three years; to a displaced homeowner who has owned a home; to a single parent (unmarried or legally separated) who has owned a home with custody of minor children; or to an individual who has owned only a mobile home. All applicants who will be on title must provide evidence of U.S. citizenship or permanent resident alien status. The buyer must obtain a home buyer education certificate from an approved provider before being approved for financing.

Income limitations: Income is limited to $52,100 for a household of one to $74,400 for a family of four. Cosigners who are not on the title and who will not occupy the property can be used for qualifying purposes on the first mortgage loan but will not be included in the determination of household income.

Location limitations: The program is limited to residents of "County of Orange unincorporated areas (not yet incorporated into a city) and the cities of Aliso Viejo, Brea, Cypress, Dana Point, La Palma, Laguna Beach, Laguna Hills, Laguna Woods, Los Alamitos, Placentia, Seal Beach, Stanton, Villa Park and Yorba Linda."

Credit requirements: There is no minimum credit score required to qualify for the program. However, you cannot have past-due credit accounts at the time the loan is recorded, outstanding unpaid judgments or involuntary liens, or bankruptcies.

Mortgage requirements: Only thirty-year fixed-rate loans are available (no ARMs). The interest rate will not be more than the current market rate. The buyer must meet underwriting and eligibility guidelines of the first mortgage lender and have a combined loan-to-value ratio (first and second mortgage added together and compared with the value of the property) of no more than 105 percent of the purchase price.

City of Buena Park, California, First-Time Home Buyer Program
Economic Development Department
(714) 562-3538

Program details: Buena Park, California, offers first-time home buyer assistance in the form of a second mortgage up to $100,000; home buyers must contribute a minimum of 3 percent of the purchase price as a down payment, and the second mortgage is repaid when the borrower sells the property, transfers title/ownership of the property, takes equity out of the property, or no longer lives in the property. Inspections of the property are required to identify violations of code and health quality standards. A sixty-day escrow is suggested to provide time for city-mandated repairs.

Who qualifies: The program is available to households displaced as a result of city, county, state, or federal government action and is open for the first sixty days from May 1, 2009, through June 30, 2009, to residents who live or individuals who are employed in the City of Buena Park at the time of application. After July 1, 2009, the program will be open to all other eligible households on a first-come, first-served basis, until funds are depleted. Applicants are required to attend a first-time home buyer seminar with the Neighborhood Housing Services of Orange County or a comparable first-time home buyer assistance program, and must provide a certificate of attendance.

Income limitations: Income is limited to $52,100 for a household of one to $74,400 for a family of four. Cosigners who are not on the title and who will not occupy the property can be used for qualifying purposes on the first mortgage loan but will not be included in the determination of household income.

Property limitations: Sales price/value of the property cannot exceed 95 percent of the area median home value in Orange County. Sales price/value cannot exceed $399,000 for condominiums or $516,800 for single-family homes.

Credit requirements: The applicant must provide a copy of the last three years of federal income tax returns, the three most recent paycheck stubs, the three most recent savings account and the six most recent checking account statements for all accounts, a copy of a credit report, proof of income for all persons living in the household, and other income documentation, including documentation of child support, alimony, Social Security, supplemental security income, retirement, disability, Aid to Families with Dependent Children (AFDC), and interest on savings/income-earning accounts.

Mortgage requirements: The second mortgage is deferred for up to thirty years at 3 percent simple interest; the city can provide funds for down payment and closing cost assistance (up to $5,000 can be used for nonrecurring closing costs).

Georgia Dream Homeownership Program
Georgia Department of Community Affairs, Office of
    Homeownership
404-679-4847 or (800) 359-HOME

Program details: The Georgia Dream First Mortgage program provides low-interest-rate mortgage loans for borrowers with moderate incomes and modest assets. With certain exceptions, borrowers must be first-time buyers. First mortgage loans require that borrowers contribute a minimum of $500 of their own funds. The Georgia Dream Second Mortgage program offers a second loan of up to $20,000 that can be used with the first mortgage loan or separately to defray the down payment, closing costs and prepaid escrow items associated with the purchase.

Who qualifies: First mortgage borrowers must be first-time buyers, with exceptions for targeted rural counties and some urban census tracts, or must not have owned a home in the past three years. Second

mortgage loans of up to $7,500 are available to protectors (fire and po-
lice), educators, health care workers, and buyers of EarthCraft Homes,
ENERGY STAR Homes, and EasyLiving Homes. Second loans of up
to $20,000 are available to individuals with disabilities and households
with disabled members. Members of the military or their surviving
spouses may qualify for second loans of up to $10,000. Applicants must
meet a housing education requirement.

Income limitations: Eligible borrowers must have a total household
income that is less than 120 percent of the area median income. That
means buyers in the Atlanta metropolitan statistical area (MSA) must
have a total annual household income of less than $68,000 (for one or
two persons) or $78,000 (for three or more persons). Buyers in the rest
of Georgia are limited to a household income of $58,000 (one or two
persons) or $67,000 (three or more persons).

Property limitations: The sales price cannot exceed $250,000 in the
Atlanta MSA or $200,000 in the rest of the state. The property must
be occupied as a primary residence within sixty days of closing.

Mortgage requirements: Borrowers must qualify with conventional,
FHA, or USDA lenders. A new offering under the Georgia Dream
Homeownership Program was funded by the Housing and Economic
Recovery Act of 2008, and it's a good example of how limited the programs can be. The Georgia Dream NSP Purchase Program provides
$14,000 to eligible borrowers purchasing foreclosed properties in eli-
gible areas. The funds are disbursed in the form of a second mortgage
that carries no interest rate and requires no monthly payments. The
second mortgage lien is released over a period of five years and six
months, and the funds can be used for repairs or down payment assistance. The program started on April 1, 2009, and all funds must be
disbursed by June 30, 2010.

Orange County, Florida, Down Payment Assistance Program
Division of Housing Development
(407) 836-5174

Program details: Qualified buyers may receive between $20,000 and $35,000 in the form of a soft second mortgage (a second loan that doesn't cost anything on a monthly basis and isn't counted toward the buyer's debt-to-income ratio) at 0 percent interest that is forgiven in fifteen years, as long as the property remains the buyer's primary residence.

Who qualifies: The program is available to buyers whose annual household income does not exceed 120 percent of the area median income. Buyers must also contribute $1,000 or 1 percent of the purchase price of the property, whichever is higher, complete a homeowner's education seminar, qualify for a first loan, and meet the residency requirement of living in the Orlando MSA (including Orange, Seminole, Lake, and Osceola Counties).

Income limitations: Annual income cannot exceed 120 percent of the area median income.

Property limitations: The property must be new or substantially rehabbed, fee simple (the most basic type of ownership, under which the owner has the right to use and dispose of the property at will) and priced at no more than $219,000.

Mortgage requirements: The first and second mortgages may not exceed 105 percent of the property's sales price.

HOW TO FIND A DOWN PAYMENT OR
MORTGAGE ASSISTANCE PROGRAM

Finding a program is as easy as doing a search on the Internet. Just search the name of the city, county, or state in which you're looking to buy and the type of program you're looking for—for example, "Chicago down payment assistance program." When I did this search in Google, about 117,000 results came up. The first was a *Chicago Tribune* article from 2006 discussing down payment assistance programs that were available all over the metro area. While it's unlikely that these programs are around today, it is very likely that the local municipalities mentioned have replaced the housing programs with other programs.

The second result of my search was the Greater Chicago and Community Development Web site, which lists housing assistance programs that are available in northeastern Illinois.

SMART PLACES TO STASH YOUR CASH UNTIL YOU'RE READY TO USE IT

When it comes to saving cash, I recommend a simple investment strategy: divide your money into short-term cash and long-term investments. Where you invest these funds depends entirely on when you'll need them, whether it's soon or maybe never.

Home buyers are sometimes confused by the difference between long-term and short-term investments—they think that "short term" means you'll use the money within a day, a week, or a month and that "long term" means anything beyond that. Ask these folks what the word "risk" means, and they'll tell you it means "reward." That's a Rorschach test, not an investment strategy.

I characterize an investment as "short term" if you'll need to use the money (*all* the money) within a time horizon of less than three to five years. If funds are short term, they need to be put in an investment that's extremely safe—one that probably won't earn any great returns (more on this in a moment).

"Long-term" investments are those that you won't need for at least ten to fifteen years—or possibly ever. This is money that should be invested in a diversified portfolio of stocks and bonds, rarely traded, checked occasionally, and basically left untouched for a long time.

What about funds that won't be needed for five to ten years? These are medium-term funds, and you can eke out a slightly larger return on them by taking some risk with some of the cash and investing the rest in supersafe investments, such as an FDIC-insured CD, or certificate of deposit.

The great stock market crash of 2008–2009 proved that sometimes the best long-term investment is a CD. Certainly, placing your cash in a supersafe investment means it'll be there when you need it—which means it's a good option if you're saving for a down payment and closing costs.

A good place to start your search for a top FDIC-insured CD or money market account interest rate is BankRate.com. You should also contact your local bank for a list of their interest rates. And online banks tend to have similar or better interest rates than brick-and-mortar banks because they have less overhead, so be sure to check out an online financial institution like ING Direct or Discover Bank (related to Discover Card). Don't be fooled by online companies that sound like FDIC-insured financial institutions but aren't. Go to FDIC.gov and look up the institution before investing with it.

Since this chapter is all about short-term money (assuming you'll need your down payment sooner rather than later), here are a few extremely safe options for investing your cash:

Checking account: There's nothing wrong with stashing cash in an FDIC-insured checking account; you just won't earn much interest on your money. But the cash is extremely liquid and available whenever you want it.

Savings account: You'll earn slightly more interest on your cash with a savings account than with a checking account, but your bank may require you to have a minimum amount invested to earn the top interest rate available (a pattern you'll see with money market accounts as well). Typically, the more you have in your savings account, the higher the rate of interest you'll earn on the funds, up to a certain amount. You may also be limited as to how many withdrawals you can make in a month.

Money market account (MMA): These accounts pay slightly more in interest than a regular savings account. You may have to maintain a minimum amount in the account, and you will be limited to a small number of withdrawals per month. On the plus side, the cash is available whenever you want it. Some investors keep most of their cash in a money market account, transferring to their checking account each month just what they need to pay bills. Make sure the money market account you choose is FDIC insured and offers ATM withdrawals, automatic bill pay, daily (versus monthly) compounding, and other features that will make your life easier.

Certificate of deposit (CD): The concept behind a CD is that you are locking up your cash for a predetermined amount of time, and in return you receive a predetermined amount of interest on that cash. For example, many FDIC-insured financial institutions offer CDs for a term of four weeks, one to eight months, or one to ten years. You can allow the interest earned to stay with the CD or transfer it to a money market account. Several months before your CD matures, your bank or financial institution should contact you to offer you renewal options. If you don't do anything, the CD should automatically renew for the same period of time and at the same rate of interest. If you opt not to automatically renew, you'll need to contact the bank or financial institution at least ten business days before the CD matures to let it know whether you're adding or removing funds, transferring funds to a different account, or changing the terms of the CD. If you buy a CD and then cancel it early, you may have to pay an early withdrawal penalty, which can be steep. Be sure you know the rules of the CD before you buy.

As the credit crisis has recently proved, you're better safe than sorry. If you have cash you won't need over the short term, then by all means invest it in a diversified portfolio of stocks and bonds. But if there's a chance you'll need this cash in the next five years, you should invest it in CDs and a money market account. Although it may kill you not to get all those extra bucks in interest, you'll feel far worse if you wake up one morning and half your savings has disappeared.

A Word of Warning about CDs

Don't be tempted to purchase a three-year CD just because the interest rate you'll receive is half a percent higher than that of the one-year CD. If you're planning to buy a house, you'll probably make that purchase sooner than three years. You'd be smarter to keep your funds more flexible and simply purchase a collection of three-month, six-month, and one-year CDs that will give you a higher rate of interest but allow your funds to be accessed easily (an investing trick known as "laddering"). One year before you plan to buy a home, you should put the one-year CDs that mature into either three-month CDs or your money market account.

A Word about the Federal Deposit Insurance Corporation (FDIC)

The FDIC will insure your checking accounts, savings accounts, retirement accounts, and CDs up to $250,000 per person per institution through December 31, 2013. Well before then, the program will be reviewed and, I believe, extended indefinitely, or perhaps the amount insured will be tied to inflation in some way.

Some FDIC-insured banks are being creative about complying with the $250,000 per person per institution rule. You can make the most of the available deposit insurance by adding another individual to the account or by creating a payable-on-death (POD) or transfer-on-death (TOD) trust account. PODs and TODs allow you to name a beneficiary for these accounts other than yourself. Because the account is held for the benefit of someone else, you will be allowed to keep up to $250,000 per institution in that individual's name. Ask your banker for details about how much you can safely stash at that institution.

To find out if your bank is FDIC insured, visit FDIC.gov, where you can also look up the relative health of your bank.

Direct-Deposit Investing

One of my former assistant editors used to have $100 per paycheck deposited in a separate, online savings account. This was her emergency savings account. Because it was an online account, it was somewhat difficult for her to gain access to the cash. She figured that if she didn't have access to the $100 per paycheck, she'd learn to live without it.

Direct-deposit investing is one of the easiest ways you can save for any financial goal, whether it's a down payment and closing costs on a home purchase or your child's college tuition. The funds are subtracted from your paycheck (after taxes are taken out) and automatically transferred into whichever account you specify.

Some folks simply do not like direct deposit; they don't trust it and like to receive their paychecks in their hands. Here's what I have to say about that: Get over it! It's far less expensive to deposit funds directly than cut a check. The cash will be in your account on payday morning (instead of you having to go to the bank to cash the check), and you don't have to do anything.

Rather than fight direct deposit, embrace it and see what it can do for you. Talk to the department that handles your paychecks and see if you can direct a portion of your paycheck into another account. Whether you set aside $100 per paycheck or something more, you'll soon see the balance growing. If you choose to deposit those savings in a money market account (instead of a checking account) at an online bank that's FDIC insured, you'll earn a higher rate of interest compared with other banks. It's a relatively painless way to save.

One more thing: If you get a tax refund each year, you should request that it be deposited directly to your bank account. You'll get it faster (within ten business days) than if you ask for it to be sent by check, it won't get lost (unless you put in the wrong account number), and you won't have to resort to an advance refund loan, a loan against your tax refund that can carry an effective interest rate of 700 percent or more.

Now that you know how much cash you'll need for your down payment and lender-required reserves, it's time to think about what kind of properties you'll want to buy, and where you can find amazing, one-in-a-lifetime deals.

SEVEN

IDENTIFYING AMAZING OPPORTUNITIES:
SHORT SALES, FORECLOSURES, FIX-AND-FLIPS,
AND BUY-AND-HOLDS

'**ve been doing** this for a lot of years, and this is the worst market I've
ever seen."

It was the summer of 2009, and Bonnie was worried about the first-
time buyers in her neighborhood. As a homeownership manager at
Affordable Housing Clearinghouse in Lake Forest, California, which
provides financing and education to low-income populations with the
goal of creating quality affordable housing, she already knew that Orange County is one of the most expensive and difficult places for first-
time buyers to purchase a home. But the housing crisis and credit crisis
had made it even more difficult, because first-time buyers were now
competing with investors for houses—and losing.

"On a $300,000 bank-owned property, there are ten to fifteen offers
coming in. And it's the investor who is offering $50,000 above list price
and paying cash and doing a thirty-day escrow," she explained. "The
poor little first-time home buyer again is being put out and can't buy a
house. Their offers aren't getting through."

She added, "I've always said that when the banks were given the bailout money, it's too bad they didn't stipulate that when they fore-closed on a property, they had to sell to a family and not to an investor. It's distorting the market. It's not helping anyone. What are these inves-tors going to do? Flip the house? Rent it out? They'll make money when they sell it, but a family would keep it."

Although Bonnie was worried that first-time buyers wouldn't be able to buy a house in this market, the truth is that right now there are amazing, once-in-a-generation opportunities to buy real estate. Whether you're an investor or a first-time buyer looking to buy a home that you can live in for a while, you'll find that the record-breaking number of foreclosures has pushed down home prices across the country. Even in the summer of 2009, as the number of homes sold started to inch back up, prices continued to feel the pressure of more foreclosures coming on the market. And with an estimated seven million additional foreclosures scheduled to hit the market by 2011, first-time buyers will have plenty of opportunity to learn how to negotiate against more skilled investors.

In my own neighborhood that summer, my husband, Sam, and I watched as a nice four-bedroom, two-and-a-half-bath house came on the market priced at $400,000—about 33 percent less than it would have been priced three years earlier. We recognized it immediately as an excellent deal—a way to get into a top school district and a lovely community at a rock-bottom price.

It would even have made a fine rental property, because it was large and in relatively good condition. If you put down 20 percent, or $80,000, you'd be able to finance $320,000 at around 5.5 percent. The monthly mortgage payment would be about $1,900, plus another $1,000 in taxes and insurance. So the costs would be around $3,000, and you could easily rent it out for $3,500 to $4,000 per month.

In less expensive communities, the deals are even better. In some parts of Atlanta, homes that might have sold in 2005 for $80,000 to

$100,000 or more are being sold for $40,000. They might require about $10,000 to $15,000 in repairs, but they're being rented out for $600 to $800 per month—more than enough to cover all the expenses and still have a healthy profit each year. Some investors are buying properties for as little as $10,500, and after doing a little fix-up work are renting them for $500 to $800 per month. If you can buy such a property with cash, you'll do even better.

The most amazing deals will be available in communities with the most foreclosures and short sales. If you don't know where these are, you should start interviewing local agents who have deep knowledge about foreclosures and strong connections with REO offices (that stands for "real estate owned," which is the area of banks that handle their foreclosures). Become a trusted client and these agents will reward your loyalty by helping you find the best deals—the ones they'd buy if they had all the money in the world.

WHAT IS A SHORT SALE? WHAT IS A FORECLOSURE?

Let's start with some definitions.

Short Sale

A short sale occurs when the seller owes more on his or her loan than the property is worth (so the property value is "short" of the full amount owed). Because the seller owes more than the property is worth, the lender has to agree to take a lesser amount as the payoff for the mortgage. (Why agree to take less? Because typically the lender will get even less if the property goes to foreclosure rather than in a short sale). The negotiation that has to take place between the seller, the agent, and the lender is one reason that short sales can take six months or longer to complete.

Once the lender agrees to the short sale, the buyer and seller can close on the property. The seller is considered by the IRS to have received as income the difference between the payoff amount to the lender and the actual balance on the loan. This is also known as "mortgage debt forgiveness." (The IRS and accountants call this "imputed income." I call it "phantom income" because it won't make your wallet get fatter but still the IRS wants you to pay income tax on it.)

Current tax law permits many sellers to avoid paying taxes on this particular type of imputed, or phantom, income, although the law is expected to end in 2013. According to IRS Publication 523, "Selling Your Home" (version 2008, for taxes paid in 2009), when it comes to mortgage debt forgiveness, "you can exclude from gross income any discharge of qualified principal residence indebtedness. This exclusion applies to discharges made after 2006 and before 2013." The maximum amount that can be excluded is $2 million for couples filing jointly or $1 million for individuals. So if your mortgage is $1 million, and you sell your home for $800,000, the amount of mortgage debt forgiveness (assuming your lender grants it) is $200,000—far less than the maximum. IRS Publication 523 includes a qualification test (yes, you have to qualify to receive mortgage debt forgiveness); you'll be able to qualify only if your short sale is directly related to a decline in the value of your personal residence or your financial condition. You can find more information online at IRS.gov (search "Publication 523" and the current tax year for updates).

As you've probably guessed, a short sale will damage a seller's credit history—even if the mortgage debt is entirely forgiven. So the seller and the lender typically have an incentive to hold out for more money. But in a market of declining values, that calculus gets thrown out the window. Holding out could mean a lender would get less money later (and certainly less if the property goes to foreclosure), which is an incentive to take what's offered now.

As a buyer, you'll want to know who qualifies for a short sale and how much mortgage debt forgiveness they're likely to get from a lender. This will inform your negotiating position.

Foreclosure

When a homeowner stops paying his or her mortgage payment, the lender has the right to "foreclose" on the loan—or close out the loan before the term is up—and take back the property, which was pledged as collateral for the loan. Once the lender forecloses on the loan, the home is said to be in foreclosure, and the bank now owns the property and can make a decision about disposing of it, either by listing it for sale or by selling it via an auction.

Once a property is in foreclosure, the process of buying it is easier in some ways: You're no longer dealing with the sellers (who may be emotional because they are losing their home); your agent has to deal only with the agent who is representing the lender—real estate owned (REO) companies typically hire real estate agents to dispose of their properties; fewer investors are involved in closing the transaction (typically the second or third mortgage holders are out of the picture by the time a foreclosure happens). Unlike a short sale, a foreclosure will typically wipe out any liens associated with the property.

However, foreclosure sales are still nearly as complicated and lengthy as short sales. We were awash in foreclosures in 2008 and 2009, and as long as the unemployment rate stays close to 9 or 10 percent, there will be millions of additional foreclosures. In fact, some industry professionals expect as many as seven million additional foreclosures to hit the market before 2012. But two problems complicate the picture: lenders don't seem to have the people power to make decisions quickly, which means foreclosures are piling up on everyone's desks; and the end investors aren't willing to take these losses, so they're dragging their heels and holding out for more.

In fact, lenders generally make more money when they agree to a short sale than when they do a foreclosure. Foreclosure experts say that lenders might agree to a 20 percent "haircut" (an investing term for a reduction in value) with a short sale but may wind up taking a 70 to 80 percent haircut with a foreclosure. In other words, on a $100,000 property, a lender might get $80,000 in a short sale but only $20,000 to $30,000 in a foreclosure.

You might be asking yourself, "Why would lenders ever agree to do a foreclosure when they could get so much more in a short sale?"

While it's easy for us to sit back and look at the market as a whole and see the trends, individual investors and lenders are caught up in a machine that treats these loans as toxic and doesn't really want to deal with them. We know they'd all be better off agreeing to short sales—and maybe they do, too. But in a declining market, where there are far more sellers than buyers, an offer for a house sometimes doesn't materialize in time, and the lender has to foreclose. Then the lender starts another game to figure out if they should wait to get another 5 to 10 percent return on their money or take an opportunity to slice another foreclosure off the books.

What I know for sure is that the total number of foreclosures is expected to rise even beyond record-setting, post-crisis levels and stay high for the next five years. Why is this happening? It's a simple matter of supply and demand. With lenders tightening their credit requirements, fewer buyers have the cash or credit necessary to buy these foreclosed homes. And with unemployment still extremely high and those who do have jobs suffering cuts in their hours (and therefore bringing in less), fewer people can afford their mortgage payments.

Since lenders can carry foreclosed homes for only five years, something will have to give: either lenders will loosen credit requirements so more people can buy mortgages, or they will cut the prices on their foreclosure inventory—or both.

And that's going to be your greatest opportunity.

A Word About the Emotional Aspect of Buying
Foreclosures and Short Sales

In a deep recession, there are families in trouble everywhere. And even after the recession is "officially" over, high unemployment levels and forced unpaid furloughs can continue to damage a family's financial stability for years. If you're a person of conscience, you can't help but feel bad when a family has a run of bad luck and faces losing its savings and its home.

But a concentration of trouble can be an excellent starting point for a real estate investor. If you're a bit softhearted, as I am, it's easy to think that you're taking advantage of someone else's troubles when you come in and bid on a house that's a short sale or is in foreclosure. There is another way to think about it: by purchasing a foreclosed house or a house via a short sale, you're taking another home off the market. (And with a short sale, you're allowing someone to regroup financially and start over.) You're taking a negative neighborhood force (a vacant home) and turning it into a positive force for the community. Every foreclosed home drags down prices. By taking these homes off the market, buyers are shoring up communities and firming up local housing markets, which will eventually raise prices for everyone.

THE SKINNY ON AUCTIONS

I had secretly been hankering to buy an investment property for a while when Sam called and asked me if I'd like to go to an auction being held nearby. One of his clients was interested in one of the properties for sale, and Sam thought I'd like to watch the process and perhaps write a story about it for my syndicated weekly column.

Entry into this particular auction required a $25,000 cashier's check and some paperwork, which is typical for real estate auctions. I looked at the list of properties being auctioned and recognized three units in a nearby apartment building. I had watched the building being built and had heard that the developer, a former manager of a nearby town, had run into some trouble. It was early 2000, and these were the last three units in the building—and they were priced far below what the others had sold for.

The rules of this auction, as with many others, were that you had to close on the property within twenty-four to forty-eight hours. That meant you had to have all your financing lined up ahead of time. Sam's client is an active developer who has lines of credit that can be tapped in cases like these, and he also works with numerous lenders who have instant cash for him—for a price. These "instant cash" lenders aren't long-term lenders; they're often referred to as "hard money lenders" because they charge credit card prices for their loans. The idea is to use them for instant cash and then refinance the property as quickly as possible with a commercial lender at a much lower interest rate.

Sam's client bid on some multiuse properties, and then the apartments came up for bid. I went over to the client, whom I've known for years, and suggested that these might be a good purchase. We discussed what would be an appropriate price and whether I'd be willing to go in as a partner with him, and before I knew it, we were bidding on a condo.

What a jolt of adrenaline! I was bidding on a $300,000 piece of property. The price went up in $25,000 increments, and then $5,000 increments, and then—*we won*!

Sam just stood there shaking his head. Later, he told me, "I couldn't believe you were there, bidding on a condo. You were supposed to be there learning about the process so you could write about it." Sure, but it's so much better to write about something you really know.

Auctions concentrate attention on properties but they can offer buyers an amazing opportunity to purchase everything from single-family homes to condos to large tracks of vacant lots in unfinished developments. In 2009, the FDIC was holding property auctions around the country to unload homes for sale. Foreclosure auctions featured properties starting for as little as $1,000. HUD offers thousands of FHA foreclosures via online auction every month. (In Atlanta, as of December 2009, HUD had more than 4,000 homes available for sale via auction.)

Sellers will auction properties because it's a cost-effective way to unload a block of properties in one fell swoop. Owners (typically banks or a government agency like the FDIC) will find it easier to manage a hundred sales over a three-hour period, even if it means coordinating a hundred open houses the week before the event. Investors and those who are looking to buy a primary residence will go to auctions looking for deals. But the concentration of interest can mean you'll pay below market value, market value, or in some cases even more than what the property is actually worth.

The process of buying property at an auction can be emotional and overwhelming—which is what the auction house is counting on. It is expecting your adrenaline to surge, causing you to keep bidding as long as someone else is there bidding against you. That's why one popular—but entirely unethical—practice is to have "straw" or fake bidders in the audience. These people are trained *not* to win but to get you to pump up the price higher than you would have otherwise paid. In some places, using straw bidders for this purpose is illegal.

I didn't know I was going to this auction until a few hours before. And I had no idea I'd be bidding on a piece of property, much less that I'd win and become an investment property owner in a matter of minutes. As such, I didn't have a chance to inspect the property or do any due diligence on it. (And even if I had, I'm not sure an inspector would have picked up on a drainage problem that would cost us an extra $25,000 and cause us to merely break even on the condo when we sold it a few years later.)

If you're going to participate in an auction, whether it's held by a local sheriff, HUD, or a private company, you'll want to do some homework to get ready:

1. **Find out the auction rules.** There are different types of auctions, and you'll want to know ahead of time what type you'll be attending and its rules. Some common types are *Dutch auction* (so called because it is used at Dutch flower auctions), where the auctioneer starts with a high price and goes lower until someone accepts the price; *open outcry auction*, where the auctioneer starts low and everyone bids up the price; *silent auction*, where you submit a sealed bid; and *with reserve*, where the auctioneer reserves the right to accept or reject the highest bid.

2. **Get your finances in order.** You may need to put up a cashier's check for $25,000, which requires going to your bank during regular banking hours. You may also need a letter of credit or reference from your banker, a current credit history or credit score, a letter from your lender, or other financial information. If you're unknown to the auction company, it may want to check your financial references before it allows you to participate.

3. **Fill out and submit your paperwork.** Sometimes paperwork has to be submitted in advance to the auction company, so find out the time line up front.

4. **Do your due diligence on the property.** If the property is open for inspection, you should be there with your digital camera and notepad in hand. Be sure to inspect the exterior and the interior of the property. If it is part of a larger complex or building, knock on the neighbor's door to ask questions about the property and how well it is run. Then go home and run an Internet search on the

property address to see if any negative information pops up; also check it out at property search sites like Realtor.com, Trulia.com, Zillow.com, and the multiple listing service. Do a public records search to find out if the property has any liens attached to it. Make sure you look up the property taxes and know what the monthly carrying costs will be. Finally, try to find out why the property is being auctioned off.

5. **Try to calculate a true value for the property.** Look up comparable properties online and visit other comparable homes for sale at weekend open houses before the auction takes place. Try to figure out how much the property is worth and whether you'll be able to get enough rent to pay the bills if you decide to hold it as an investment property.

6. **Decide in advance how much you're willing to pay.** Whenever you face the possibility of a multiple-bid situation, you should decide in advance the maximum amount you're willing to pay. Write that number down on a piece of paper and keep looking at it during the bidding process. It's easy to get caught up at an auction and pay more than you want to, or than you should. Stay on budget and remember that there will always be another property.

7. **Have a plan B.** If you're interested in several properties at a single auction, you should decide which property you most want to purchase. Hopefully, that property will come up first, so if you don't get it you can move on to plan B and bid on your second-favorite property. But if the plan B property comes up first and you can't afford to buy them both, you'll have to forgo bidding until your favorite property comes up.

8. **Go to another auction for practice.** Auctions are usually open to the general public, although only registered buyers can participate. Visiting a few auctions ahead of time will help familiarize you with the process and the adrenaline rush you'll feel. (If you get

a huge rush even when you're not bidding, expect the rush you'll feel when you do to be ten times as strong.)

9. **Understand all the costs.** One way auction companies make money is to take a percentage of the sale price of the property. Sometimes they charge as much as 10 percent of the price. The question you need to answer is: Who pays this fee? Sometimes the seller pays, sometimes the buyer pays, and sometimes the buyer and seller split the fee. There may also be flat dollar fees associated with participating in an auction. Be sure to find out how much you'll have to pay and add that into the total cost of the purchase.

10. **Be ready to close before going to the auction.** The paperwork you sign as part of your entry into the auction essentially says that you guarantee you'll close on the property within twenty-four to forty-eight hours after submitting the winning bid. In other words, you can't start looking for financing the morning after the auction—that's supposed to be your closing day. Instead, you have to line up your financing, the title insurance, and other pieces of the closing ahead of time. If you have a home-buying team in place, you'll be able to pull it off. (See the section on putting together a home-buying team later in this chapter.)

11. **Be at your personal best for the auction.** Get a good night's sleep the night before. Don't overeat and don't drink anything alcoholic before the auction—you don't want to impair your judgment when you're dealing with something as high stakes as purchasing real estate. Before you start the bidding process, remember to pull out the piece of paper with your maximum price on it, take a deep breath—and go for it!

12. **Remember that auctions don't always deliver the lowest price.** Just because something is selling at an auction doesn't mean it's going to be at the cheapest price. Auctions are designed to get national and even international exposure for properties and to whip up

speculation and frenzy, which is then used to crank up the price. Auction companies know that the more excited bidders are about a property and the higher the level of perceived interest, the more competition for the property and the higher the dollar value.

13. **Run the numbers for all contingencies.** We bought our property at auction in 2000. It came with a tenant, who paid enough in rent each month to cover our expenses. We expected we'd be able to continue to get that kind of rent, and allow the property to essentially pay for itself, while letting the price rise. And then came September 11, 2001. Companies stopped transferring employees, people stopped buying and selling, and the country went into a recession (albeit a small one, by comparison to the credit crisis of 2008). Our property was vacant for about half the time we owned it after that; we had trouble getting tenants and had to pay an agent to find tenants for us. We took some short-term losses on the property and then got hit with that $25,000 bill to fix the drainage system. The building had so many units for sale at one time that the homeowners association forbade any "for sale" signage to be placed in front of the property, which, I think, hindered sales. Ultimately, the properties listed for sale in the building were sold, the competition for buyers evaporated, and we were able to sell ours and break even.

Looking back, I realize that this particular investment property was hardly the home run I thought it would be. The property was worth about $100,000 more than what we paid, which would have been a nice amount of profit had we not had the $25,000 drainage problem and the tenant issues after September 11. But that's how it goes when you're investing in real estate. Sometimes you win and sometimes you don't. You can be as smart and as well prepared as possible, and still sometimes you'll lose money for reasons that fall outside of your control.

Finding Reputable Auction Companies

Auction companies advertise online and in the real estate sections of local newspapers. Before going to an auction, do your due diligence on the company to be sure it's reputable. You can search for it online at the Better Business Bureau (bbb.org/us) and at the National Auctioneers Association (auctioneers.org). The federal government and quasi-governmental entities often auction off properties that have been foreclosed. You can learn more at the Web sites of these agencies: the Department of Housing and Urban Development (HUD.gov), the Department of Veterans Affairs (VA.gov), the Department of Agriculture (resales.usda.gov), Fannie Mae (FannieMae.com), and Freddie Mac (FreddieMac.com).

WHY BUY THIS HOUSE OVER THAT HOUSE? LEARNING SELECTIVITY

First-time and repeat home buyers often feel as if they are looking for that one elusive property that can only be the house of their dreams. It's as if they're looking for a needle in a haystack. The reality is so much better than that: there are plenty of needles and plenty of haystacks. Unlike your parents or grandparents, you probably will not live the rest of your life in the first house you buy. You'll move two, three, or four times or more over the years because of a transfer or a promotion or because you want different amenities or a different neighborhood.

Experienced investors understand that there are many properties that fit their particular financial parameters and can work as successful and profitable investments over time. But understanding why one property will work as an investment and another will not is a skill that you'll want to develop over the years.

If you're buying a home to live in, you'll want to spend some time figuring out what you want in a house and what you can't live without, and hand those lists over to your agent. If you're buying for investment, you should think about what level of amenities and size are most desired in a particular neighborhood and how much you will need to spend to get a home in rentable shape.

You should get these thoughts on paper, too, and hand them over to your agent who can help you scour the neighborhood looking for homes that are for sale and figure out which ones best meet your needs. If your agent is doing her job, she'll present you with a bunch of properties that meet all of the items on your reality check and include at least some of the items on your wish list. In a strong buyer's market, that list of properties could number in the hundreds, depending on where you live. In a strong seller's market, there could be just a handful.

Being able to differentiate between desirable properties is a quality I call "selectivity." You have to be able to look beyond the decorating (which is notoriously difficult) and decide if the house meets enough of your wants and needs to work for you over the time span you have in mind. The time issue is key: if you're going to live in the property, you have to know about how long you plan to live in the home and then add or subtract a few years to account for changes beyond your control, such as transfers or housing market crashes; if you're going to rent it out, you'll need to know how long you plan to own it, how much you can get in rent, and whether you can get someone to sign a multiyear lease to develop a cash flow projection you can count on.

How can you narrow down a handful of choices so that you select the one property that will work best for you and your family? Ask yourself these questions:

1. **What's happening in the neighborhood?** Neighborhoods change, but they tend to change slowly. And once a neighborhood finds its

niche, it tends to go generations without changing at all. On Chicago's North Shore, where I live, the small communities of Evanston, Kenilworth, Wilmette, Winnetka, Glencoe, Highland Park, Highwood, and Lake Forest haven't changed much over the past fifty to eighty years. Sure, old houses have been torn down to make way for new houses, and there's been some retail development and strengthening of the city centers in the bigger communities. But overall, the character of these towns hasn't changed at all.

On the other hand, Chicago's Near South Side and Near East Side have risen out of nothing. These are communities that didn't exist thirty years ago, and now they are vibrant, beautiful places to live.

Take a look at your neighborhood of choice. Ask your agent what the community was like five, ten, even twenty years earlier. Is it improving? Is the quality of life better? Does it have more amenities, shops, restaurants, transportation options, recreational opportunities, and public facilities? Are the houses well maintained? Has the infrastructure (such as the sewer system) grown as the neighborhood has? Has crime decreased? Are the schools improving? Is the community investing in itself?

Some people crave stability. Others thrive on change. For real estate pioneers who like taking risks and moving into neighborhoods that aren't yet established, a changing neighborhood could mean huge profits—or big losses, if the neighborhood doesn't change as quickly as you expect or doesn't change at all. Truly stable neighborhoods tend to have solid home price appreciation over the years.

2. **What's going on with the street?** It's not enough just to get a good feel for the neighborhood; you also need to educate yourself about the specific street where the property is located. And even beyond that, you need to evaluate the position of the prop-

erty on that street. Houses in the best locations on a street will appreciate faster than houses in less desirable locations. The best location may be in the middle or on the corner; it may be the narrow but deep lot or the evenly proportioned one—your agent should help you figure out which one is right for you, but you can also get a good idea of value by looking at how homes are priced for sale and the prices at which different homes sold on the same block.

The same idea holds true for townhomes, single-family homes in subdivisions, and even condo and co-op buildings. Think of your condo or co-op building as a vertical block. On that block, the penthouse might be the most prized, because higher units are generally more valuable than lower units. Units facing the "preferred" view (whatever that may be—water or city, sky or trees) will be more valuable than units facing the other way. Remember that your preference for a view or location, while important, shouldn't cancel out what your agent tells you is the preferred view or location. The general preference will help you figure out how the property will be valued by future buyers. (The time to think about selling a property is before you even buy it.) Of course, there may be one big reason to select the less preferred view or location: price. (We'll get to that in a moment.)

3. **Do the near neighbors take care of their property?** When you're trying to decide between two or three properties, you should look at how well your future neighbors take care of their property.

Take a walk around the property. Look at your near neighbors' landscaping, home exteriors, driveways, and alleys. This will tell you a lot about how they value their homes and property. Of course, a person's property may not tell the whole story—neglect may be the result of personal challenges, such as a job loss or a sick child. And it's also true that conscientious neighbors move and are replaced by less responsible ones. But it's important to keep in mind that if everyone in the neighborhood takes good care of their property, it will attract future buyers who want to live in that kind of a community.

4. **How adaptable is the property?** When you walk through the homes you're thinking of buying, you should imagine yourself in different circumstances and consider the property's flexibility. Lifestyles change, and the more flexibility you have with your property, the more valuable it will be to you. While you may not plan on it, you can expect to confront some kind of life-changing milestone every few years or so, and you want your property to be able to accommodate those changes. Getting married, having children, starting a home-based business, or taking in an aging or sick relative—all of these may require an adaptation to your home. Can the property you're considering support that?

The truth is that some houses are more flexible than others. For example, a first-floor spare room with a full bathroom could serve as a home office for you or your kids; a suite for a live-in parent, if he or she can't manage stairs; or a guest room, if most of your family lives out of town. If you don't have this space now and you don't need it right away, that's fine; but can you expand the space as your family or needs grow? Is it flexible enough that you could stay in it for twenty years, if necessary? Not having to move to accommodate these changes could save you a lot of money down the line.

The house Sam and I bought in 1994 was a two-and-a-half-bedroom (the half bedroom was a tiny room without a closet that is now an upstairs laundry room), one-and-a-half bath farmhouse that hadn't been renovated in at least forty years. But it sat on a big enough piece of land that we knew we could always add on to create the house of our dreams— which we did five years later. It's now been nearly sixteen years since we purchased the property and it's still a wonderful place to live and raise our family, while being flexible enough to meet our changing needs.

5. **How do the houses compare physically to each other?** Think about how you are going to live in the house, and then compare room sizes, amenities, recent home improvements and upgrades (how long it's been since the upgrade and how successful it was), square footage, total lot size, backyard space, garage space, and so on. Is one house substantially larger than the other? Weigh the costs and benefits of heating, cooling, and cleaning a bigger or smaller space. How is the view from each of the major rooms of the home? Is it on a quiet street or a busy one?

    If you're deciding between two homes, you'll want to buy the one that's in better physical condition. Look at the age and condition of the mechanical systems, including the electrical, plumbing, cable, heating, and air-conditioning systems. In addition, check out the underside of the roof (from the attic), the exterior walls, and the windows. If you're evaluating potential investments, and one house has five bedrooms and the other has four, and you know that five-bedroom houses rent much more quickly, you should think seriously about buying the bigger home, even if it needs more work.

6. **How closely does each house meet your wish list and reality check?** After you've examined all of these details, you should pull out your wish list and reality check and compare each house to each of the points on your lists. This is the time to apply your most objective filters to each property and see how they match up. The house that matches the most items on your wish list and reality check (assuming you've prioritized them) *should* be the house in which you will be most comfortable.

    But there's always that je ne sais quoi, that unknown factor that can complicate even the most deliberate actions. In that case, ask yourself one final question . . .

7. **How happy will I be living here?** This is a question that no one can answer but you. You have to know in your heart of hearts that you'll be comfortable and content in this new house, whether you're sitting in the living room reading the paper on a Sunday morning, cooking spaghetti and meatballs for the kids on a Tuesday night, or serving Thanksgiving dinner in the dining room each November.

Some buyers know instantly that a property is right for them. You might need four or five showings to figure out which house will be a right one for this point in your life. It doesn't matter how long it takes you to decide, as long as you figure it out eventually. (I say *"a* right house" rather than *"the* right house" because I firmly believe that there are many houses that would meet your wish list and reality check and would be a good move. I've seen many buyers lament the loss of a particular house only to find a "better" one next time.)

INVESTORS: BUYING A FIX-AND-FLIP OR A BUY-AND-HOLD PROPERTY

Part of figuring out whether a piece of real estate is an amazing opportunity or just a so-so investment is knowing what you're going to do with the property after you close.

Real estate investors have two choices: they can fix up the property and sell it for quick profit—a process known as "flipping"—or they can buy it and hold it for long-term price appreciation and rental income. Each property you see will have a highest and best use, but whether or not it will work for you depends on where you are financially and what goals you have for the future.

Are you looking to boost your income now? Then flipping property might work for you. Are you looking to build a stable of income-producing properties for the future, even if you don't have positive cash flow now? Then buying and holding might be right for you. Do you want to be a landlord? If not, then fixing and flipping homes will make a lot more sense than buying and holding.

Different strokes for different folks

- Mike, the investor in Atlanta, is building a stable of investment properties by buying and holding. He buys at the very low end of the foreclosure market, does minimal fixing up, and then rents out the properties for cash flow and long-term price appreciation. He believes he has built up several million dollars in equity in just a year and a half.
- In the wake of the 2008 credit crisis, a West Coast investor spent millions of dollars buying up thousands of just-foreclosed homes and then began renting them back to their former owners. He figures that he can offer the occupants a far better deal, since he bought their homes for less than thirty cents on the dollar. Eventually, he can offer the tenants a rent-to-own option, allowing them to buy back their own homes and collecting fat profits along the way.

Buying a home, fixing it up, and flipping it is a strategy that was extremely popular during the early 2000s, when homes were easier to sell. Since the housing crisis, this strategy has proven much tougher to implement, because so many competing homes are available and property values have declined. To be successful with this strategy, you have to be able to spot homes whose needed improvements are cosmetic and not structural; to purchase the home at a price far below those of other comparable homes in the neighborhood; to make smart, cost-effective improvements; and to put the property back on the market at a price that's competitive with the other homes that are for sale locally. If you're creative and have the resources, it's doable. But you have to make sure that you buy properties at a price that allows you to know going in that there will be a profit on the other side.

When looking for properties to fix and flip, scan the Web, newspaper ads, and signage for phrases such as "fixer-upper," "needs work," "diamond in the rough," "vacant home," "motivated seller," "must sell," "owner being transferred," and others that convey the kind of work that must be done. Another way to generate leads is to connect with savvy real estate agents and let them know you'll work with them if they send you properties that fit your needs. Successful fix-and-flip companies, such as We Buy Ugly Houses, use signs, billboards, and ads, and even pass out flyers in neighborhoods to get house referrals. You just have to get the word out about what you're doing.

What you don't want is to get stuck with a "white elephant." In real estate lingo, this is a property that has been upgraded beyond what the neighborhood or local housing market will support. It's the gorgeously outfitted home in a sea of fixer-uppers. If you fix up a home to that level, not only is it unlikely that you'll get your money out of the home, but the carrying costs might also send you to the poorhouse.

Remember this: If you're buying a foreclosure in a neighborhood of foreclosures, it's unlikely that you'll be able to fix and flip the property, since its value will continue to be dragged down until the other homes are sold and some time has passed. And if you're in a neighborhood where few homes are for sale, it's unlikely that you'll get such an amazing deal that you'll be able to flip the property for a huge profit.

As my mother, Susanne, a top real estate agent in Chicago likes to say, "It's really hard to buy low and sell high in the same market at the same time."

Calculating Home Improvement Costs

Before you buy an investment property, you should think about what kind of work has to be done to get it into either rentable or salable condition. There is a difference between those two standards: renters don't expect their home to be in perfect shape (unless they're paying top dollar for it) but will be happy if the place is clean and freshly painted and offers a few nice amenities, such as a washer and dryer in the space; a buyer is going to want everything in perfect condition—to the point of perhaps seeming unreasonable. (The attitude depends on the condition of other properties for sale in the neighborhood and the price you're asking for your property.)

The difference in what it will cost to fix and flip a house versus buy and hold it may help you decide which route to go with it. How do investors know how much a home improvement project will cost? Usually, years of paying to fix up homes will help them determine how much it will cost to paint a room, install a new toilet, or upgrade the landscaping. If you're new to the game, you can talk with a few contractors you trust about the general costs to do various projects (such as installing a new roof, doing a basic bathroom renovation, doing a kitchen upgrade versus a gut job, and so on), or you can go to a home improvement store and price the materials you'll need and the time it will take to do the job yourself (the least costly option unless you really bungle the job).

Some jobs are great for DIYers with a lot of time on their hands: sanding, painting, wallpapering, and installing crown molding, curtains, and some kinds of floor or wall tile. You can also replace appliances yourself (most stores will install them for a fee) and hire a plumber for a day's worth of work changing out toilets, sinks, and faucets—or do it yourself.

But if the property you're buying needs a new roof, gutters, windows, or doors, you may feel more comfortable calling in a pro to eyeball the property and give you a "back of an envelope" calculation of the dollars you can expect to spend getting the place into shape. This may be especially helpful if you'll be expanding the property out or up, or if you have to do some structural work in the basement.

If you plan to buy investment properties regularly and build a stable of them, you may want to add a contractor to your home-buying team (see "Building the Perfect Home-Buying Team" later in the chapter).

Don't Forget about Taxes

When deciding whether to fix and flip or buy and hold a property, you may find that the taxes you'll pay come into play as well.

If you fix and flip a property within a year of purchase, you'll have to pay taxes at your marginal tax rate (the highest tax rate you qualify for). If you hold the property for at least a year, you'll pay capital gains tax, which will be at a far lower rate. If you decide to do a 1031 tax-free exchange and defer taxes by purchasing another investment property that costs at least the same as the one you're selling, this issue may not be as important. (To find out more about 1031 tax-free exchanges, see chapter 8.)

Tax mistakes often kill an investor's profits. Take a look at "Six Tax Mistakes Real Estate Investors Often Make" in the appendix and information online at ThinkGlink.com to learn how to avoid some of these common tax mistakes.

CREATING AN AMAZING OPPORTUNITY CHECKLIST

For some buyers, having a detailed wish list and reality check is not enough to help them decide on a home to buy. These buyers take a more nuanced approach to home buying: they understand that compromises are involved, and may be willing to make trade-offs in the property they choose if they can adapt it to meet their needs in the future. For these buyers, a checklist to remind them of their goals and help them see opportunities where others might not can be extremely helpful. I call this checklist the Amazing Opportunity Checklist. If you apply it to a property you're considering and find you answer yes to most, if not all, of the questions, most likely it's an opportunity that can't be missed.

The Amazing Opportunity Checklist goes a step beyond the wish list and reality check and assesses unusual community, location, and pricing considerations. For example, let's say you really want to live in neighborhood A. But in neighborhood A, you can only afford to buy a two-bedroom, one-and-a-half-bath house on a small lot—and your reality check says you need a three-bedroom, two-and-a-half-bath house. According to your reality check, squeezing into a two-bedroom home really won't work for you (unless there is a way to live in the home for a while and add on a few years later, which we'll get to in a moment).

However, there are plenty of houses that meet your wish list and reality check priorities and fall within your price range in neighborhood B. Most real estate agents would encourage you to start shopping for a property in neighborhood B, but if you really think neighborhood A is the only one for you, you can use the Amazing Opportunity Checklist to help you figure out a way to live there (such as buy a larger house that is a fixer-upper, or a foreclosure or short sale).

Admittedly, this Amazing Opportunity Checklist will make some real estate agents crazy. But there will be some who understand that buying real estate is about wanting to achieve something great: You're looking for a place that represents your version of the American Dream—or that could, given time and resources.

I get this approach, because it's the leap Sam and I took back in 1994 when we traded up from our vintage three-bedroom, three-bath co-op on Lake Shore Drive to a dilapidated two-and-a-half-bedroom, one-and-a-half-bath farmhouse on Chicago's North Shore. The farmhouse, while it needed work, had land on which we could expand and was in a great community for raising children (which we didn't have at the time). So we put everything we had into buying this house that even our real estate agent (not to mention my mother) thought was a teardown. Five years later, we gutted it and doubled its size. The property has truly become our dream home. Not only has the community been a marvelous place to live, but the house has been a terrific financial investment, even in the wake of the housing crisis.

It won't always work out that you'll get the house you want in the location you want. But if you're willing to think creatively, try using this checklist to find that amazing opportunity:

Your Amazing Opportunity Checklist

1. **Is this your dream location?** Why is it so much better than neighborhoods B or C?

2. **Can you afford to buy a property that will work for you in your dream location?** How does the property compare to properties in other neighborhoods that also meet your wish list and reality check priorities?

3. **Can you live in what you can afford to buy until you can save enough to fix it up?** Some people can't live in a run-down house, no matter what.

4. **Are you willing to live with construction and do some of the work yourself?** Some people can't do this kind of work for health or other reasons.

5. **Is there a way to buy a better property for less money in your dream location?** Does the neighborhood offer foreclosures, short sales, properties selling at auction, rent-to-own options?

6. **Does the community offer any home-buyer down payment assistance or mortgage assistance programs?** You may be able to

qualify on income or on location, and may not need to be a first-time buyer.

7. **Do you have an agent who understands what you're trying to do?** If your agent doesn't get your approach, he or she could become frustrated by the process and not be able to truly be your partner in this purchase.

8. **Are you willing to wait for a home in your dream location?** If you wait a year or more, you may have to do more of the work on your own. Some agents may think you're wasting your time—and theirs—and won't want to work with you.

If you've answered yes to these questions, you may be facing one of those can't-miss opportunities.

Still, the saying is true: you can't get blood from a stone. If the property you need doesn't exist (or can't be created) in your dream neighborhood, you can search for fifty years and it won't turn up. At some point, you'll need to fine-tune your priorities, go back to the wish list and reality check you've created, or find a way to bring more cash to the table. But going through this checklist will help you picture exactly what circumstances and what housing opportunity will let you take the leap, and that's extraordinarily valuable.

BUILDING THE PERFECT HOME-BUYING TEAM

After more than twenty years of writing about real estate and personal finances, I'm convinced that a little planning goes a long way toward paving the road to opportunity.

When it comes to real estate, planning means figuring out how much you can afford to spend before you make an offer or hire a contractor. (Sam's favorite question is "What's the budget?") But it also means knowing who your go-to people will be for any move you make.

Whether you're buying your first house or your third investment property, you need a community of experts to help make the purchase happen. Having this team in place before you make an offer will save you

- **Time:** You won't have to scramble at the last minute to find people to help you when you're ready to move on a property.
- **Money:** By shopping ahead of time, you'll have the flexibility to negotiate better prices or do a cost comparison—unlike when you're under the gun and may be at risk of overpaying.
- **Angst:** If you get into a bidding situation, the stress and aggravation will only be increased by not having a support system of people who've been through it all before. There will be angst even in the easiest deal—but if you don't have your team in place, you'll find that no deal goes very well.

Deciding on the Members of Your Home-Buying Team

If you've bought real estate before, you're probably already familiar with the most common team members: real estate agent, mortgage lender, real estate attorney (in some states), professional home inspector, and escrow or closing agent or title company. This core group of professionals can help guide you to the appropriate piece of real estate and then make sure you're being protected during the purchase and closing process.

Real estate agent: Your real estate agent is the person who will start and finish the home-buying process with you, helping you identify the right properties and serving as your eyes and ears on the ground. He or she will also be the liaison to the seller and provide necessary support and documentation. In addition, the agent should be at the home inspection, the bank appraisal, and in most states, at the closing.

When you work with a traditional real estate agent, you will be asked to sign an agency disclosure agreement. This acknowledges that your agent is working with you as a buyer's agent, meaning that he or she has a fiduciary duty to you, the buyer. If you were selling a piece of real estate, the agency disclosure agreement would state that the agent is working with you as a seller's agent, with a fiduciary duty to the seller.

What you need to keep in mind is that even if the agent is working with you as a buyer's agent, he may also have real estate listings that he is trying to sell. Often, a real estate agent working as a buyer's agent will show one of his own listings to the buyer; if the buyer then wants to make an offer, the agent will represent both sides of the transaction. This situation can and does work, but if you want to avoid any conflict of interest, you have another option.

Exclusive buyer agent: An exclusive buyer's agent (EBA) never lists property for sale and so never gets into a situation where she's representing both the buyer and the seller in a single transaction. The downside of working with an EBA is that they typically don't work in a single market area. They might represent buyers over half a metro area, so their knowledge of an area might not be as complete as that of a traditional agent who works every day in one or two neighborhoods. You can locate an EBA in your area by doing a search on the National Association of Exclusive Buyer Agents Web site, NAEBA.org.

Mortgage lender: Price is important, but don't discount how important good service is to a successful closing. When it comes to mortgage lenders, having an excellent reputation for customer service is rarer than you'd imagine, particularly in the case of a mortgage broker (who represents a variety of different lenders) rather than a mortgage banker (who lends the company's own funds for mortgages, although these may later be sold to other investors).

Sam recently had two home purchases close with the same online mortgage brokerage firm funding the transactions. The company didn't send the final closing numbers until the *morning of the closings* (typically, these are sent a few days ahead of time so the buyer has time to get a cashier's check, wire funds, and so on), and at one of the closings, the company wired funds to the wrong bank and made a few other errors.

This is not what I'd call good customer service. It's not even close to being good. But both buyers chose this company based solely on price. While both deals eventually closed, sometimes they don't in cases like this. Or you might have what's known as a "dry" closing, in which the funds are in transit—either getting from one place to another or being sent from the wrong place and redirected to the right one. In such a situation, you technically own the property, but you may not be able to move in on time.

When you're shopping for a lender, be sure to ask friends, family members, and colleagues about their experience with the company: Did the company seem on top of your loan application? Did the process go smoothly? Did the lender seem to backtrack on promises made? A top-quality financing partner is crucial when buying property, especially if you plan to buy a lot of real estate.

Real estate attorney and closing attorney: In many states, the only attorney in the deal is a closing attorney who is hired by the mortgage company and represents the mortgage company's interests, not yours—even though you foot the bill. These states don't require a real estate attorney to close a residential transaction.

You have to ask yourself: Why is the transaction important enough for the mortgage company to have an attorney but not for me to hire one to represent my own interests? In my mind, you should hire your own real estate attorney to help you close the deal, even if you live in a state where attorneys are not typically hired to close residential transaction. Why? This is the single largest purchase of your life and it's fraught with obstacles and hidden dangers that you, as someone who doesn't buy and sell real estate every day, may not even know exist. The attorney's job is to protect you from these dangers, which can cost you big-time down the road. (Full disclosure: My husband, Sam, is a real estate attorney. After years of listening to his real estate closing horror stories, I have become a big believer in spending a few hundred bucks to protect yourself during this process.)

If you have to or want to hire a real estate attorney, you should ask your family, friends, and colleagues for a recommendation. You can also call your local bar association and ask for the person who heads up the real estate committee; when you contact that person (who will also be a real estate attorney), explain your situation and ask for a referral (if he or she isn't the right fit). Interview the real estate attorney about how he works, the fees he charges, any other fees he receives (such as title agent fees—the cash some attorneys are paid by the title insurance company to review your title, a process that takes very little time), where the transaction will close, and so on. Some real estate attorneys will send you an engagement letter, which specifies how much you'll be charged and what is covered in that fee. Typically, real estate attorneys will negotiate and charge a flat fee for a house closing. If you're being charged by the hour (which is common when making a commercial or investment property purchase) the attorney will inform you of that, as well.

No matter where you live, you should hire a real estate attorney if you're buying investment property, a foreclosure, or a short sale. Foreclosures and short sales can be extremely complicated transactions. They can have unresolved hidden lien issues (such as unpaid property taxes) that should be uncovered and dealt with before the closing. And often banks like to deal with an attorney rather than an agent in a foreclosure or short sale. If several lenders are involved in a short-sale purchase, an attorney may be able to make more headway than you in negotiating with the parties for a successful resolution. With an investment property, there may be other issues—such as setting up a limited liability company or using an unusual financing arrangement—in which a skilled real estate attorney will be extremely helpful in figuring out how to make it work.

Professional home inspector: A home inspector will charge anywhere from about $350 for a small condo to upward of $1,500 to inspect a mansion with outbuildings. But a good home inspector is worth every penny.

Ask your real estate agent and attorney to give you the names of the top home inspectors they've worked with. Then interview the inspectors: Ask them how long the inspection should take, how they charge, if they provide you with an online report, how long it takes to get the report. If the inspector tells you he or she will spend less than three hours inspecting the home, find someone else. A thorough inspection should take longer than that.

Want to know what a good home inspector looks for? My Web site, ExpertRealEstateTips.net, features more than twenty videos showing how a great home inspector inspects an old house. I've known Jamie Dunsing for years and worked with him on several home inspections, and Sam has recommended him to dozens of clients over the years. We spent a day with Jamie inspecting a century-old house in Evanston, Illinois, and the videos that we took show how everything from mechanical systems to fireplaces to faucets should be inspected.

Escrow or closing agent and title company: In some states, escrow companies close real estate transactions and in others, closings take place at title companies. Whether called an escrow or closing agent or a title closer, this function is the same.

Of all the members of the home-buying team, the title insurance company and the escrow or closing company remain the least understood. That's because home buyers typically don't choose the closing company (who chooses? The seller, seller's attorney, or buyer's lender), fees differ all over the country, and there is so little transparency about costs and fees that buyers are often confused about the process. Buyers will choose whether to purchase an owner's title insurance policy in addition to the lender's policy their mortgage company will require.

(Watch for title company fees and escrow or closing agent fees to become more transparent as Web sites like Closing.com begin to shed light on these transactions. I believe that HUD will also become more involved over the next few years in bringing transparency to this part of the home-buying process.)

Currently, four major title companies control about 80 percent of the business. When it comes to choosing a title company or an escrow or a closing company (if you get to make the choice), you want to make sure that it is in good standing and will be there on the day you close.

Additions to the home-buying team for real estate investors: If you're buying investment property, you may want to add these professionals to the team we've just discussed:

- **1031 exchange company:** Finding a high-quality 1031 company to act as a qualified intermediary is extremely important if you'll be buying and selling investment properties. (See chapter 8 for my list of what you should look for in a top 1031 exchange company.)
- **Appraiser:** When you purchase residential real estate, the lender will hire the appraiser to figure out your property's true current market value. (Actually, with the new HVCC legislation, a third-party company will hire an appraiser to do the appraisal, as we've discussed.)
- **Contractor:** If you don't know how much it will cost to replace the roof on a prospective new rental property, or how much you'll have to spend to shore up the foundation, you may want to have a contractor on call who can inspect the property and give you some

ballpark figures. Accurate rehab figures should guide your offer and inform your negotiating position.

Best tip: At an event I hosted in 2009 called "How to Profit from Foreclosures," I had a group of real estate professionals on the stage discussing how to build a successful real estate investing team. One of the panelists suggested hosting a barbeque so that your team members can get to know one another in a more informal setting. That's a great idea because as everyone munches on hot dogs and hamburgers, they can learn more about you and your investing goals, as well as figure out where each team member's expertise lies. By getting to know one another, your team members will hopefully feel comfortable enough to contact one another, working more efficiently and effectively on your behalf.

SEVEN WINNING CONTRACT NEGOTIATION STRATEGIES

No matter what type of property you're buying, these contract negotiation strategies should serve you well.

1. **Know what the true value is in your neighborhood of choice.** If you haven't done your homework, you risk overpaying for a piece of property. You need to do an exhaustive survey of properties that have sold, looking not just at original list price but also at most recent list price and final closing price, to understand what's going on with local housing values. You should also determine the average number of days on the market for the local housing stock so you understand the state of mind of local sellers.
2. **Know how much you're willing to pay for a property before making an offer.** Only you can decide how much you'll pay for a

piece of real estate, a number that should be based on what you now know is the true value for the neighborhood. Write down that number and keep it in a place where you can see it during the negotiation so it reminds you to stay within your budget.

3. **Get your financing in place before you make your offer.** Sellers today want to know that the buyer already has financing in place; they want to know you're not going to disappear and force them to stay on the market until another buyer materializes. If they know you have a loan commitment in place, they'll treat you as a very serious buyer, even if your initial bid comes in below what they were expecting.

4. **Make your offer based on facts, not fiction.** If the property is priced at $500,000 and every other similar property is selling for $400,000, don't think you'll be able to waltz in and offer $300,000—and expect the seller to simply meet you in the middle. If comparable properties are selling for $400,000, you should think about making an initial offer at 5 to 8 percent below, or anywhere from $368,000 to $380,000—and be prepared to back up your offer with verification of the purchase price of similar houses.

5. **Treat the contract negotiation as the game it is.** A contract negotiation is like a game of chess: Every move by the buyer and the seller is a carefully thought-out defensive or offensive move. Map out your strategy by thinking about what you'll do if the seller moves in one of three ways: doesn't respond to your offer; doesn't come down enough in price; or accepts your offer. Don't let the seller psych you out—if you lowball, the seller may either ignore you (giving you the opportunity to put in a higher offer) or come down only a token $1 (essentially inviting you to try again, but letting you know that he doesn't think his price is as high as you do). If the seller engages you by dropping the price significantly, you can respond by coming up close to or even at your maximum

purchase price. (I'd try to come in just below so you have a little room to maneuver.) Try to understand each of the seller's moves and not take them personally. Remember that this is just a business transaction, even if it is the house of your dreams.

6. **Be flexible and fair.** If you're focused on price, it may be hard to imagine that the seller is not. But he or she may be concentrating on more important factors. He may not have found another place to live and needs extra time. Or she may be losing her house in a short sale, and so emotions are ruling the day. If you've hit your maximum price, try to be flexible on other issues, such as the closing date. (Who knows? By compromising on the closing date, you may get the price you want.)

7. **Know when to fold 'em.** If you wind up in a situation where you're negotiating with someone who just doesn't get it, you're best off bowing out gracefully. For example, Sam recently had a closing with a seller who had turned down an offer for the property a year earlier for $50,000 more than what he was now getting. The seller held out, ignoring the signs of market collapse and thinking he could get even more, and the result was that he ended up losing $100,000—the $50,000 from the higher offer plus the $50,000 it cost to carry the property for another year. And then he had to come to the closing table with thousands of dollars in cash to pay off the lender. Sometimes, you just can't make a deal work, and it's best to walk away.

NEGOTIATING WITH A LENDER FOR A SHORT SALE

If you're negotiating with a lender for a short sale in today's market, know that things have drastically changed. Here are some new rules of thumb for negotiating these kinds of transactions:

- **Several people have to approve your short-sale offer.** As with a traditional sale, your offer first has to be accepted by the seller. Then it has to be approved by the lender (and then the second lender, if there is one—some sellers have taken out multiple home equity loans and lines of credit on their property, and each of these lenders must be negotiated with and give their approval for a short sale to close). Note that it can be extremely difficult to get the second lender to approve a short sale, because that lender (and any others) typically won't see any cash from the deal. Let's say a seller receives an offer for $100,000 for his property. But he owes $120,000 to his primary lender and $30,000 on his home equity line of credit, for a total of $150,000. After closing costs and fees, the first lender might collect $95,000 of the $100,000 sales price. But even though there's nothing left for the second lender, that lender still has to sign off on the deal—and has little or no incentive to do so.

- **Approval of a short sale can take months.** Short sales used to take a few weeks, but with the huge number of short-sale properties on the market and understaffed banks overwhelmed with distressed mortgage loans, these sales can take up to six months or longer. Short-sale agents and attorneys have to continually prod the lender to move things along. Denise, an agent who specializes in short sales in Florida, says she finds files will be passed around a lender's office several times because no one is comfortable making the final decision to accept a short-sale offer—which means a hefty loss for the lender.

- **You'll need a seller in true hardship and a strong agent to buy a short sale.** A common misperception is that any seller can get a short sale approved. Before accepting a deal, a lender will want to know why a short sale is the seller's only option for relief. If the seller doesn't have a good enough reason (such as job loss, medical expenses, divorce, and so on) or has funds available to pay off the remaining balance, the short sale might be denied. If you're looking specifically to buy a short sale, work with an agent who does them all the time and knows the local players. It helps if he or she is a relentless negotiator who can almost bully the bank into accepting the right offer.

- **You might not know if the property has other offers.** The selling agent has a fiduciary responsibility to the bank, so he or she may not tell you if there are other offers—but you definitely won't know how high of an offer you have to make to beat them. Just remind yourself of your maximum offer price and stay grounded. If the bank won't accept your price, it may not be the property for you.

- **The bank will shop around even after you make an offer.** The bank will continue to look at other offers until it believes the numbers work. That's another reason the time line drags.

- **You may not get the cheapest price.** Depending on where you live, short-sale properties may only provide you with a 5 percent discount from the market price. As Jim, a loan officer in northern California, puts it, you're not the only buyer looking to save on your purchase, and low-priced homes are priced based on demand.

- **Short sales may need more work.** If a seller can't afford her mortgage, it's likely that she hasn't kept up with the maintenance required on the house. Keep those costs and expenses in mind while drafting your offer.

- **Look for hidden liens and other financial traps.** In a foreclosure, most (if not all) of the liens are wiped out. In a short sale, you might find mechanics' liens or tax liens that survive the sale and become the buyer's responsibility after closing. If you know about these liens, you can negotiate around them and make sure they get paid off at the closing. This is why having a good real estate attorney on your team is essential.

When shopping around for a short sale, remember that you won't get a good deal simply because it's a short sale—it still has to be the right property for you, and the lender has to agree to the price.

NEGOTIATING WITH A LENDER FOR A FORECLOSURE

Many of the rules of thumb for short sale negotiations also apply to foreclosures. But here are a few extra things to keep in mind:

- **The foreclosure information on the Internet may be misleading.** If you're using the Internet to search for foreclosures on the market, remember that it's hard to keep listings 100 percent up to date. Make sure you work with an agent who is skilled in verifying what's available and what's been sold. According to Rick Sharga, a senior vice president at RealtyTrac, most states do a reasonably good job of collecting the information. Very few do a good job of making it accessible to consumers. California, Florida, Washington, and Arizona do about the best job with posting information, but other states are starting to do better. Also, Sharga notes that just because a property owner is ninety days delinquent doesn't mean that this home automatically goes into foreclosure. And just because a home is in foreclosure doesn't automatically mean it's for sale. Working with a professional who understands the ins and outs of foreclosures in your neighborhood of choice is essential. Your best bet will be to find a great agent who helps customers buy foreclosures every day and is successful closing on them.
- **Many foreclosure properties are in poor condition.** The previous owners may have taken everything they could, even if it was nailed down. Buyers may get discouraged seeing abandoned home after

abandoned home, but agents say there are still plenty of foreclosure properties out there that are ready to be lived in—it just takes some hunting to find the right one.

- **You may be able to negotiate for a repair loan on top of the loan to purchase the property.** A foreclosure property is only a great value if you don't have to spend a lot of money on repairs to make it livable (and remember that that's the goal—you don't want to overspend and end up with the white elephant on the block). Figure out how much you'll have to spend to repair a property to make it livable and then ask the bank if it will lend you the cash to get there. You might want to look at an FHA203k loan, which will give you up to 125% of the purchase price to rehab and repair the property. Find out more at ThinkGlink.com/203k.
- **It's all about what the bank will net after the sale.** The bank has up to five years to sell a foreclosed property—that's a lot of time to filter through offers to find the best price it can get from the asset. You just have to know that the bank isn't going to give the property away and factor that into your offer.
- **Just because a property is foreclosed doesn't mean it's priced right.** According to Jim, the former president of a large luxury real estate company in Chicago, the home could still be priced on the loan amount that's owed rather than what it's truly worth, because the lender just wants to make its money back.

While some metropolitan areas certainly have more amazing deals than others, there are so many opportunities to make money in real estate everywhere. You just need to take the first step outside your comfort zone. Each purchase will teach you new lessons and make you a savvier consumer of real estate. And pretty soon, you'll be ready to buy something else.

EIGHT

THE ART OF SAVVY REAL ESTATE INVESTING

As the housing crisis gets further into the past and life returns to normal (or the *new* normal), there will be people who boast of making millions on the back of the "Great Recession" of 2007–2009. We'll hear stories of fortunes being made even as the net worth of average Americans plummeted, their home values decimated, and record numbers of people went into foreclosure and bankruptcy.

With the Great Depression, we remember the 25 percent unemployment rate and lines forming in the street around banks with padlocked doors. We recall stories of stockbrokers who, having lost a fortune, threw themselves out of their office windows and others who sold apples and pencils in the street to try to scrape together enough for a meal for their family. But even through all that, some folks worked harder and smarter and created demand for their products and services out of thin air. It's an art, this fortune making.

How can you be one of those savvy investors? You can watch trends and figure out a way to turn a trend into an opportunity. These trends exist in all areas of life, but we'll focus here on real estate. If you're looking for a way to make money by investing in real estate, you need savvy: You have to know how to spot a golden opportunity, how to act on it, and how to profit from it.

PROFITING FROM TRENDS AND OPPORTUNITIES

Over the past few years, thousands of residential and commercial areas across America have been devastated by foreclosures, short sales, and other destructive forces (such as homegrown meth labs). The opportunity exists to go into these neighborhoods, buy up some or many of these homes, multifamily properties, strip shopping malls, commercial office buildings or other types of commercial property, and become a stabilizing force. Once neighborhoods stabilize, property values will start to rise.

How do you cash in? If you want to be a landlord, you have an amazing opportunity to buy investment property, fix it up, and rent it out for profit. There are more than 300 million people in the United States, and the country is growing. All of these people need somewhere safe to live and raise their families. They need to go to work somewhere, or have a place to launch their own business. (I met a woman recently who started baking in her house and within a year had grown so much that she now rents space at a local commercial kitchen about three miles from where she lives.) Many of us want to own our piece of the American Dream, but about 30 percent will be happy renting a home for years to come.

This trend means there is plenty of opportunity for you to buy, for example, an apartment building with two to four units and still qualify for Fannie Mae or Freddie Mac financing. Or you can buy a building with sixty to one hundred units and find commercial financing. You can buy single-family homes one at a time, fix them up, and rent them. You can buy any number of vacant and abandoned strip malls in New

Orleans, Atlanta, Phoenix, Las Vegas, and other devastated communities, fix them up, rent out the stores, and make money while you help bring life back to the neighborhood. Eventually—though it may take years—the millions of foreclosures will be absorbed, fixed up, and resold, and home buyers and home sellers will roughly balance out again in number. The market will normalize, and prices will start to rise.

So many people don't see an opportunity until it hits them in the face. They're so busy worrying about their daily lives and putting one foot in front of the other that they never look up and out into the world to see what else is going on. By the time an opportunity comes up on their radar, the people who knew where to look and spotted it early have collected their profits and moved on to the next big thing.

When Sam and I decided it was time to move out of our vintage co-op on Lake Shore Drive, we spent a long time (months, in fact) discussing what was driving our decision to move so that we could figure out what we were looking for in a new home. Did we want a small house in the city or something else? And what would that "something else" be? Eventually, we decided that, like a lot of DINKs (double income, no kids), we would ultimately want to have children, and that should be the main factor in our decision about what and where to buy.

The public schools in the areas where we were looking were lousy, and options for private schools were slim. We didn't want our kids to go to those public schools, but we also knew that spaces were limited in the good private schools. We reasoned that since space was limited at those schools and not many people could afford to spend—or would choose to spend—upward of $25,000 per child per year on private school tuition, there would be a flight to great public school districts both in the city and in the suburbs.

Spotting that trend—DINKs needing good school districts for the kids they would have—was life changing for us. We knew we wanted to live near Lake Michigan, so we started driving north of the city along the lake to see what we could find. After visiting several lovely communities that were out of our price range, we found a suburb where the housing stock hadn't yet popped in price, the grade schools were phenomenal, and the high school district was our district of choice. It was near enough to Lake Michigan to stroll over on a pleasant summer evening and close enough to town to walk to get a cup of coffee. It was within a mile of a major expressway and on a major train line that would allow Sam to get to the office in thirty minutes. And there wasn't a strip mall in sight. We loved the tall trees and the sense of history conferred by a village founded in the 1860s. We started looking at the houses that were for sale and ultimately settled on our small farmhouse.

When we started looking, in 1993, the young, childless couples hadn't yet begun moving in waves to the suburbs. They were still enjoying city life. But we could see that their relocation was coming. Young couples with young families were starting to buy the old houses in the communities along the lake just north of the city and either fix them up or tear them down and build new. Slowly, neighborhood by neighborhood, community by community, the HGTV-watching fixer-uppers were moving north. The community where we bought just hadn't been discovered quite yet. More than fifteen years later, we're still enjoying the fruits of that trend spotting: the house we bought and later renovated has been satisfying on every level.

When it came time to purchase an investment property, we went through the same thought process: What would the demand be for the various different types of properties in our neighborhood (single-family house, townhome, and condominium), and under what circumstances would people rent from us? When we went to the auction and noticed the condos were on the table, Sam and I discussed how families would need a place to live while renovating their properties or if being transferred from one location to another. For a later property, purchased near Northwestern University in Evanston, Illinois, we discussed the type of student who might be able to afford a two-bedroom plus den, two-bath condo with a beautiful view of Lake Michigan. It turns out that older MBA students with families are the ideal tenants for that particular property.

Each property is different. One investor suggested that each of her twenty-five properties is like a child—unique. But just because each property is an individual ownership experience doesn't mean you can't use trends to spot opportunities.

Exercise: Spot Real Estate Trends

So how do you spot a real estate trend? If you've never turned a critical eye toward the real estate you know best, you might find it hard to see it in the future. Here are some questions to ask as you wander around your neighborhood:

1. Is the neighborhood stable or changing? How is it changing?
2. Are young people moving into the neighborhood? Where are they moving, and what are they buying or renting?
3. Are rental rates stable? Are they rising or falling? Why?
4. Are homeowners taking care of their property? Are parts of the community being better taken care of than others?
5. Are people of a certain age group or in a certain cycle of life moving into or out of the community? Why?
6. Looking at the larger community, what kinds of real estate are not "hot" at the moment? (Real estate is cyclical, meaning that what's desired now will eventually not be desired, and out-of-favor property will eventually become popular, or "hot," again. Neighborhoods function the same way.)
7. Are there a lot of foreclosures in the neighborhood, a handful, or very few? Is there vacant land that could be improved?
8. What do real estate experts in the community think about how the

area is changing and growing? (Talk to real estate agents, mortgage lenders, and home inspectors who work in the area about their experiences with it. Their information can inform your trend spotting.)

9. Could the neighborhood use any amenities it doesn't currently offer (a retail store, restaurant, coffee shop, or service that caters to the people who are moving into the neighborhood)? Are people looking to start businesses in the area and in need of rental space?

10. Are there regional or national real estate trends (such as lack of water or drought conditions in the South, or rising or falling mortgage interest rates and home prices in the country) that affect your local community?

11. Is there continuing rental demand for commercial or industrial properties in your area? Can you buy a foreclosed commercial or warehouse property from a bank, fix it up, rent it and profit from the cash flow each month? If you live in an area that has many failed commercial properties, now may be the right time to swoop in and pick up properties at ten or twenty cents on the dollar and hold them for the long term.

To spot a real estate trend in your area, you need to think bigger and wider. Look beyond what you need and where you live now to consider other people's needs and wants; what's going on in your city, state, and country; and what the future may hold. It may take some time for your vision to expand in this way, but when it does, you stand to profit.

FINDING MONEY FOR REAL ESTATE INVESTMENTS

Spotting a trend is just the first step, albeit an important one, to investing in real estate. Once you're ready to act on a real estate trend and invest accordingly, you'll need to have your financial ducks in a row. If you've read this book from the start, you know that one of the biggest changes since the housing crisis is that lenders everywhere have dramatically tightened their requirements for getting a loan. Getting financing is a significant challenge, so it's worth repeating the two most important rules in the new world of mortgage finance:

1. **You need skin in the game.** If you're buying real estate, particularly investment or commercial real estate, you'll need cash to put down: at least 25 percent if you're buying a house as an investment, and 30 to 40 percent if you're buying a large-scale commercial property.
2. **Great credit is an absolute MUST.** Gone are the days when anyone with a pulse could get 100 percent (or more than 100 percent) financing.

Most folks don't have hundreds of thousands of dollars just sitting in a bank account waiting for the right investment. What do you do if you don't have cash on hand for a down payment? It might not be easy to find cash with which to invest in real estate in today's market, but you do have options. (Just keep in mind that even if you do have cash, some lenders won't approve your loan application if you don't have commercial or investment real estate experience. They want to back a sure thing—and you may not be there yet.) Here are some ideas you might want to consider:

- **Self-directed IRAs:** A self-directed IRA is a special kind of qualified individual retirement account that permits you to use funds to buy commercial or investment property. IRS rules stipulate that you cannot live in the property you purchase with IRA funds as a personal residence. In addition, a third-party company must act as the facilitator, making sure that transactions are aboveboard and meet IRS rules and regulations.

Warning: You may have to move some of your IRA funds into a particular type of self-directed IRA that permits this sort of investment. This sort of self-directed IRA often charges higher fees for the management of the account and the investment. You'll also have to pay the third-party company to act as your qualified intermediary to make sure the transaction is considered "arm's length" according to IRS rules. Before you move your funds, be sure to do your due diligence on the companies that claim to offer self-directed IRAs. Do an Internet search for the company's name, make sure the company is properly licensed, and has not had any complaints to any attorney general's office or to the state agency that licenses it.

- **Seller financing:** As we've discussed, sometimes sellers are willing to finance the purchase of their property in order to create a steady stream of income that's greater than what they could get from another investment but carries less perceived risk. When you identify a commercial, an industrial, residential, or a retail real estate opportunity, ask the broker if the owner would entertain a seller-financing deal. Or ask the seller him- or herself, if you're just knocking on doors.

Warning: Seller financing carries some very real risks for the buyer and the seller. As a buyer, you need to make sure that all related documents are properly and completely recorded. The seller, in turn, must understand that a buyer could stop making payments or wreck the property—in which case, the buyer would essentially be wrecking the collateral for the loan, and the seller would have to walk in and try to salvage the situation. Still, if properly documented and managed (get your real estate attorney involved and consider using a site like VirginMoney.com to process the payments), seller financing can work out well for everyone.

- **P2P lending:** As we discussed in chapter 6, you may want to tap into social lenders for small amounts of cash needed to help finance deals.

  Warning: Most of the major P2P lenders currently limit the size of the loan to $25,000. You may also run into a problem if not enough people sign on to finance part of the loan purchase— you could wind up paying much higher interest rates in order to "sell out" subscriptions for your loan. And if you don't have a high enough credit score, you might not get any takers at all.

- **Small Business Administration (SBA) loans:** The SBA works through commercial banks, guaranteeing loans for small business owners. The application process for an SBA commercial real estate loan is similar to getting a regular business loan. You'll need copies of your business and personal tax returns, a profit and loss statement, other financial papers, and proof of your assets.

  Warning: While commercial banks will require 25 to 30 percent down for some of their commercial real estate loans, SBA loans require as little as 10 percent down. That's the good news. Unfortunately, the government doesn't do creative financing. SBA loans are fully amortized over 25 years. You can borrow as much as $5 million, depending on the loan program, but the loans can be difficult to get, even though they're backed by the federal government. Another problem is that the SBA loan program sometimes runs out of money. You'll find more resources at the beginning of a year than at the end. Sometimes, programs run out of money midyear. Find out more at SBA.gov.

- **Local lenders:** Community banks, S&Ls, Federal Home Loan Banks, and other local lenders might say yes when big banks say no. Why? Most of these banks often have loan officers on staff who know a lot about the immediate community, and they also take the time to get to know their depositors. Community banks also have an impetus to lend locally, especially on smaller commercial loans that wouldn't be profitable enough for the large, national banks.

Local lenders can be a good resource for investors for the same reasons. I've chosen to bank at a small bank in my hometown (part of a larger, regional finance company that owns more than thirty local banks). I see the vice president and manager of the branch all the time; she invites me and my family to bank events and helps me out personally with the management of my business accounts. If I wanted to buy a piece of local real estate, I'd certainly talk to her, because she knows me, knows the surrounding area, and probably knows the seller of the property I want to buy.

Local lenders also keep these kinds of loans in their own portfolio of investments, which allows them to be more flexible in terms of which applications get approved.

If your project offers housing for low-income or moderate-income families, you may have an even better chance of getting financing with a local lender. In 2009, the federal government published a rule called "Community and Economic Development Entities, Community Development Projects, and Other Public Welfare Investments" that, according to the Office of the Comptroller of the Currency, "authorizes national banks and their subsidiaries to make public welfare investments directly or indirectly if the investments primarily benefit low- and moderate-income individuals, low- and moderate-income areas, or other areas targeted by a governmental entity for redevelopment, or if the investment would receive consideration under the Community Reinvestment Act regulation as a 'qualified investment.'" In short, banks and local lenders have an incentive to help finance projects that help low- to moderate-income families and neighborhoods.

Warning: Many community banks were burned in the housing crisis and credit crisis and as a result have an overwhelming number of toxic loans in their portfolio. Since the full extent of the commercial loan crisis isn't yet known, you might have to talk to a lot of community banks before you find someone willing to take a risk on you.

- **Alternative lenders:** While your local banker might approve your application for a commercial real estate loan, he or she probably isn't going to give you 100 percent financing—or anything close to it. Instead, you might be offered a 60 or 65 percent loan, and your lender will tell you whether the financing will allow you to find subordinate financing (a second loan) for another piece of the loan amount.

If you need more of your purchase financed, you can find lenders who will charge a higher interest rate than a bank but less than a credit card. As you expand your circle of experts who guide you in your real estate investment ventures, ask for leads from your real estate attorney, accountant, mortgage broker, commercial real estate broker (a residential real estate broker may not have these kinds of contacts to share), personal banker, and even contacts at the title company. You may need to pursue several leads until you wind up with the right person at the right company, one who is willing to do the kind of deal you're looking for, a process that won't necessarily be quick or easy. These alternative lenders (who will charge you more than a commercial bank, but less than a true hard-money lender) will want to see that you're established in the real estate world, with either equity or some sort of track record. Since many of these lenders base their decisions on personal relationships (in addition to financials), you'll need to spend some time getting to know the lender and developing a relationship that you can build on in the future.

Warning: You have to make sure that the property you want to buy has enough cash flow to make a loan with a higher interest rate work. Do your due diligence on the lender, and be sure to hire a qualified real estate attorney who can explain the fine print in the loan documents. Don't try to do one of these loans without a team of qualified people supporting and protecting you. When dealing with alternative lenders, you may have to put up additional collateral or agree to harsher loan terms. You'll want an experienced real estate attorney to negotiate this contract for you.

- **Hard-money lenders:** There is a thriving business for commercial real estate lenders who charge credit card interest rates but don't take your firstborn as collateral. Still, you don't want to mess around with them, because if you don't have the cash flow to support a 23 percent interest rate, signing on with these lenders is a one-way trip to bankruptcy court.

Hard-money lenders (a term that the industry uses to describe itself) work with real estate developers to put together last-minute, short-term, or permanent financing, usually at extremely high interest rates. The best use for these sorts of loans is as an interim financing move. That means you have to have your exit strategy in place before you sign on the dotted line. If you don't know that you can immediately refinance the property or if you don't have the cash flow to support that kind of monthly payment, a hard-money loan simply won't work.

When might a hard-money lender work well? If you can get a community bank to finance 65 percent of the purchase price of a one-hundred-unit building, for example, and the bank will agree to subordinate financing for another 10 percent of the purchase price, you might be able to finance that 10 percent with a hard-money lender and still be able to make the payments from the cash the property throws off.

You'll want to have a top-notch accountant on hand who can help you realistically run the numbers (accounting for catastrophic events) and a great real estate attorney who can draw up the paper-work and protect you.

How do you find a hard-money lender? As with alternative lenders, you'll need to ask around. The relationships you develop with top real estate attorneys, accountants with extensive experience helping real estate developers, commercial real estate brokers, title company officers, and even mortgage brokers (who often place financing with these kinds of companies, charging big, fat fees as well) will help you find them—and then it's about finding the right fit and a situation with which you're comfortable.

Warning: There are a lot of crooks and scam artists who pose as legitimate hard-money lenders. You can avoid getting scammed out of your investment (or worse) by taking the time to find quality people who can help you achieve your goals. If you build your community of advisers with high-quality professionals, they will lead you to other high-quality professionals.

- **Real estate syndication:** With a typical real estate syndication deal, you have a managing partner who controls the deal and owns the biggest piece of the pie, and a lot of people who own shares. The people who own shares in the syndicate pay cash for them, and the return is usually twofold: ongoing (by means of cash generated by the investment) and one-time (when the property is sold, hopefully for a higher price than what it was purchased for).

As managing partner in a syndicate, you are able to borrow a little bit of money from a lot of different people and still retain control of the investment as the manager or general partner (depending on the legal entity you choose to form). You get to decide how to manage the property, improve it, rent it out, and ultimately sell it. Everyone else is a silent partner. Here's how it can work: you find a property you want to buy. You then go to your friends, relatives, and colleagues and ask them if they want to invest in it with you. Your attorney draws up the legal document, and you outline the business deal. If the people you approached go for it, you essentially set up an investment fund that will have the means to purchase property.

Warning: Creating a real estate syndicate is a complicated, expensive effort. You can expect to shell out thousands of dollars for the attorney and accountant who will help you put the syndicate package documents together. Then you have to go out and find people who are willing to take a risk on investing with you. But if it works, and you can raise enough to buy and manage the property for at least a year, you could be on your way to building a successful real estate investment portfolio.

PRICING INVESTMENT PROPERTY: LEARNING HOW TO CALCULATE THE CAP RATE

Real estate investment pricing is often based on something called a "cap rate." Here's the formula:

Gross Rental Income – Operating Expenses = Net Operating
   Income
Cap Rate = (Net Operating Income/Purchase Price) x 100

Let's say you purchase an investment property for $1 million that generates $150,000 in revenue per year. If the property's expenses are $50,000, your net operating income is $100,000. Divide $100,000 by $1 million, and you have 0.10. Multiply by 100, and you have a cap rate of 10.

If your real estate agent or broker tells you that a property has a cap rate of 8, it means the property is priced at eight times the net operating income. Of course, you'll want to run the numbers yourself before making an offer. Many investors will look only at properties that have a cap rate of 10 or higher.

Ideally, you'll want the highest possible cap rate on your investment property. One way to get that is to pay less for the property. You won't always be able to do that, but in the wake of the housing crisis, property prices have dropped significantly while rents haven't declined as quickly, which effectively boosts the cap rate for the property. In essence, the property becomes more valuable to you because you're paying less for it up front, but the cash flow will be a higher percentage of the price you paid.

Verifying Property Revenue

If you are buying a commercial building or other type of investment property, you'll want to verify all the income streams and expenses for the property. One way to do this is to request copies of all the leases for the property as well as a building budget. Typically, this verification comes after you've made an offer that has been accepted. But sometimes it happens before—it all depends on the property owner, the broker, and how big or complicated the deal is. Regardless of when the verification takes place, you'll want to have a qualified real estate attorney and accountant help you.

When you're figuring out what to offer for a particular piece of commercial or investment property, think about where rents are going and how much you'll be able to get from a new tenant versus one who renews his or her lease. If rents are trending downward, you don't want to get into a situation where your income isn't enough to pay the mortgage, taxes, and insurance on the property.

Return on Investment (ROI) Versus Cap Rate

A lot of investors talk about the returns they are earning on their investment, also known as the "ROI." You might make the mistake of thinking that your ROI is the same thing as the cap rate of the property. But they measure different things. Determining the cap rate for a property helps you figure out the value and what you want to pay for it. If you know you want a cap rate of 10 on all of your properties, you can work backward to figure out how much to pay for the property (ignoring how much the seller is asking).

The ROI is a more complete look at how much net income the property generates after closing. It compares the net income with your purchase price. For example, let's assume you paid the $1 million in cash in our example. If your net operating income is the same, your return on investment would be 10 percent. But if you put down only $250,000, or 25 percent, and your net operating income is $100,000, your return on investment would be 40 percent. Depending on what kind of tax write-off you'll get, your ultimate ROI might even be higher.

UNDERSTANDING 1031 EXCHANGES

A 1031 tax-free exchange, sometimes referred to as a "Starker Trust" or "Starker Exchange," is a tax code mechanism that allows you to sell an investment property and purchase a replacement investment property, deferring any taxes you would owe on the sale of the property (including the recapture of any depreciation—or income tax on the disposed asset when depreciation has been deducted—and long-term or short-term capital gains) as long as you own the replacement property.

Section 1031 of the Internal Revenue Code has strict rules that must be followed if you want to defer paying tax on the sale of one business-producing property by buying another: The property you purchase must cost at least as much as the property you're selling. You must identify the replacement property within forty-five days of selling your current investment property, and you must close on the new property within 180 days. There are no exceptions to the rule—if you blow the 1031 timetables, you'll lose your ability to defer any taxes owed on the sale of your investment property. You must also use a third-party 1031 exchange company as a qualified intermediary to hold your funds.

These exchanges are generally used for real estate transactions but can also be used for other types of investments, including airplanes, cars, trading cards, gold coins, and even musical instruments. They just have to be true investments, and the sale of one of these assets must be followed by the purchase of a like-kind investment: a real estate asset for another real estate asset, or an airplane for an airplane.

By continuing to do 1031 exchanges, you can defer any taxes owed on a property forever. After you die, your heirs will inherit the property at its stepped-up basis, and all of the depreciation you've taken and recapture you might have owed will effectively disappear. (Your accountant, enrolled agent, or tax preparer can help you with this tax strategy, as well as with other new and changing estate tax rules.)

What to Look for in a 1031 Exchange Company

According to Scott, a senior executive with a top 1031 exchange company that acts as a qualified intermediary, security isn't a high priority for some 1031 exchange companies, which are basically unregulated. "Making sure that taxpayers' 1031 funds are secure is expensive and time-consuming," Scott says, "so a lot of 1031 exchange companies don't do it."

If you're looking to hire a 1031 exchange company, you'll want to make sure it has a long track record of satisfied clients and zero complaints. (Search the company's name at the Better Business Bureau (bbb.org/us) and in a major search engine to find any complaints.)

Companies that aren't well capitalized can also run into trouble, putting your funds in jeopardy.

To ensure that the company you hire is legitimate and your funds will be safe and secure, get the answers to these questions:

- **Where will the funds be held?** The only answer you want to hear is in an FDIC-insured bank.
- **How will the funds be held?** The right answer is that they'll be held in a special escrow trust account, so that if the bank goes under, the funds are safe—even if you have more than $250,000 in the account (the current FDIC-insured limit through 2013). Scott says it takes an extra day to get funds out of a special trust account.
- **Does the company have a fidelity bond, and can you get a copy of it?** A fidelity bond is like a financial insurance policy that protects a company—and, by extension, the company's customers—against dishonest acts by its employees. Scott says his company has a $55 million fidelity bond to protect customers.
- **Does the company carry errors-and-omissions insurance on each exchange?** The answer you're looking for is yes, because the E&O policy covers mistakes such as funds being wired to the wrong location.

During the 2008 credit crisis, the faltering economy and slowing real estate market spelled trouble for many 1031 exchange companies that weren't quite on the up-and-up. Investors lost millions of dollars to Ponzi schemes and companies that made poor investment decisions. These investors blew the terms and dates of their 1031 exchanges, so they ended up owing the IRS the tax dollars they were hoping to defer.

"The IRS is unforgiving on this issue, because they say you have the right to choose any 1031 exchange company you want. If you choose a company that turns out to be a bunch of crooks, the IRS says it's your problem," Scott explains. You still owe the taxes even if you can't buy a replacement property and have lost your money.

How much could you owe? If you fail to complete the 1031 exchange for any reason, you'll owe capital gains tax on your profit, any state taxes that would have been due, and the recapture of any depreciation you took. In short, you could easily be completely wiped out, especially if you have been doing 1031 exchanges over and over again, deferring hundreds of thousands of dollars or more in profits.

Many investors use their life savings to make real estate deals, and yet "they never ask these important questions about security," says Scott. "What we are often asked is why we're going to keep the funds in a trust account that only earns 2 percent. They keep asking if there isn't a place where we could earn a little more." But when it comes to a 1031 exchange, what you really want is safe.

For more information on 1031 exchanges, go to my Web sites, ThinkGlink.com and ExpertRealEstateTips.net, and check out all the articles and videos that explain the process in depth. Start your search at ThinkGlink.com/1031. Look for a special eBook on real estate investing and 1031 exchanges in the ThinkGlink.com store.

STARTING A REAL ESTATE INVESTING BUSINESS: WHEN LLCS MAKE SENSE

There are several legal vehicles you can use to start a real estate investing business, including a limited partnership (LP), a corporation, and a limited liability company (LLC). Real estate attorneys and experienced investors agree that, for the purposes of real estate, LLCs give their organizers the most flexibility with regard to structure and income taxes. An LLC shields its members from claims from creditors and litigation matters, and permits its tax benefits to flow directly to its members, so you avoid being taxed twice.

But you can run into problems financing property that is being purchased through an LLC or is owned by an LLC. Lenders often want buyers to personally guarantee the loan in addition to using the property as collateral, but the whole point of putting property inside an LLC is to create a legal layer of protection that takes away your personal liability. (It is possible to pierce the corporate veil of an LLC, but that goes beyond my scope here. If you're worried about this, talk to your real estate attorney before drafting the documents for your LLC.)

Over the years, I, along with my husband, Sam, have answered dozens of questions from real estate investors about when it makes sense to set up an LLC. Here's a sample of the most-asked questions we receive and answers for those who are considering creating an LLC.

Q: Why do some real estate investors create an LLC?

A: When investors have more than a handful of properties, they may decide that the liability has become too great. If they have personally guaranteed the properties, a problem with one property could put the others in jeopardy. Creating an LLC for each investment property separates the risks of the individual properties, removing this potential. Just remember that LLCs are like trusts: if you don't retitle the investment property into the name of the LLC, it will be ineffective.

Q: I own some investment properties and wanted to protect my personal assets, so I formed an LLC and transferred the title to the properties into the LLC. My mortgage states that the lender can accelerate the repayment of my debt because of this transfer. I didn't think the lender would find out unless someone told them, which I wasn't going to do. But now my insurance company is going to notify my lender to change the insurance policy to be in the name of the LLC. I am the only member of this LLC. What should I do?

A: It would have been smart to call the lender before setting up the LLC and transferring title to the new company, since it's likely the lender has a policy for this situation, and you could have been aboveboard.

The lender may not care that your properties are now held within an LLC, particularly since you are its sole member, but if the lender does care, you'll have to explain why you transferred title to the LLC and hope that the lender does not accelerate the debt. Most, if not all, mortgages have a clause stipulating that if a property is sold or if title to the property is transferred, the lender has the right to "call" the loan—or demand repayment of the loan in full. The lender reasons that it made a loan to a particular borrower and wants to make sure that borrower always has an interest in the home; if the borrower sells the home, the lender wants the right to quit the arrangement and get repaid.

If you knew in advance that your lender would not approve the transfer and you did it anyway, you're playing with fire. I hope you have enough cash on hand to repay the loan or can refinance the property quickly, if you run out of other options.

Q: What's my best option when it comes to transferring a property to an LLC and avoiding the due-on-sale clause?

A: A due-on-sale clause is the provision in a mortgage that states that if the owner of the property sells the home, the lender has the right to call the loan. The idea behind the due-on-sale clause is that the lender was willing to give the loan to a specific owner of a specific piece of property, and if that owner sells or transfers the property, the lender is entitled to discontinue the loan arrangement. In the residential marketplace, lenders can't trigger the due-on-sale clause under certain circumstances, including the death of one of the owners, a conveyance from one spouse to another, and certain other family arrangements.

In your case, you want to convey a property to an LLC. Let's assume that you're the sole member of the LLC and therefore its owner. Many people transfer properties to LLCs either for liability purposes or for flexibility in their investment strategies or estate planning. If you're transferring the property to an LLC for these reasons, and the property will generally be financed through a residential lender, keep in mind that many, if not most, residential lenders will require you to have the property in your own name to finance or refinance the property. You may encounter a residential lender that will tell you that you can transfer the title to the property to an LLC after you refinance, but it will not modify the documents to eliminate the due-on-sale clause. You have two choices: transfer the property and risk that the lender will decide to call the loan, or wait until you need to refinance the property and then transfer it to an LLC as part of the transaction.

If your property is commercial and the loan documents contain a standard due-on-sale clause, any transfer can trigger the due-on-sale clause, giving the lender the right to call the loan. But commercial lenders are more used to LLCs and have more flexibility to consent to the transfer.

Q: My brother and I own some rental property and have set up an LLC. Can we do a quit claim deed to transfer our personal interest into the LLC? I have a quit claim deed form but have no idea how to fill it out properly so that it's legal. Is there anything else we should worry about?

A: A quit claim deed allows you to transfer whatever interest you have in a property to someone else. A real estate attorney or title officer can help you fill out a quit claim deed and make sure it is recorded correctly.

You can use a quit claim deed to transfer your personal interest into the LLC; just be aware that by transferring title to the LLC, you may lose any coverage you had on the title insurance policy you received when you purchased the property. The LLC will be considered a new buyer not covered under your existing policy. In this case, you might consider transferring title to the new LLC and having the title company issue a new policy to cover the LLC as the owner of the property. Along the way, the title company may also offer to help you find someone to fill in and complete the deed (and any other documentation there may be) for you. Also, remember to record your deed. Recording your quit claim deed puts the world on notice that this claim has been filed. Find a quit claim deed form at Thinkglinkstore.com/document-forms.html.

Q: **My husband and I personally own rental properties that have mortgages. These loans have affected our debt-to-income ratios, and we were recently turned down for a mortgage for another real estate acquisition. We set up a limited liability company to separate our personal and business real estate properties. Will this help us finance new properties?**

A: You may have entered a black hole of real estate ownership. While you probably have good cash flow from the homes or buildings you own, your income has likely been reduced by the depreciation you take in owning these properties. In other words, the tax benefits you get from owning a property, which allow you to reduce your tax liabilities each year, cause your income to go down. The more investment real estate you own, the bigger the effect on your tax return. In short, if you own enough investment real estate, you might have plenty of cash flow but show no income—and pay no income taxes (you may even show a loss on your taxes). That's the good news.

Now for the bad news: if you don't show enough—or any—income, a residential mortgage lender won't be able to lend you a dime on your properties.

As for transferring title of the properties from your name to your LLC to help you qualify for more financing, your efforts will be in vain if the lender still requires you to personally sign the loans.

If the LLC secures financing without your personal guarantees, that will help you obtain loans for other investment properties. But if the company's structure is such that the losses and gains flow directly to you and your income tax return, you may end up in the same place. Your tax return will show you having little income to justify new loans.

While you may find a residential lender willing to lend you money, you'll probably have better luck with a commercial lender or a local bank that has these sorts of loans in its portfolio. If you plan on adding to your investment properties, you might want to start cultivating a network of mortgage brokers or bankers who are interested in financing companies like yours.

Q: **Our investment properties have mortgages with prepayment penalties. If we transfer the properties into an LLC, will we have to pay the penalties because of the change of ownership?**

A: It depends on the terms of the prepayment penalty. If the terms of the penalty state that you do not have to pay the penalty if you sell the home, your transfer of title may not satisfy this requirement, because the lender would be looking for a true sale of the property and not a transfer of title from your name to an entity you control.

You need to review the terms of the prepayment penalty and have a discussion with your lender to determine if the penalty can be waived under your circumstances. You might also want to speak with your real estate attorney.

Q: Do I have to file a separate tax return for an LLC?

A: Each LLC you own requires a separate tax return. That's why having a separate LLC for each individual rental property you own can quickly become expensive. Talk to your tax preparer about the requirements of an LLC (you will need a separate checking and savings account as well and will have to keep detailed records of expenditures and revenue). Make sure you understand what you have to do to stay on the right side of the IRS.

ONWARD AND UPWARD

Late in 2009, I held an event in Atlanta called "How to Profit from Foreclosures." Nearly 400 people bought tickets to the event, and many came at seven o'clock in the morning, a full hour before registration opened, in order to get good seats. In the ballroom next door, a huge foreclosure auction was being held, with properties offered at prices starting at $1,000. The week after our event, the hotel was hosting an enormous two-day FDIC foreclosure auction. I told the audience, "Today, you're learning how to identify a real estate opportunity, and figure out whether it works for you. Next week, you can come back and get started."

In the wake of the credit crisis and housing crisis, with unemployment extremely high and perhaps staying high through 2010 and 2011, there will be millions of homeowners in extreme financial distress.

Millions of properties will fall into foreclosure or be sold for less than the mortgage balance. Commercial loans are equally distressed, and those properties are also falling into foreclosure, forcing banks to write down billions of dollars in losses. We aren't going to see the financial world fix itself overnight.

The opportunity to buy distressed property, either to live in or as an investment property, is as good as it can get. Once the economy does right itself and this period of foreclosures leaves us, I don't think we'll see an opportunity this good for decades to come. If you're going to buy property, now is the time to figure out what you want, where you want it, how you're going to finance it, and who is going to help you put it all together and support you in your real estate adventures.

In the coming years, my latest venture, RealWorldSeminars.com, will host savvy seminars around the country on real estate and personal finance, featuring top-notch experts who will share with you their smarts and their experiences rather than selling at you from the stage. In 2010, we'll be doing events in Atlanta, Chicago, and other cities.

If you'd like me to bring a Real World Seminar to your city, if you have an idea for a topic we haven't covered, or if you'd like to share your experiences or ask me a question, feel free to e-mail me at Ilyce@thinkglink.com.

This chapter is just the tip of the iceberg when it comes to real estate investing. Please check the store at ThinkGlink.com, where you can find a special package of eBooks that will give you more information on finding and financing properties, tax and legal issues, 1031 exchanges, and how to manage your tenants.

One final thought: today is the best day to buy a piece of property, as long as you purchase the right property, at the right price, with the right financing. It isn't optimism, it's just good business.

Appendix I

Top Ten Mistakes We're Now Making in the New World of Real Estate

With rules, laws, and fees changing daily, it's easy to make a mistake when shopping for a home or a loan. Here are some of the most common mistakes I see buyers make in the new world of real estate:

1. NOT UNDERSTANDING THE NEW WAY OF DOING BUSINESS

What's changed in real estate? The details. While you still go out and shop for a home, make an offer, find financing and close on the property, the details of how this process works today are vastly different from the way we went about buying real estate five, ten, or twenty years ago.

If you've read this book cover to cover, you should now be familiar with some of the ways life has changed. If you picked up the book and flipped back to the Appendix, you'll have to go back and read the good stuff.

But understand this: if you attempt to wade in without familiarizing yourself with the new way of doing business, you'll find yourself blocked at almost every turn. Finding good partners (see below) can help, but you have to be prepared to provide more information and evaluate more factors in order to close successfully on a new home.

2. FAILING TO BUILD A TOP REAL ESTATE TEAM

If you buy and sell property for a living, you know that it's a team sport. By that I mean you can't do everything on your own. Even if you're a real estate agent, you'll still need a good lender, inspector, title or escrow company, and attorney to assist you in completing this purchase successfully.

But some buyers think they can do it on their own. In today's new real estate world, that's a mistake. For example, even in states where real estate attorneys aren't generally used to close house deals, using an attorney to help you negotiate a foreclosure or short-sale purchase can mean the difference between closing and sitting in limbo. Real estate agents who intimately know the foreclosure market or have colleagues who represent real estate owned (REO) properties for banks and other financial institutions can help you find the right property faster. Get on their short list as an investor with cash to spend and they'll give you extra time and attention.

Taking the time to build a great real estate team will pay off in spades. Not putting this team together ahead of time is a mistake you don't want to make.

3. NOT RESPONDING TO YOUR LENDER'S REQUEST FOR ADDITIONAL DOCUMENTATION

Lenders have tightened up credit requirements and are taking the time to verify every piece of information you submit. In fact, when you apply for a mortgage today, you should expect to provide reams of documentation both with your application and during the verification process.

It's quite likely that some of your information will disappear during the process, and you'll be asked to replace various documents or augment your documentation. When these requests come in, you should take them seriously and respond quickly. If you don't, you could be putting your financing in jeopardy.

4. NOT CLEANING UP YOUR CREDIT BEFORE APPLYING FOR A LOAN

One of the ways lenders are tightening credit requirements is by raising the minimum credit score necessary to be approved for a mortgage. Prior to the credit crisis, lenders might have charged one interest rate if you had a 680 credit score—today you might need a credit score of 720 to get the same rate. When it comes to government-backed loans, FHA originally didn't have a minimum acceptable credit score limit, but it has now instituted tougher standards that require a credit score floor of at least 600 (or higher) in order to get a loan.

That's why is extremely important that you spend time cleaning up your credit history and score *before* you apply for a loan.

5. PAYING MORE THAN YOU SHOULD FOR PROPERTY

Although home buyers are enjoying the strongest buyers' market in recent memory, some buyers are paying more than they should for properties. Why? There seems to be a fear growing in some areas of the country that if you don't buy now, you'll miss out on a once-in-a-lifetime opportunity to "get in at the bottom."

While it's true that in some markets "bottom feeders" are coming in and swooping up properties by the dozen, fear is the wrong emotion to drive the real estate market. The housing bubble formed because too many folks were thinking about real estate as an investment and not about the other parts of the equation. They were afraid to wait, believing that property prices would go up at 8 to 10 percent per year.

We now know that property prices can tank as well as soar. The trick is to understand what the real value is in a neighborhood and not overpay for property. Don't be pressured into making a move before you're ready.

6. BELIEVING WHAT YOU READ AND SEE ON THE INTERNET

Scam artists love the Internet, and there will always someone trying to scam you in some way, shape, or form. And when it comes to real estate, it's even easier to get ensnared in someone's web.

But even if you don't get scammed, it's easy to get fooled by what you read or see on the Internet. If you shop for a home only on the Internet, and never go to see the property in person, you might be surprised to find that the house looks different, or the neighborhood is not as it was represented. Perhaps the property backs up to a dump or the train tracks that you didn't notice when you did your Google search.

The smartest thing you can do is take everything you see on the Internet with a grain of salt—and then take the time to see the property in person.

7. NOT UNDERSTANDING THE TRUE RISKS OF A SHORT SALE

The housing crisis has produced millions of foreclosures. But it has also spawned millions of homeowners who owe more than their homes are worth—and are offering them for sale for less than the mortgage amount.

There are some risks involved when you buy a home through a short sale: The property might have years of deferred maintenance (because if you can't afford your mortgage, you probably can't afford to maintain your home either); there may be hidden liens lurking in a short sale that will cause problems after the closing; and you may have to negotiate with several lenders, which could take months.

If you're shopping for a short sale, you'll need to be patient. But above all, you'll need to realize that even though you've spent months negotiating a deal, it could fall apart overnight—and you'll have to start all over again.

8. FORGETTING TO BUY AN OWNER'S TITLE INSURANCE POLICY

When you purchase property, your lender will require you to buy a lender's title insurance policy. But unless you also purchase an owner's title insurance policy, only the lender will be made whole financially if something goes wrong.

And there are so many things that can go wrong when it comes to title. Not only can a former owner pop out of the woodwork, but mechanics' and tax liens can "magically" appear—especially if you're buying a short sale.

Don't risk it. Order an owner's title insurance policy when you order the lender's policy. If you're buying with cash, don't forget to order your owner's policy well in advance of the closing date.

9. BELIEVING YOU HAVE TO PAY MORE TO GET A PROPERTY

As we move into the second decade of this century, there's a feeling that if you don't buy a home or investment property now, prices will only rise. I can understand how anyone looking at the 70 percent stock market bounce-back (March to November, 2009) might imagine that housing prices are about to skyrocket as well. But there are some other issues to consider.

First, while the number of houses for sale (known as the "housing inventory") has dropped somewhat, there are still plenty of houses for sale. Also, housing experts expect another 7 million foreclosures to come on the market in 2010 and 2011, plus millions of homes listed by sellers who waited until the housing market got stronger. With so many homes on the market, prices may well fall instead of rise over the next few years, so if you don't pony up enough to win the first property, take heart in knowing that there will be plenty of others on which to bid.

Second, home prices will not rebound as quickly as the stock market. After the Southern California housing market crashed in 1988, it took home prices about six years to reach the previous level. This time, home prices across the nation have fallen anywhere from 15 to 53 percent. It's unlikely that home prices will return to 2005 levels until the middle of this decade, especially in places like South Florida, Nevada, Arizona, and parts of the greater Atlanta metropolitan area.

Third, don't try to compete with real estate investors who are bottom feeding. While it sounds great to say that you bought a foreclosure for $25,000, it's very difficult to compete with professional investors who are scooping up those properties at record low prices. These folks think about real estate investing all day, every day. If you attempt to play their game, you'll probably lose out or pay more than you want for a property. On the other hand, if you aim a little higher, you should find plenty of homes to buy at prices that make sense whether you're going to live there or rent it out. As I write this, for example, there are plenty of homes in the Atlanta metro area priced around $40,000 to $50,000 that will prove to be profitable for some savvy investor.

The most important thing you can do to protect yourself is to arm yourself with knowledge: You need to know what people are paying for properties in your neighborhood of choice, and where you—and your investing style—fit in.

10. NOT CONSIDERING A HUD HOME

At a "How to Profit from Foreclosures" event I held in Atlanta in October, 2009, I learned that there were more than 4,000 HUD homes for sale. (A HUD home is simply a foreclosure that had FHA financing.) I learned that there are clever ways of searching for an agent who is more than just HUD-certified, but who really knows how to put in an offer on a HUD home. (You must have a HUD-certified agent put in your offers for HUD homes.) I learned that home buyers who plan to live in the house have a two-week advantage over real estate investors. And I learned that with FHA financing about 20 to 25 percent of all homes purchased, there will be plenty of HUD homes for sale over the next few years.

There are thousands of HUD homes for sale across the country, in most neighborhoods. If you're not thinking about buying HUD homes, you should.

Appendix II

Do You Qualify for a Home-Buyer Tax Credit?

Last November, President Obama signed legislation that extended the $8,000 first-time home buyer tax credit and expanded it to give a $6,500 tax credit to existing homeowners who qualify. Do you qualify for a home-buyer tax credit? Here are some of the principal terms and conditions for the tax credit:

- You must have a contract in place by April 30, 2010 and close on the property by June 30, 2010.
- The property may not cost more than $800,000.
- You must not earn more than $125,000 as an individual, or $225,000 as a married couple.
- The tax credit is limited to 10 percent of the purchase price, up to $80,000 for first-time buyers and $65,000 for existing homeowners. For example, if you purchse a home for $50,000, you will receive a $5,000 tax credit.
- To qualify as an existing homeowner, you must have lived in your current residence for five years (or 60 months straight) out of the

past eight years. The IRS counts houseboats and mobile homes as residences if you owned them, even if they are registered as vehicles and you rent the dock to which it is tethered or the land on which it sits.

- To qualify as a first-time home buyer, you must not have owned a home in the past three years. Your spouse must not have owned a property, either.
- You cannot claim the credit if you are buying a vacation home or an investment property.
- You must be at least eighteen years of age. If you're under the age of eighteen, but are married and your spouse is at least eighteen, you would qualify for the tax credit.
- Members of the U.S. armed forces, military intelligence, or foreign service on qualified extended duty get an extra year to take either credit. And if you or your spouse has been deployed overseas for ninety days or more in 2008 or 2009, you have until April 30, 2011 to claim the tax credit.
- You must use the home you buy as your primary residence for the next three years—or you'll have to pay back the tax credit.
- You can't buy a house from a close relative. The IRS defines close relative as a spouse, parent, grandparent, child, or grandchild.
- If you inherit a portion of a property from someone else, you can purchase the remaining part of the property and qualify for the tax credit. The inheritance is treated as a long-term investment property—even if you inherit it from a parent or grandparent.
- You can claim the tax credit on your 2009 or 2010 tax return. You will need the HUD-1 settlement statement and a completed IRS Form 5405 to submit with your federal tax return.
- You may also qualify for state tax credits. Check with your local and state housing authority for more information.
- Find out more about the tax credits at IRS.gov.

Will the home-buyer tax credits be extended and expanded again? My sense is that they won't. This latest extension and expansion of the tax credit will cost the U.S. Treasury more than $17 billion. While that is a small amount relative to the immense amount of debt the country has taken on to deal with the "Great Recession," there is a growing backlash against taking on more debt.

But it will all depend on what is happening in 2010, and whether the Treasury Department feels that the U.S. housing market is ready to stand on its own.

Appendix III

Six Tax Mistakes Real Estate Investors Often Make

nvesting in real estate takes time. You need time to understand how the system works, time to put the right team together, time to find the right property, and time to plan your investing strategy. Real estate investing can be complicated, even tricky. It's not hard to believe many novice real estate investors don't allot enough time to figure it all out before signing an offer to purchase. When you rush, you're going to make mistakes. Here are six tax mistakes novice real estate investors often make:

1. **Not Taking the Time to Plan Your Investment Lifecycle**
   Often, novice real estate investors decide to spend big bucks before figuring out what they're going to do with the property or what their exit strategy will be. If you don't have a game plan, you'll almost certainly wind up paying more in taxes than you would otherwise. So take the time to figure out how you're going to buy the property, own the property, pay the property's ongoing maintenance expenses and how you're going to sell it—before you plunk down your cash.

2. Not Deciding How to Hold Title Before You Close

Knowing how you plan to hold title to your properties will affect all of your business decisions down the line. Spend some time with your tax preparer to figure out what will be the smartest course of action for the type of real estate investor you are (or plan to be). You'll need to decide whether you'll hold title in an S-Corporation, a C-Corporation, a limited liability company (LLC) or if you'll purchase investment properties in your own name. There are positives and negatives to each type of business structure, and each will have a direct impact on how you pay taxes to Uncle Sam.

3. Failing to Decide Whether You're an Active or Passive Investor

If you make the decision to actively invest and manage your real estate investments, you will be treated one way by the IRS. If you merely buy real estate as an investment as you would a stock or other investment, you will be treated as a passive real estate investor. Active real estate investors get to take advantage of various tax benefits and can take tax losses but passive real estate investors are limited in the tax losses they can take on their federal income tax returns. You won't become an active investor solely based on the time you spend trying to buy properties and managing those properties. You may have to make real estate your business to substantiate your claim that you are an active investor in real estate. This can be confusing for many rental property managers and investors who also hold full-time jobs outside of real estate. But understand this distinction—or pay for it on April 15.

4. Thinking Depreciation Is Optional

The major difference between owning your personal residence and owning investment property is depreciation, or the fixed amount that a rental or investment property owner is allowed to deduct from their federal income taxes each year. The depreciation that active real estate investors can take is a fixed, deductible cost that reduces the amount of income you would otherwise report to the IRS by sheltering the income the investment property generates. It has the net effect of reducing the amount you pay in federal income taxes each year. If you own ten properties and each has the same amount of depreciation, you might wind up generating a tremendous amount of cash flow from the properties, but reporting no income to the IRS and paying no federal income taxes.

The total depreciation deduction you take during the years you own the property is recaptured (that is, repaid to the IRS) when the property is resold. The reason you take the deduction now is that the money might be worth more to you today than ten years down the road. And if you use deferral mechanisms upon the sale of investment real estate (such as a 1031 Exchange), you might defer paying real estate taxes for quite some time or even forever.

The mistake real estate investors often make is thinking that taking depreciation is optional. In fact, you're required to take it on your investment assets. Although some find the concept of depreciation to be confusing, you've got to figure it out—the tax penalties you'll pay otherwise are quite steep.

5. **Blowing Your 1031 Deadlines**
If you want to use a 1031 Exchange to defer taxes owed on the sale of an investment property, you'd better make sure you don't blow the timing. From the day you sell your existing investment property, you'll have forty-five days to identify the new investment property you want to purchase and must close within 180 days. There are almost no exceptions to the 45/180 day rule. If you're even one day late, you'd better be prepared to pay your tax bill. For

more information on 1031 Exchanges, see IRS Publication 544 and IRS forms 8824 and 4797. (You can download these forms at IRS.gov.)

6. **Using IRA Funds to Buy Property You Plan to Use Personally**
The only way to use IRA funds to buy a personal residence is if you're a first-time buyer and take a withdrawal of up to $10,000. You'll pay taxes on the withdrawal, but no 10 percent penalty (if you're under the age of 59 ½).

However, you can use funds in a special self-directed IRA account to invest in property. The mistake some real estate investors make is thinking they can buy investment property (say, a beachfront condo) with IRA money and then somewhere along the line turn it into a personal residence. My advice: Don't try this.

Of course, there are many other tax mistakes real estate investors make. If you're going to be a great real estate investor, find yourself a great tax preparer and educate yourself on the tax consequences before you start looking for investment properties.

Glossary of Real Estate Terms Every Home Buyer or Real Estate Investor Should Know

A

Abstract (of title) A summary of the public records affecting the title to a particular piece of land. An attorney or title insurance company officer creates the abstract of title by examining all recorded instruments (documents) relating to a specific piece of property, such as easements, liens, mortgages, etc.

Acceleration clause A provision in a loan agreement that allows the lender to require the balance of the loan to become due immediately if mortgage payments are not made or there is a breach in your obligation under your mortgage or note.

Addendum Any addition to, or modification of, a contract. Also called an amendment or rider.

Adjustable-rate mortgage (ARM) A type of loan whose prevailing interest rate is tied to an economic index (such as one-year Treasury Bills), which fluctuates with the market. There are three types of ARMs, including one-year ARMs, which adjust every year; three-year ARMs, which adjust every three years; and five-year ARMs, which adjust every five years. When the loan adjusts, the lender tacks a margin onto the economic index rate to come up with your loan's new rate. ARMs are considered far riskier than fixed-rate mortgages, but their starting interest rates are extremely low, and in the past five to ten years, some people have done very well with them.

Agency A legal term used to describe the relationship between a seller and a broker, or a buyer and a broker.

Agency closing The lender's use of a title company or other party to act on the lender's behalf for the purposes of closing on the purchase of a home or refinancing of a loan.

Agent An individual who represents a buyer or a seller in the purchase or sale of a home. Licensed by the state, an agent must work for a broker or a brokerage firm.

Agreement of sale This document is also known as the contract of purchase, purchase agreement, or sales agreement. It is the formal written arrangement by which the seller agrees to sell you his or her property if you pay a certain price. It contains all the provisions and conditions for the purchase, must be written, and is signed by both parties.

Amortization A payment plan that enables the borrower to reduce his debt gradually through monthly payments of principal and interest. Amortization tables allow you to see exactly how much you would pay each month in interest and how much you repay in principal, depending on the amount of money borrowed at a specific interest rate.

Annual percentage rate (APR) The total cost of your loan, expressed as a percentage rate of interest, which includes not only the loan's interest rate, but factors in all the costs associated with making that loan, including closing costs and fees. The costs are then amortized over the life of the loan. Banks are required by the federal truth-in-lending statutes to disclose the APR of a loan, which allows borrowers a common ground for comparing various loans from different lenders.

Application A series of documents you must fill out when you apply for a loan.

Application fee A one-time fee charged by the mortgage company for processing your application for a loan. Sometimes the application fee is applied toward certain costs, including the appraisal and the credit report.

Appraisal The opinion of an appraiser, who estimates the value of a home at a specific point in time.

Articles-of-agreement mortgage A type of seller financing that allows the buyer to purchase the home in installments over a specified period of time. The seller keeps legal title to the home until the loan is paid off. The buyer receives an interest in the property—called "equitable title"—but does not own it. However, because the buyer is paying the real estate taxes and paying interest to the seller, it is the buyer who receives the tax benefits of home ownership.

Assumption of mortgage If you assume a mortgage when you purchase a home, you undertake to fulfill the obligations of the existing loan agreement the seller made with the lender. The obligations are similar to those that you would incur if you took out a new mortgage. When assuming a mortgage, you become personally liable for the payment of principal and interest. The seller, or original mortgagor, is released from the liability, and should get that release in writing. Otherwise, he or she could be liable if you don't make the monthly payments.

B

Balloon mortgage A type of mortgage that is generally short in length but is amortized over twenty-five or thirty years, so that the borrower pays a combination of interest and principal each month. At the end of the loan term, the entire balance of the loan must be repaid at once.

Broker An individual who acts as the agent of the seller or buyer. A real estate broker must be licensed by the state.

Building line or setback The distance from the front, back, or side of a lot beyond which construction or improvements may not extend without permission by the proper governmental authority. The building line may be established by a filed plat of subdivision, by restrictive covenants in deeds, by building codes, or by zoning ordinances.

Buy-down An incentive offered by a developer or seller that allows the buyer to lower his or her initial interest rate by putting up a certain amount of money. A buy-down also refers to the process of paying extra points up front at the closing of your loan in order to have a lower interest rate over the life of the loan.

Buyer broker A buyer broker is a real estate broker who specializes in representing buyers. Unlike a seller broker or conventional broker, the buyer broker has a fiduciary duty to the buyer, because the buyer accepts the legal obligation of paying the broker. The buyer broker is obligated to find the best property for a client and then negotiate the best possible purchase price and terms. Buyer brokerage has gained a significant amount of respect in recent years since the National Association of Realtors has changed its code of ethics to accept this designation.

Buyer's market Market conditions that favor the buyer. A buyer's market is usually expressed when there are too many homes for sale and a home can be bought for less money.

C

Certificate of title A document or instrument issued by a local government agency to a homeowner, naming the homeowner as the owner of a specific piece of property. At the sale of the property, the certificate of title is transferred to the buyer. The agency then issues a new certificate of title to the buyer.

Chain of title The lineage of ownership of a particular property.

Closing The day when buyers and sellers sign the papers and actually swap money for title to the new home. The closing finalizes the agreements reached in the sales agreement.

Closing costs This phrase can refer to a lender's costs for closing on a loan, or it can mean all the costs associated with closing on a piece of property. Considering all closing costs, it's easy to see that closing can be expensive for both buyers and sellers. A home buyer's closing costs might include: lender's points, loan origination, or loan service fees; loan application fee; lender's credit report; lender's processing fee; lender's document preparation fee; lender's appraisal fee; prepaid interest on the loan; lender's insurance escrow; lender's real estate tax escrow; lender's tax escrow service fee; cost for the lender's title insurance policy; special endorsements to the lender's title insurance policy; house inspection fees; title company closing fee; deed or mortgage recording fees; local municipal, county, and state taxes; and the attorney's fee. A seller's closing costs might include: survey (which in some parts of the country is paid for by the buyer); title insurance; recorded release of mortgage; broker's commission; local municipal, county, and state transfer taxes; credit to the buyer for unpaid real estate taxes and other bills; attorney's fees; FHA fees and costs.

Cloud (on title) An outstanding claim or encumbrance that adversely affects the marketability of a property.

Commission The amount of money paid to the broker by the seller (or, in some cases, the buyer) as compensation for selling the home. Usually the commission is a percentage of the sales price of the home, and generally hovers in the 5 to 7 percent range. There is no "set" commission rate. It is always and entirely negotiable.

Condemnation The government holds the right to "condemn" or take back land for public use, even against the will of the owner. The government, however, must pay fair market price for the land. Condemnation may also mean that the government has decided a particular piece of land, or a dwelling, is unsafe for human habitation.

Condominium A dwelling of two or more units in which you individually own the interior space of your unit and jointly own common areas such as the lobby, roof, parking, plumbing, and recreational areas.

Contingency A provision in a contract that sets forth one or more conditions that must be met prior to the closing. If the contingency is not met, usually the party who is benefiting from the contingency can terminate the contract. Some common contingencies include financing, inspection, attorney approval, and removal of toxic substances.

Contract to purchase Another name for Agreement of Sale.

Contractor In the building industry, the contractor is the individual who hires the tradespeople needed to build the property. He or she erects the structure and manages the subcontracting (to the electrician, plumber, etc.) until the project is finished.

Conventional mortgage A loan for the purchase of real property, underwritten by banks, savings and loans, or other types of lending companies. There are also certain limitations imposed on conventional mortgages that allow them to be sold to private institutional investors (such as pension funds) on the secondary market. As of 1993, the loan must be less than $203,500, otherwise it is considered a "jumbo" loan. Also, if you are buying a condominium, conventional financing decrees that the condo building be more than 70 percent owner-occupied.

Co-op Cooperative housing refers to a building, or a group of buildings, that is owned by a corporation. The shareholders of the corporation are the people who live in the building. They own shares in the corporation that owns their building—which gives them the right to lease a specific unit within the building—and pay monthly maintenance assessments for the expenses associated with living in the building. Co-ops are relatively unknown outside of New York, Chicago, and a few other cities. Since the 1970s, condominiums have become much more popular.

Counteroffer When the seller or buyer responds to a bid. If you decide to offer $100,000 for a home listed at $150,000, the seller might counter your offer and propose that you purchase the home for $140,000. That new proposal, and any subsequent offer, is called a counteroffer.

Covenant Assurances or promises set out in a deed or legally binding contract, or implied in the law. For example, when you obtain title to a property by warranty, there is the covenant of quiet enjoyment, which gives you the right to enjoy your property without disturbances.

Credit report A lender will decide whether or not to give you a loan based on your credit history. A credit report lists all of your credit accounts (such as charge cards), and any debts or late payments that have been reported to the credit company.

Cul-de-sac A street that ends in a U-shape, leading the driver or pedestrian back to the beginning. The cul-de-sac has become exceptionally popular with modern subdivision developers, who use the design technique to create quiet streets and give the development a nonlinear feel.

Custom builder A home builder who builds houses for individual owners to the owners' specification. The home builder may either own a piece of property or build a home on someone else's land.

D

Debt service The total amount of debt (credit cards, mortgage, car loan) that an individual is carrying at any one time.

Declaration of restrictions Developers of condominiums (or any other type of housing unit that functions as a condo) are required to file a condominium declaration, which sets out the rules and restrictions for the property, the division of ownership, and the rights and privileges of the owners. The "condo dec" or "homeowner's dec," as it is commonly called, reflects the developer's original intent, and may only be changed by unit-owner vote. There are other types of declarations, including homeowners' association and town house association. Co-op dwellers are governed by a similar type of document.

Deed The document used to transfer ownership in a property from seller to buyer.

Deed of trust A deed of trust or trust deed is an instrument similar to a mortgage that gives the lender the right to foreclose on the property if the borrower stops making the payments required.

Deposit Money given by the buyer to the seller with a signed contract to purchase or offer to purchase, as a show of good faith. Also called earnest money.

Down payment The cash put into a purchase by the borrower. Lenders like to see the borrower put at least 20 percent down in cash, because lenders generally believe that if you have a higher cash down payment, it is less likely the home will go into foreclosure. In recent years, however, lenders have become more flexible about cash down payments; recently, lenders have begun accepting cash down payments of as little as 5 percent.

Dual agency When a real estate broker represents both the buyer and the seller in a single transaction, it creates a situation known as dual agency. In most states, brokers must disclose to the buyer and to the seller whom they are representing. Even with disclosure, dual agency presents a conflict of interest for the broker in the transaction. If the broker is acting as the seller broker and the subagent for the seller (by bringing the buyer), then anything the buyer tells the broker must by law be brought to the seller's attention. If the broker represents the seller as a seller broker and the buyer as a buyer broker in the same transaction, the broker will receive money from both the buyer and the seller, an obvious conflict of interest.

Due on sale clause Nearly every mortgage has this clause, which states that the mortgage must be paid off in full upon the sale of the home.

E

Earnest money The money the buyer gives the seller up front as a show of good faith. It can be as much as 10 percent of the purchase price. Earnest money is sometimes called a deposit.

Easement A right given by a landowner to a third party to make use of the land in a specific way. There may be several easements on your property, including for passage of utility lines or poles, sewer or water mains, and even a driveway. Once the right is given, it continues indefinitely or until released by the party who received it.

Eminent domain The right of the government to condemn private land for public use. The government must, however, pay full market value for the property.

Encroachment When your neighbor builds a garage or a fence, and it occupies your land, it is said to "encroach on" your property.

Encumbrance A claim or lien or interest in a property by another party. An encumbrance hinders the seller's ability to pass good, marketable, and unencumbered title to you.

Escrow closing A third party, usually a title company, acts as the neutral party for the receipt of documents for the exchange of the deed by the seller for the buyer's money. The final exchange is completed when the third party determines that certain preset requirements have been satisfied.

Escrow (for earnest money) The document that creates the arrangement whereby a third party or broker holds the earnest money for the benefit of the buyer and seller.

Escrow (for real estate taxes and insurance) An account in which monthly installments for real estate taxes and property insurance are held—usually in the name of the homebuyer's lender.

F

Fee simple The most basic type of ownership, under which the owner has the right to use and dispose of the property at will.

Fiduciary duty A relationship of trust between a broker and a seller or a buyer broker and a buyer, or an attorney and a client.

First mortgage A mortgage that takes priority over all other voluntary liens.

Fixture Personal property, such as a built-in bookcase, furnace, hot water heater, and recessed lights, that becomes "affixed" because it has been permanently attached to the home.

Foreclosure The legal action taken to extinguish a home owner's right and interest in a property, so that the property can be sold by the lender to satisfy a debt.

G

Gift letter A letter to the lender indicating that a gift of cash has been made to the buyer and that it is not expected to be repaid. The letter must detail the amount of the gift and the name of the giver.

Good faith estimate (GFE) Under RESPA (below), lenders are required to give potential borrowers a written good faith estimate of closing costs within three days of an application submission.

Grace period The period of time after a loan payment due date in which a mortgage payment may be made and not be considered delinquent.

Graduated-payment mortgage A mortgage in which the payments increase over the life of the mortgage, allowing the borrower to make very low payments at the beginning of the loan.

H

Hazard insurance Insurance that covers the property from damages that might materially affect its value. Also known as "homeowners insurance."

Holdback An amount of money retained at closing by the lender or the escrow agent until a particular condition has been met. If the problem is a repair, the money is kept until the repair is made. If the repair is not made, the lender or escrow agent uses the money to make the repair. Buyers and sellers may also have holdbacks between them, to ensure that specific conditions of the sale are met.

Homeowners' association A group of homeowners in a particular subdivision or area who band together to take care of common property and common interests.

Homeowners insurance Coverage that includes hazard insurance as well as personal liability and theft.

Home warranty A service contract that covers appliances (with exclusions) in working condition in the home for a certain period of time, usually one year. Homeowners are responsible for a per-call service fee. There is a homeowner's warranty for new construction. Some developers will purchase a warranty from a company specializing in new construction for the homes they sell. A homeowner's warranty will assure the good working order of the appliances and workmanship of a new home for between one and ten years; for example, appliances might be covered for one year while the roof may be covered for several years.

Housing and Urban Development, Department of Also known as HUD, this is the federal department responsible for the nation's housing programs. It also regulates RESPA, the Real Estate Settlement Procedures Act, which governs how lenders must deal with their customers.

I

Inspection The service performed when an inspector is hired to scrutinize the home for any possible structural defects. May also be done in order to check for the presence of toxic substances, such as lead paint or lead in water, asbestos, radon gas, or pests, including termites.

Installment contract The purchase of property in installments. Title to the property is given to the purchaser when all installments are made.

Institutional investors or lenders Private or public companies, corporations, or funds (such as pension funds) that purchase loans on the secondary market from commercial lenders such as banks and savings and loans. Also sources of funds for mortgages through mortgage brokers.

Interest Money charged for the use of borrowed funds. Usually expressed as an "interest rate," it is the percentage of the total loan charged annually for the use of the funds.

Interest-only mortgage A loan in which only the interest is paid on a regular basis (usually monthly), and the principal is owed in full at the end of the loan term.

Interest rate cap The total number of percentage points that an adjustable-rate mortgage (ARM) might rise over the life of the loan.

J

Joint tenancy An equal, undivided ownership in a property taken by two or more owners. Under joint tenancy there are rights of survivorship, which means that if one of the owners dies, the surviving owner rather than the heirs of the estate inherits the other's total interest in the property.

L

Landscape The trees, flowers, planting, lawn, and shrubbery that surround the exterior of a dwelling.

Late charge A penalty applied to a mortgage payment that arrives after the grace period (usually after the 10th or 15th of a month).

Lease with an option to buy When the renter or lessee of a piece of property has the right to purchase the property for a specific period of time at a specific price. Usually, a lease with an option to buy allows a first-time buyer to accumulate a down payment by applying a portion of the monthly rent toward the down payment.

Lender A person, company, corporation, or entity that provides money to a borrower for the purchase of real estate.

Letter of intent A formal statement, usually in letter form, from the buyer to the seller stating that the buyer intends to purchase a specific piece of property for a specific price on a specific date.

Leverage Using a small amount of cash, say a 10 or 20 percent down payment, to purchase a piece of property.

Lien An encumbrance against the property, which may be voluntary or involuntary. There are many different kinds of liens, including a tax lien (for unpaid federal, state, or real estate taxes), a judgment lien (for monetary judgments by a court of law), a mortgage lien (when you take out a mortgage), and a mechanic's lien (for work done by a contractor on the property that has not been paid for). For a lien to be attached to the property's title, it must be filed or recorded with local (county) government.

Listing A property that a broker agrees to market for sale in return for a commission.

Loan An amount of money that is borrowed by an individual, who agrees to repay it plus interest.

Loan commitment A written document that states that a mortgage company has agreed to lend a buyer a certain amount of money at a certain rate of interest for a specific period of time, which may contain sets of conditions and a date by which the loan must close.

Loan origination fee A one-time fee charged by the mortgage company to arrange the financing for the loan.

Loan-to-value ratio The ratio of the amount of money you wish to borrow compared to the value of the property you wish to purchase. Institutional investors (who buy loans on the secondary market from your mortgage company) set up certain ratios that guide lending practices. For example, the mortgage company might only lend you 80 percent of a property's value.

Location Where property is geographically situated. "Location, location, location" is a broker's mantra that states that where the property is located is its most important feature, because you can change everything about a house except its location.

Lock-in The mechanism by which a borrower confirms the interest rate that will be charged on a particular loan. Usually, the lock lasts for a certain time period, such as thirty, forty-five, or sixty days. On a new construction, the lock may be much longer.

M

Maintenance fee The monthly or annual fee charged to condo, co-op, or townhome owners, and paid to the homeowners' association or corporation, for the maintenance of common property. Also called an assessment.

Mortgage A document granting a lien on a home in exchange for financing granted by a lender. The mortgage is the means by which the lender secures the loan and has the ability to foreclose on the home.

Mortgage banker A company or a corporation, such as a bank, that lends its own funds to borrowers in addition to bringing together lenders and borrowers. A mortgage banker may also service the loan (that is, collect the monthly payments).

Mortgage broker A company or individual that brings together lenders and borrowers and processes mortgage applications.

Mortgagee A legal term for the lender.

Mortgagor A legal term for the borrower.

Multiple listing service (MLS) A computerized listing of all properties offered for sale by member brokers. Buyers may only gain access to the MLS by working with a member broker, but similar information is available at a multitude of Web sites, including Realtor.com.

N

Negative amortization A condition created when the monthly mortgage payment is less than the amount necessary to pay off the loan over the period of time set forth in the note. Because you're paying less than the amount necessary, the actual loan amount increases over time. That's how you end up with negative equity. To pay off the loan, a lump-sum payment must be made.

O

Option When a buyer pays for the right to purchase property for a given length of time, without having the obligation to actually purchase the property.

Origination fee A fee charged by the lender for allowing you to borrow money to purchase property. The fee—which is also referred to as points—is usually expressed as a percentage of the total loan amount.

Ownership The absolute right to use, enjoy, and dispose of property. You own it!

P

Package mortgage A mortgage that uses both real and personal property to secure a loan.

Paper Slang usage that refers to the mortgage, trust deed, installment, and land contract.

Personal property Moveable property, such as appliances, furniture, clothing, and artwork.

PITI An acronym for principal-interest-taxes-and-insurance. These are usually the four parts of your monthly mortgage payment.

Pledged account Borrowers who do not want to have a real estate tax or insurance escrow administered by the mortgage servicer can, in some circumstances, pledge a savings account into which enough money to cover real estate taxes and the insurance premium must be deposited. You must then make the payments for your real estate taxes and insurance premiums from a separate account. If you fail to pay your taxes or premiums, the lender is allowed to use the funds in the pledged account to make those payments.

Point One percent of the loan amount.

Possession Being in control of a piece of property, and having the right to use it to the exclusion of all others.

Power of attorney The legal authorization given to an individual to act on behalf of another individual.

Prepaid interest Interest paid at closing for the number of days left in the month after closing. For example, if you close on the 15th, you would prepay the interest for the 16th through the end of the month.

Prepayment penalty A fine imposed when a loan is paid off before it comes due. Many states now have laws against prepayment penalties, although banks with federal charters are exempt from state laws. If possible, do not use a mortgage that has a prepayment penalty, or you will be charged a fine if you sell your property before your mortgage has been paid off.

Prequalifying for a loan When a mortgage company tells a buyer in advance of the formal application approximately how much money the buyer can afford to borrow.

Principal The amount of money you borrow.

Private mortgage insurance (PMI) Special insurance that specifically protects the top 20 percent of a loan, allowing the lender to lend more than 80 percent of the value of the property. PMI is paid in monthly installments by the borrower.

Property tax A tax levied by a county or local authority on the value of real estate.

Proration The proportional division of certain costs of home ownership. Usually used at closing to figure out how much the buyer and seller each owe for certain expenditures, including real estate taxes, assessments, and water bills.

Purchase agreement An agreement between the buyer and seller for the purchase of property.

Purchase money mortgage An instrument used in seller financing, a purchase money mortgage is signed by a buyer and given to the seller in exchange for a portion of the purchase price.

Q

Quit-claim deed A deed that operates to release any interest in a property that a person may have, without a representation that he or she actually has a right in that property. For example, the first lady may use a quit-claim deed to grant the president her interest in the White House in Washington, D.C., although she may not actually own, or have any rights to, that particular house.

R

Real estate Land and anything permanently attached to it, such as buildings and improvements.

Real estate agent An individual licensed by the state who acts on behalf of the seller or buyer. For his or her services, the agent receives a commission, which is usually expressed as a percentage of the sale price of a home and is split with his or her real estate firm. A real estate agent must either be a real estate broker or work for one.

Real estate attorney An attorney who specializes in the purchase and sale of real estate.

Real estate broker An individual who is licensed by the state to act as an agent on behalf of the seller or buyer. For his or her services, the broker receives a commission, which is usually expressed as a percentage of the sale price of a home.

Real Estate Settlement Procedures Act (RESPA) This federal statute was originally passed in 1974, and contains provisions that govern the way companies involved with a real estate closing must treat each other and the consumer. For example, one section of RESPA requires lenders to give consumers a written good faith estimate within three days of making an application for a loan. Another section of RESPA prohibits title companies from giving referral fees to brokers for steering business to them.

Realtist A designation given to an agent or broker who is a member of the National Association of Real Estate Brokers.

Realtor A designation given to a real estate agent or broker who is a member of the National Association of Realtors.

Recording The process of filing documents at a specific government office. Upon such recording, the document becomes part of the public record.

Redlining The slang term used to describe an illegal practice of discrimination against a particular racial group by real estate lenders. Redlining occurs when lenders decide certain areas of a community are too high risk and refuse to lend to buyers who want to purchase property in those areas, regardless of their qualifications or creditworthiness.

Reserve The amount of money set aside by a condo, co-op, or homeowners' association for future capital improvements.

S

Sale-leaseback A transaction in which the seller sells property to a buyer, who then leases the property back to the seller. This is accomplished within the same transaction.

Sales contract The document used to purchase property. Also known as the purchase contract or a contract to purchase.

Second mortgage A mortgage that is obtained after the primary mortgage, and whose rights for repayment are secondary to the first mortgage.

Seller broker A broker who has a fiduciary responsibility to the seller. Most brokers are seller brokers, although an increasing number are buyer brokers, who have a fiduciary responsibility to the buyer.

Settlement statement A statement that details the monies paid out and received by the buyer and seller at closing.

Shared appreciation mortgage A relatively new mortgage used to help first-time buyers who might not qualify for conventional financing. In a shared appreciation mortgage, the lender offers a below-market interest rate in return for a portion of the profits made by the home owner when the property is sold. Before entering into a shared appreciation mortgage, be sure to have your real estate attorney review the documentation.

Special assessment An additional charge levied by a condo or co-op board in order to pay for capital improvements or other unforeseen expenses.

Subagent A broker who brings the buyer to the property. Although subagents would appear to be working for the buyer (a subagent usually ferries around the buyer, showing him or her properties), they are paid by the seller and have a fiduciary responsibility to the seller. Subagency is often confusing to first-time buyers, who think that because the subagent shows them property, the subagent is "their" agent, rather than the seller's.

Subdivision The division of a large piece of property into several smaller pieces. Usually a developer or a group of developers will build single family or duplex homes of a similar design and cost within one subdivision.

T

Tax lien An encumbrance attached to property if the owner does not pay his or her real estate taxes or federal income taxes. If overdue property taxes are not paid, the owner's property might be sold at auction for the amount owed in back taxes.

Tenancy by the entirety A type of ownership whereby both the husband and wife each own the complete property. Each spouse has an ownership interest in the property as their marital residence and, as a result, creditors cannot force the sale of the home to pay back the debts of one spouse without the other spouse's consent. There are rights of survivorship whereby upon the death of one spouse, the other spouse would immediately inherit the entire property.

Tenants in common A type of ownership in which two or more parties have an undivided interest in the property. The owners may or may not have equal shares of ownership, and there are no rights of survivorship. However, each owner retains the right to sell his or her share in the property as he or she sees fit.

Title Refers to the ownership of a particular piece of property.

Title company The corporation or company that insures the status of title (title insurance) through the closing, and may handle other aspects of the closing.

Title insurance Insurance that protects the lender and the property owner against losses arising from defects or problems with the title to property.

Torrens title A system of recording the chain of ownership for property, which takes its name from the man who created it in Australia in 1858, Sir Robert Torrens. While that system was popular in the nineteenth century, most cities have converted to other, less cumbersome, systems of recording.

Trust account An account used by brokers and escrow agents, in which funds for another individual are held separately, and not commingled with other funds.

U

Underwriter The individual who makes sure that a borrower qualifies for a mortgage. Your lender will have an investor underwrite your loan.

V

Variable interest rate An interest rate that rises and falls according to a particular economic indicator, such as Treasury Bills.

Void A contract or document that is not enforceable.

Voluntary lien A lien, such as a mortgage, that a homeowner elects to grant to a lender.

W

Waiver The surrender or relinquishment of a particular right, claim, or privilege.

Warranty A legally binding promise given to the buyer at closing by the seller, generally regarding the condition of the home, property, or other matter.

Z

Zoning The right of the local municipal government to decide how different areas of the municipality will be used. Zoning ordinances are the laws that govern the use of the land.

Acknowledgments

I started writing about real estate and money over twenty years ago. As I look back at the real estate market in the late 1980s, 1990s, and early part of this new century, I am amazed at the progress we have made in helping home buyers, home sellers, and homeowners buy, sell, fix up, and finance their homes.

But in all the years I have been writing about real estate, I have been stunned by the pace of change since the housing bubble burst in 2005. The latter half of this decade has seen an unprecedented slide in home values, a "Great Recession" that is widely viewed as the worst economic crisis since the Great Depression, and a collapse of everything most Americans thought was true about homeownership.

Staying on top of all that is new, different, and changing is a full-time task, one that requires plenty of help. Over the years, I have spoken with countless real estate agents and brokers, mortgage lenders, appraisers, inspectors, contractors, real estate investors, attorneys, developers, economists, buyers, sellers, homeowners, and others who are involved in the residential real estate market. Untold numbers of spokespeople from various trade associations, lobbying firms, and governmental and quasi-governmental organizations and housing agencies have provided everything from off-the-record insights to hard-core data. All of these people have generously shared their time, experiences, and expertise with me, and I am grateful for their help.

Every year, I receive thousands of e-mails from home buyers, sellers, and homeowners. Whether our conversations were on or off the record, you should know that your experiences have enriched my understanding of how the world of real estate works on Main Street and Wall Street, and have informed my reporting, hopefully for the better. Although I no longer have the ability to respond personally to every comment or letter, please know that I read everything you send, and am grateful that you've taken the time to write. You can always reach me at Ilyce@thinkglink.com.

For this book, we interviewed dozens of people who work in the real estate industry and dozens of home buyers, sellers, and homeowners. My deep thanks to those who went above and beyond the call to answer questions, clarify concepts, share stories, and enlighten me, including Mark Akchin, Frank Alexander, Jim Alexander, Wendy Alley, Curtis Arnold, Don Atkinson, Michael Barry, Renee Beidler, Terry Bersach, Megan Bhatia, John Bisney, Suzanne Boas, Amy Bonitatibus, Merry Brodie, Chris Brown, David Brown, Doug Brown, Matthew Buck, Rick Burch, Chet Burgess, Stan Cameron, Tammy Chan, Steve Cook, Amy Crews Cutts, Gail Cunningham, Katie Curnutte, Linda Bauer Darr, Edward Delgado, Samantha DiMatteo, John Donovan, Bruce Dorpalen, Rick Druker, Jamie Dunsing, Jim Eberle, Steve Ely, Brian Faith, Lynda Fernandez, Dan Frahm, Michael Frenkel, Brad German, Dan Gjeldum, Herb Gomez, Doug Gooch, Melanie Green, Erin Griffin, Aaron Hultigren, Gene Jones, Katy Jones, Shannon Judd, Millie Kanyar, Carolyn Kemp, Mark and Anne Lackey, Lyndra Lea, Dick Lepre, David Lereah, Natalie Lohrenz, Mark Luscombe, Shannon Lukas, Dave Mace, Chris Marcotte, George McCarthy, Steven McKenna, Walter Molony, Bonnie Morris, Bill and Jenny Chang Muller, Scott Nathanson, Bill Nemeth, Brad Nix, Lee Norville, Ricky Novak, Krista Obenza, Jonathan Otto, Jim Pair, Anita Paul, Jessica Petrucci, Tom Pool, Frank Riddick, Maria Romano, Mike Rose, David Rubinger, Jeanne Salvatore, Faith Schwartz, Scott Scredon, Leslie

Sellers, Rick Sharga, Aleis Stokes, Kelly Surmacewicz, Michelle Velcheck, Donna Vilar, Tanisha Warner, Kevin Waetke, Sheridan Watson, Jason Weber, Stephanie White, Will Wille, Cate Williams, Demitra Wilson, Mark Zandi, Shea Zimmerman, and others who asked to remain anonymous.

I'd be half as productive and not nearly as accurate without the contributions of current and past members of the ThinkGlink team, who assisted me with some of the research for this project and carried the ball for a few other things we do in the office, including Kate Bernot, Matthew Cozza, Jennifer Freeman, Heidi Hill, Melanie Rogers, Sarah Schaale, and Claire Young. My radio show executive producer Crystal Wheeler leads the ThinkGlink/ WSB team and does an amazing job getting our show on the air each week. I also want to thank my WSB family, including Pete Spriggs, Greg Moceri, Condace Pressley, Clark Howard, Walter Reeves, Herman Cain, Alan Hunt, Clint Reed, Eric Lauer, and many others at CoxRadio who are so supportive of the content we bring to you each week on the radio. Thanks to Dave Muleahey and the amazing team at Tribune Media Services, who make sure my "Real Estate Matters" columns are delivered on time and in great shape each week. The terrific CBSMoneyWatch.com team, including Eric Schurenberg, Rachel Elson, Rich Eisenberg, and others, helped me start my "Home Equity" blog in 2009 and encouraged me to take risks with it. Thank you for your support and guidance.

I am also grateful for the friendship, counsel, and support of: Leo Shaw and Gene Galperin, Sarah and Michael Alter, Ellen Fiedelholtz and Michael Silverman, Lane and Ruth Epstein, Thea Flaum and Bob Hill, Ellyn Rosen and Susanna Darwin, Lance and Ellen Gams, Chris and Elise Klein, Pamela and Jon Anderson, Ruth Peterman and Dwight Yackley, and Josh Lowitz. Alice Martell has represented me with aplomb since my first book was sold, in 1993. I am thrilled that my HarperCollins editor, Henry Ferris, who took that first book proposal and helped shape it into a fabulously useful book, agreed to take on this project. He, Danny Goldstein, and so many others on the HarperCollins team have been fantastic to work with, and I look forward to our next project.

I often say that a house is just four walls, a ceiling, and a floor. It's family that makes it a home. I am thankful for my extended family's love, support, and encouragement: Stan and Margo Tamkin, Linda and Simon Waller, Mitch and Alice Tamkin, Brad and Maru Tamkin, Marya Flood and Peter Frenkel, Erika Erhart, Helene Mayer and Ken Virgile, Beth Mayer and Rob Elkin, Sherri and Rick Swiman, and Pamela Mayer; my sisters, Shona Glink Kitei and Phyllis Glink Harris, and their husbands Jon and Ian, have been especially wonderful (and forgiving!) as I raced to keep up with it all. My mother, Susanne Kraus Glink, a top agent with more than twenty-five years of experience in real estate, continues to share her secrets, change-agent strategies, and still-surprising (and sometimes shocking!) stories about what goes on in her profession. My children, Alex and Michael, always make me smile. I am in awe of their many talents and am enjoying watching them grow as citizens of the world.

Finally, I would have never finished this book without the unstinting help of my husband, business partner, and best friend, Samuel J. Tamkin, the world's best real estate attorney, technology guru, and one hell of an editor— who cowrites our weekly nationally syndicated "Ask the Lawyer" column— and who continues to believe all my wildest dreams will come true.

Index

About the Author

ILYCE GLINK is the author of more than ten books, including *100 Questions Every First-Time Home Buyer Should Ask,* which have sold nearly a million copies in total. Her nationally syndicated column, "Real Estate Matters," appears four times a week in more than 125 newspapers and Web sites including the *Washington Post,* the *Los Angeles Times,* and the *Detroit Free Press.* She hosts the online video series "Expert Real Estate Tips," as well as a two-hour radio program every Sunday on Atlanta's top news/talk station and writes the Home Equity blog at CBS's MoneyWatch.com. She owns a number of popular Web sites, including ThinkGlink.com, ExpertRealEstateTips. net, and HouseTask.com and publishes a widely-read free weekly newsletter about money and real estate. Each year, thousands of consumers attend her Real World Seminars (RealWorldSeminars. com) events to learn more about real estate investing, money management, credit improvement and entrepreneurship. Her company, Think Glink Publishing, designs and creates unique online and offline content solutions for corporations and nonprofits. A popular speaker, Glink also consults with companies on their media and content strategies. Find her online at ThinkGlink.com, at Twitter (@Glink), and Facebook.com/IlyceGlink.